THE ENCYCLOPEDIA OF
FAMILY
COOKING

HUNDREDS OF TEMPTING RECIPES, WITH LOTS OF NEW IDEAS TO TRY

Grange
BOOKS

© 1993 Orbis Publishing Ltd

Published by Grange Books
An Imprint of Grange Books PLC
The Grange
Grange Yard
LONDON
SE1 3AG

Published 1993

ISBN 1 85627 337 7

Printed in Hungary

CONTENTS

CONVENTIONAL COOKING

This section provides a wealth of recipes cooked by conventional methods to help you prepare tasty meals for all occasions and to suit all tastes — be it a simple snack, a brunch time treat, or a special meal for family and friends.

The overall recipe timings are a great help to those who have busy work schedules, demanding families who often eat at different times, or for when unexpected guests arrive. A quick flick through the recipes and you are sure to find a suitable dish that makes use of everyday store cupboard ingredients that can be turned into an attractive and nutritious meal in minutes rather than hours.

All the recipes give an indication of recipe servings and indicate those which are suitable for freezing. Why not make up some of these in advance and freeze them so you have a selection of dishes to fall back on should you be rushed for time. It will make entertaining so much easier and keep last-minute preparation to the minimum, giving you more time to spend with family and friends.

All the recipes make use of foods which are easily obtainable and economic to use. Many give serving suggestions. The greatest bonus, however, is the fact that each delicious dish is illustrated, making meal planning so easy. You can at a glance take into account contrasts in shape, consistency, colour and texture. The illustrations inspire new ideas for garnishing and serving so you can plan a meal that not only tastes good and is nutritious to eat, but looks quite delightful too.

Hungarian cabbage soup

Overall timing 2 hours

Freezing Suitable: add flour and soured cream when reheating.

To serve 4

8 oz	Onions	225 g
1	Garlic clove	1
3 tbsp	Oil	3x15 ml
12 oz	Stewing beef	350 g
12 oz	Canned sauerkraut	350 g
½ teasp	Fennel seeds	2.5 ml
½ teasp	Coarse salt	2.5 ml
3½ pints	Stock	2 litres
4 oz	Streaky bacon	125 g
2	Frankfurters	2
1 tbsp	Paprika	15 ml
2 tbsp	Plain flour	2x15 ml
4 tbsp	Water	4x15 ml
2 tbsp	Soured cream	2x15 ml

Peel and slice onions; peel and crush garlic. Heat 2 tbsp (2x15 ml) oil in large saucepan. Add onions and garlic and fry over moderate heat till golden. Cut beef into small cubes, add to pan and brown all over.

Add drained canned sauerkraut, fennel seeds and coarse salt to the pan. Cover with the stock (made with 2 stock cubes if necessary) and simmer gently for 1 hour or till meat is tender.

Derind and roughly chop the bacon. Fry bacon in remaining oil in a frying pan till crisp, then add the sliced frankfurters and paprika. Cook for 5 minutes, then remove and add to the saucepan.

Blend flour with cold water in a bowl till smooth, then stir into the soup mixture and cook for a further 5 minutes. Stir in the soured cream, adjust the seasoning and serve at once with slices of black bread.

Savoury dumpling soup

Overall timing 2½ hours

Freezing Suitable: add dumplings after reheating

To serve 6–8

1	Onion	1
4 oz	Carrots	125 g
3 oz	Parsnips	75 g
5	Stalks of celery	5
3 oz	Butter	75 g
2 tbsp	Plain flour	2x15 ml
3 pints	Chicken stock	1.7 litres
1 lb	Cooked chicken joints	450 g
Dumplings		
4 oz	Fresh breadcrumbs	125 g
2 oz	Streaky bacon	50 g
4 oz	Calf's liver	125 g
4 oz	Minced beef	125 g
1	Onion	1
1	Egg	1
½ teasp	Dried marjoram	2.5 ml
	Salt and pepper	
1 tbsp	Chopped parsley	15 ml

First make dumplings. Soak breadcrumbs in ½ pint (300 ml) water for 15 minutes. Derind and chop bacon and fry till crisp. Mince liver. Add beef, squeezed out breadcrumbs, chopped onion, drained bacon, egg, marjoram, seasoning and parsley. Shape into small dumplings.

Peel and chop onion, carrots and parsnips; chop celery. Melt butter, add onions and cook for 2–3 minutes. Add carrots, celery and parsnips, cover and cook till tender. Sieve vegetables and return to pan. Stir in flour then 1 pint (560 ml) stock. Simmer until thickened. Add remaining stock.

Skin, bone and chop chicken. Add to soup with dumplings and simmer for 15 minutes.

Scotch broth

Overall timing 2½ hours

Freezing Not suitable

To serve 4

4 oz	Pearl barley	125 g
2 lb	Scrag end of neck of lamb	900 g
2 oz	Butter	50 g
2	Onions	2
4	Stalks of celery	4
1 tbsp	Plain flour	15 ml
4 pints	Water	2.2 litres
1 teasp	Sugar	5 ml
	Salt and pepper	
1 lb	Potatoes	450 g
4	Carrots	4
1	Leek	1

Wash the barley and drain thoroughly. Wipe and trim the lamb and cut into pieces. Melt the butter in a saucepan or flameproof casserole. Add the lamb and fry over a high heat till browned on all sides.

Peel and chop the onions; trim and slice the celery. Add to the meat and fry till transparent. Add the barley and cook for 2 minutes. Sprinkle in the flour and cook, stirring, till flour begins to brown. Gradually add the water and bring to the boil, stirring constantly. Add the sugar, salt and pepper. Cover and simmer for about 1½ hours.

Peel and quarter the potatoes; scrape and slice the carrots. Add to the soup and simmer for a further 30 minutes.

Wash and finely chop the leek and add to the soup. Simmer for 3 minutes more. Taste and adjust the seasoning. Serve immediately with toast or granary rolls and butter.

Tregaron broth

Overall timing 1 hour

Freezing Not suitable

To serve 6

1 lb	Streaky bacon	450 g
1 lb	Shin beef	450 g
1 oz	Butter	25 g
1	Large leek	1
1 lb	Potatoes	450 g
8 oz	Carrots	225 g
8 oz	Parsnips	225 g
1	Small swede	1
3 pints	Water	1.7 litres
1	Small white cabbage	1
2 oz	Fine or medium oatmeal	50 g
	Salt and pepper	

Derind the bacon and cut into 1 inch (2.5 cm) pieces. Trim the beef and cut into chunks. Melt the butter in a large saucepan and fry the bacon and beef for 5 minutes.

Meanwhile, trim and slice the leek. Peel the potatoes, carrots, parsnips and swede. Cut into chunks. Add vegetables to pan and fry for 5 minutes. Add the water and bring to the boil.

Shred the cabbage and add to the pan with the oatmeal and seasoning. Cover and simmer for 45 minutes. Adjust the seasoning to taste before serving.

Turkish soup with meatballs

Overall timing 1¾ hours

Freezing Not suitable

To serve 4–6

1	Knuckle of veal	1
1 lb	Shin of beef	450 g
1	Large onion	1
2	Large carrots	2
1	Stalk of celery	1
	Parsley stalks	
	Salt and pepper	
2	Eggs	2
3 tbsp	Lemon juice	3x15 ml
Meatballs		
1 lb	Minced beef	450 g
4 oz	Cooked long grain rice	125 g
1	Egg	1
1 tbsp	Chopped parsley	15 ml
¼ teasp	Grated nutmeg	1.25 ml
	Salt and pepper	
1 oz	Butter	25 g
2 tbsp	Oil	2x15 ml

Chop knuckle in half lengthways. Dice beef. Peel and chop onion and carrots; chop celery. Put meat and vegetables into a saucepan with 4 pints (2.2 litres) water, parsley stalks and seasoning. Cover and simmer for 45 minutes.

Meanwhile, mix beef with rice, egg, parsley, nutmeg and seasoning to a stiff paste and shape into small balls.

Heat butter and oil in a frying pan. Add meatballs and fry till browned all over.

Strain stock, discarding meat and vegetables. Return to pan and bring back to boil. Add meatballs and simmer for 15 minutes.

Put the eggs and lemon juice into a tureen and gradually stir in soup.

Chicken, lemon and egg drop soup

Overall timing 2 hours 10 minutes

Freezing Suitable: add eggs after reheating

To serve 6

1 lb	Knuckle of veal	450 g
3½ pints	Water	2 litres
3 lb	Boiling chicken with giblets	1.4 kg
1	Lemon	1
2	Onions	2
2	Cloves	2
	Salt and pepper	
2	Eggs	2

Place knuckle in saucepan with the water. Bring to the boil, then cover and simmer for 1 hour.

Meanwhile, chop the chicken into joints and remove skin if liked. Wash giblets. Grate the rind of the lemon and squeeze out the juice. Reserve both. Peel onions and spike each with a clove. Add chicken, giblets, lemon rind, spiked onions and seasoning to pan. Cover and cook gently for 1 hour till chicken is tender.

Strain the stock into a clean pan. Cut meats into small pieces, discarding bones, skin, giblets and onions. Skim stock, add meats and bring to the boil. Stir in lemon juice, then taste and adjust seasoning.

Beat the eggs in a small bowl. Remove saucepan from heat and pour soup into tureen. Drizzle egg in a thin stream into soup, stirring continuously. Serve.

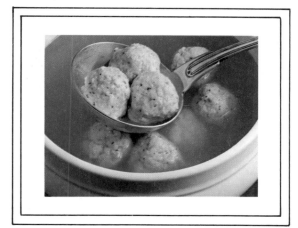

Chicken noodle soup

Overall timing 10 minutes

Freezing Not suitable

To serve 4

2½ pints	Chicken stock	1.5 litres
3 oz	Fine egg noodles	75 g
2 tbsp	Lemon juice	2x15 ml
	Salt and pepper	
2 tbsp	Chopped parsley	2x15 ml

Put the stock into a large saucepan. Bring to the boil and add the noodles. Boil for 3–4 minutes till tender.

Add the lemon juice and seasoning and sprinkle with chopped parsley. Serve with a side dish of grated mature Cheddar cheese.

Bacon dumpling soup

Overall timing 2¾ hours

Freezing Suitable: add dumplings to stock after thawing

To serve 4

12 oz	Stale white bread	350 g
½ pint	Milk	300 ml
2 oz	Lean bacon rashers	50 g
1 oz	Butter	25 g
1	Onion	1
1	Garlic clove	1
1 tbsp	Chopped parsley	15 ml
¼ teasp	Dried marjoram	1.25 ml
	Salt and pepper	
3	Eggs	3
4 oz	Self-raising flour	125 g
2 pints	Stock	1.1 litres

Remove crusts from bread, then soak in milk for 2 hours. Derind and chop bacon. Fry in butter till crisp.

Peel and finely chop onion. Peel and crush garlic. Put both into bowl with bread, bacon, parsley and marjoram. Season and add eggs. Mix together well. Sift in flour and stir until absorbed.

Heat the stock in a large saucepan. Make the bacon mixture into 1 inch (2.5 cm) balls and roll them in a little flour so they don't fall apart when cooking. Add the dumplings to the stock and simmer for 15 minutes. Serve hot.

Tuscan vegetable soup

Overall timing 2 hours plus overnight soaking

Freezing Not suitable

To serve 6

8 oz	Dried beans	225 g
1¼ lb	Cabbage	600 g
1	Onion	1
1	Large leek	1
1	Stalk of celery	1
1	Carrot	1
1	Garlic clove	1
3 tbsp	Oil	3x15 ml
1	Bay leaf	1
3	Sprigs of oregano	3
	Sprig of rosemary	
	Salt and pepper	
2 tbsp	Tomato purée	2x15 ml
3 pints	Light stock	1.7 litres

Soak beans in cold water overnight. The next day, drain beans, put into a large saucepan and cover with fresh cold water. Bring to the boil and simmer for about 1½ hours till tender.

Meanwhile, shred cabbage. Peel and thinly slice onion; trim and slice leek and celery. Scrape and chop carrot. Peel and crush garlic. Heat oil in a large saucepan and fry vegetables, except cabbage, with garlic and herbs till lightly browned. Add cabbage and seasoning and fry for a further 5 minutes.

Remove herbs from pan and add the tomato purée, drained beans and stock. Bring to the boil and simmer for a further 15 minutes. Taste and adjust the seasoning and pour into warmed individual bowls.

Watercress soup

Overall timing 40 minutes

Freezing Suitable: add cream after thawing

To serve 4

1	Large onion	1
2	Large floury potatoes	2
1 oz	Butter	25 g
3	Bunches of watercress	3
1¾ pints	Chicken stock	1 litre
	Salt and pepper	
4 fl oz	Double cream	113 ml

Peel and finely chop onion. Peel and chop or grate potatoes. Melt butter in a saucepan, add onions and potatoes and turn till coated in butter. Cover and cook gently for 10 minutes.

Wash, dry and chop watercress leaves and stalks, reserving some whole leaves. Add to pan with stock and bring to boil. Cover and simmer for 15 minutes.

Rub soup through sieve or purée in blender. Return to pan, add reserved watercress leaves and reheat. Taste and adjust seasoning. Serve immediately with side dish of whipped cream, or cool, stir in cream and chill well before serving.

Rice and cabbage soup

Overall timing 45 minutes

Freezing Not suitable

To serve 6–8

1	Large onion	1
8 oz	Streaky bacon	225 g
1	Garlic clove	1
2 oz	Butter	50 g
8 oz	Long grain rice	225 g
3 pints	Light stock	1.7 litres
	Salt and pepper	
	Bouquet garni	
1 lb	Green cabbage	450 g
4 oz	Cheese	125 g

Peel and chop the onion; derind and finely dice the bacon. Peel and crush garlic. Melt the butter in a saucepan and add the onion, bacon and garlic. Fry gently for 5 minutes without browning.

Add the rice and cook, stirring, for 2 minutes till coated with butter. Add the stock, seasoning and bouquet garni. Bring to the boil and simmer for 15 minutes.

Meanwhile, coarsely shred the cabbage. Add to the pan, bring to the boil again and simmer for 5 minutes.

Remove pan from the heat and discard the bouquet garni. Grate cheese, stir into soup and adjust seasoning. Pour into a tureen and serve immediately with rye bread.

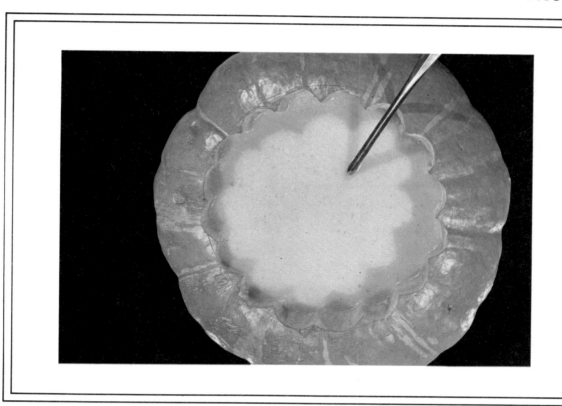

Pumpkin soup

Overall timing 50 minutes

Freezing Not suitable

To serve 6

2 lb	Pumpkin or other squash	900 g
½ pint	Water	300 ml
	Salt and pepper	
1½ pints	Milk	850 ml
1 teasp	Sugar	5 ml
¼ teasp	Grated nutmeg	1.25 ml
1	Egg yolk	1
4 tbsp	Single cream	4 x 15 ml

Prepare the squash, discarding fibrous centre and seeds. Cut the flesh into chunks, put into a saucepan with the water and salt and bring to the boil. Simmer for about 30 minutes till tender, then purée in a blender or food mill. Place purée in saucepan with milk, sugar and nutmeg. Heat through gently till almost boiling, stirring occasionally.

Beat the egg yolk and cream together in a bowl and pour in a little of the hot soup, stirring constantly. Pour back into the pan and stir over a low heat for 3 minutes – do not boil. Taste and adjust seasoning, then serve immediately with toasted rye bread.

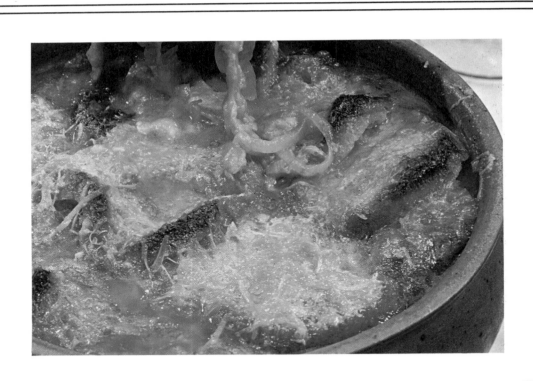

Onion soup with wine

Overall timing 45 minutes

Freezing Suitable: pour soup over bread and add cheese after reheating

To serve 4

3	Large onions	3
2 oz	Butter	50 g
1 tbsp	Plain flour	15 ml
½ teasp	Brown sugar	2.5 ml
2½ pints	Water	1.5 litres
8	Slices of French bread	8
2 tbsp	Dry white wine	2x15 ml
	Salt and pepper	
2 oz	Gruyère or Cheddar cheese	50 g

Peel and slice onions. Melt half the butter in a large saucepan and cook onions till transparent. Sprinkle onions with flour. Cook, stirring, until flour colours. Add sugar, then gradually stir in water. Simmer for 20 minutes.

Preheat the oven to 450°F (230°C) Gas 8.

Fry bread in remaining butter. Place bread slices in bottom of individual bowls or ovenproof soup tureen. Add wine and seasoning, then pour soup over bread. Grate cheese and sprinkle it into the bowls. Bake for 5–10 minutes to melt the cheese.

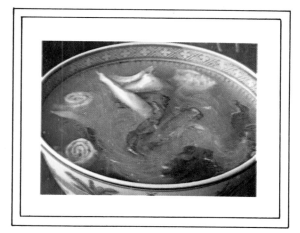

Mushroom soup

Overall timing 30 minutes

Freezing Not suitable

To serve 4

2	Stalks of celery	2
8 oz	Mushrooms	225 g
2 teasp	Oil	2x5 ml
12 oz	Cooked chicken meat	350 g
1 tbsp	Soy sauce	15 ml
1 tbsp	Dry sherry	15 ml
8	Water chestnuts	8
1¾ pints	Chicken stock	1 litre
4 oz	Bean sprouts	125 g
	Salt and pepper	
1	Egg	1

Finely chop celery. Thinly slice mushrooms. Heat oil in a saucepan and stir-fry vegetables for 5 minutes.

Cut chicken into small pieces and sprinkle with soy sauce and sherry. Quarter or dice water chestnuts.

Add stock to pan with water chestnuts. Bring to the boil, then add chicken and soaking juices. Simmer for 10 minutes. Add bean sprouts and cook for 2 minutes. Taste and adjust seasoning.

Beat egg. Remove pan from heat and trickle in beaten egg, stirring constantly. Divide soup between individual soup bowls and serve.

Chicken vermicelli soup

Overall timing 40 minutes

Freezing Not suitable

To serve 6

1 oz	Chinese dried mushrooms	25 g
2½ pints	Chicken stock	1.5 litres
6 oz	Cooked chicken meat	175 g
2	Lettuce leaves	2
4	Eggs	4
	Salt and pepper	
1 oz	Butter	25 g
2 oz	Chinese vermicelli	50 g
2 tbsp	Dry sherry	2x15 ml

Soak mushrooms in warm water for 30 minutes. Drain, discard woody stalks and put into saucepan with stock. Bring to the boil and simmer for 10 minutes.

Meanwhile, cut chicken into strips. Shred lettuce. Beat eggs with seasoning. Melt half butter in frying pan, add half egg mixture and make a thin omelette. Remove from pan and reserve. Use remaining butter and egg mixture to make another omelette. Roll up both omelettes and cut into thin slices.

Add noodles and chicken to saucepan and simmer for 2 minutes. Remove from heat and add sherry, omelette strips and lettuce. Serve immediately.

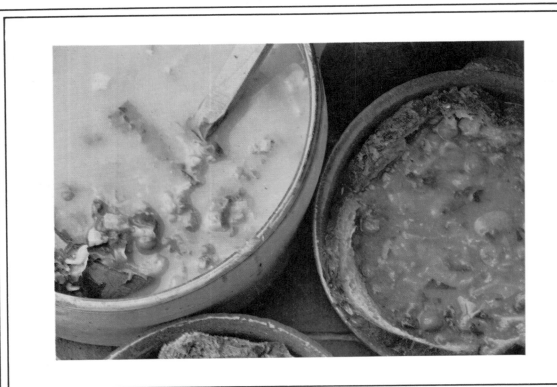

Majorcan vegetable and bread soup

Overall timing 1½ hours

Freezing Not suitable

To serve 6

8 oz	Continental lentils	225 g
3 pints	Water	1.7 litres
4 oz	Streaky bacon rashers	125 g
1 lb	Fresh broad beans	450 g
1 lb	Fresh peas	450 g
1 lb	Cabbage	450 g
8 oz	Fresh spinach	225 g
	Salt and pepper	
18	Thin slices of brown bread	18

Wash and pick over the lentils and put into a saucepan with the water. Bring to the boil and simmer for 45 minutes.

Meanwhile, derind and dice the bacon. Shell the beans and peas. Shred the cabbage and spinach.

Rub the lentils with their cooking liquor through a sieve or purée in a blender. Return to the saucepan and add seasoning, bacon and vegetables and bring to the boil. Simmer for about 25 minutes till the vegetables are tender.

Taste and adjust the seasoning. Arrange three slices of bread in each soup bowl and pour the soup over. Serve immediately.

Irish celery soup

Overall timing 35 minutes

Freezing Suitable: add cream when reheating

To serve 4

1 lb	Celery	450 g
2	Potatoes	2
2	Onions	2
2 oz	Butter	50 g
	Salt and pepper	
1	Bay leaf	1
1	Garlic clove	1
	Grated nutmeg	
1¾ pints	Chicken stock	1 litre
¼ pint	Carton of single cream	150 ml

Cut off base of celery, then wash and chop stalks and leaves. Peel and finely chop potatoes and onions. Melt butter in saucepan over a low heat. Add celery stalks and leaves, potatoes and onions, cover and cook for 5 minutes, stirring to prevent colouring.

Sprinkle with salt and pepper, add the bay leaf, peeled and crushed garlic, pinch of nutmeg and hot stock (made with 2 cubes if necessary). Cover and simmer for 20 minutes.

Remove bay leaf. Push soup through sieve into a bowl, or liquidize, then return to saucepan and add the cream. Heat through without boiling. Adjust seasoning, then serve with croûtons (diced bread fried in oil till brown).

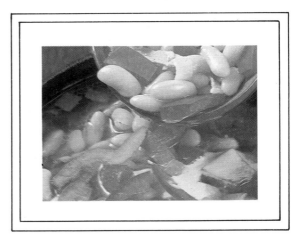

Cheese soup

Overall timing 30 minutes

Freezing Not suitable

To serve 4–6

1	Onion	1
3 oz	Butter	75 g
1½ pints	Light stock	850 ml
¼ pint	Dry white wine	150 ml
4 teasp	Cornflour	4x5 ml
½ pint	Milk	300 ml
	Salt and white pepper	
4 oz	Cheddar cheese	125 g
4 oz	Parmesan cheese	125 g
	Croûtons	

Peel and finely chop the onion. Melt the butter in a saucepan, add onion and fry till transparent. Stir in the stock and wine and bring to the boil slowly.

Blend the cornflour with a little water and add to the pan, stirring constantly. Bring back to the boil, stirring, and cook for 3 minutes. Add the milk, salt, pepper and grated cheese. Stir over a very low heat till the cheese has completely melted. Taste and adjust seasoning, then pour into a warmed tureen. Serve immediately garnished with lots of croûtons.

Bean soup

Overall timing 30 minutes

Freezing Suitable: add soured cream after thawing

To serve 4

4 oz	Streaky bacon	125 g
1	Red pepper	1
1	Green pepper	1
1¾ pints	Strong beef stock	1 litre
12 oz	Can of butter beans	340 g
	Tabasco sauce	
	Salt	
4 tbsp	Soured cream	4x15 ml

Derind and chop bacon and fry it lightly in a frying pan till the fat runs. Place in a deep saucepan.

Deseed and finely chop half the red and green peppers and add to the pan with the stock (made up with 3 stock cubes if necessary) and drained beans. Bring to the boil and simmer for 20 minutes.

Add Tabasco sauce and salt to taste.

Slice remaining peppers and blanch for 5 minutes in boiling water. Drain well.

Remove soup from the heat and stir in the soured cream. Garnish with pepper slices and serve with a bowl of grated cheese and fresh wholemeal bread.

Barley and mushroom soup

Overall timing 3 hours 50 minutes

Freezing Suitable: add butter and cream after reheating

To serve 4

3 oz	Pearl barley	75 g
	Salt	
2	Carrots	2
2	Celery stalks	2
1	Leek	1
1	Onion	1
2	Bay leaves	2
10	Black peppercorns	10
1	Sprig of parsley	1
1½ oz	Dried mushrooms	40 g
2 tbsp .	Vinegar	2 x 15 ml
2 oz	Butter	50 g
¼ pint	Carton of single cream	150 ml

Wash barley, then cook in lightly salted, boiling water for 2½ hours till very soft and gelatinous.

Meanwhile, scrape and chop carrots. Wash and slice celery and leek. Peel and quarter onion. Put all vegetables into a saucepan with bay leaves, salt, peppercorns, parsley, mushrooms and 9 fl oz (250 ml) water. Cover and simmer gently for 1 hour.

Strain stock into a bowl. Reserve mushrooms and discard remaining vegetables. Slice mushrooms and return to pan with strained stock.

Drain barley and crush with a potato masher, or partly liquidize in a blender. Add barley and vinegar to stock, heat through and season.

Cut butter into small pieces and put in bottom of a warmed soup tureen. Pour in soup, stir in cream and serve.

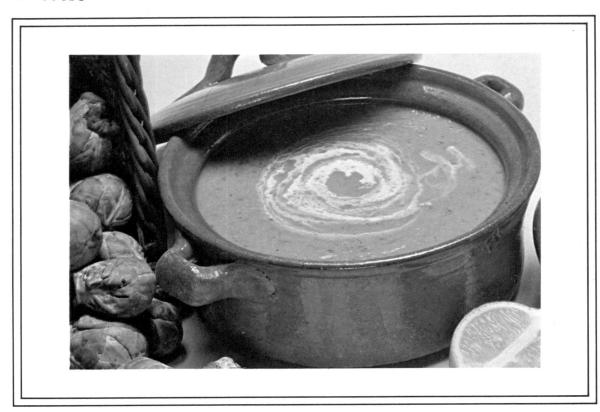

Brussels sprout soup

Overall timing 1¼ hours

Freezing Suitable: add cream and egg yolk mixture when reheating

To serve 4

1 lb	Brussels sprouts	450 g
3 oz	Butter	75 g
1¾ pints	Hot beef stock	1 litre
	Salt	
1 oz	Plain flour	25 g
	Grated nutmeg	
6 tbsp	Single cream	6 x 15 ml
1	Egg yolk	1

Trim sprouts. Cut a cross in base of each. Melt 2 oz (50 g) butter in a saucepan, add sprouts and cook for 3 minutes, stirring continuously. Add stock and salt. Cover and cook for 40 minutes.

Sieve sprouts into a bowl, or liquidize.

Melt remaining butter in a pan. Add flour and cook, stirring, for 3 minutes. Remove pan from heat and gradually add sprout purée. Return to heat and cook for 10 minutes over low heat. Season with salt and pinch of nutmeg.

Mix cream with egg yolk. Off heat, stir cream mixture into soup to thicken.

Baked eggs in potatoes

Overall timing 2 hours

Freezing Not suitable

To serve 4

4x10oz	Potatoes	4x275g
2oz	Butter	50g
	Salt and pepper	
2oz	Cheese	50g
4	Small eggs	4
4 tbsp	Double cream	4x15ml
2 teasp	Chopped chives	2x5ml

Preheat the oven to 400°F (200°C) Gas 6.

Scrub and dry the potatoes and push a metal skewer lengthways through each one. Place on a baking tray and rub a little of the butter over the skins. Bake for 1–1¼ hours.

Remove from the oven. Increase the temperature to 450°F (230°C) Gas 8.

Cut a slice lengthways off each potato and scoop out the insides, leaving a shell about ½ inch (12.5mm) thick. Mash the scooped-out potato (plus any from the lids) in a bowl with the remaining butter and seasoning. Grate cheese and beat into potato mixture.

Press the mixture back into the potato shells, leaving a hollow in the centre large enough for an egg. Place on baking tray. Carefully break an egg into each potato. Season and spoon the cream over. Return to the oven and bake for 8–10 minutes till the eggs are lightly set. Sprinkle the chives over and serve hot.

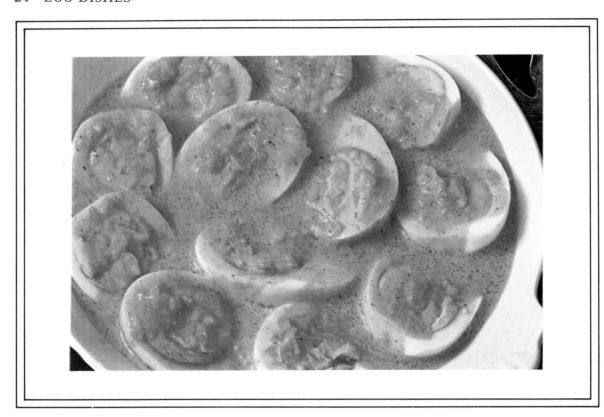

Curried eggs

Overall timing 35 minutes

Freezing Not suitable

To serve 4

6	Eggs	6
2	Onions	2
2 oz	Butter	50 g
2 teasp	Curry powder	2x5 ml
1 pint	Chicken stock	560 ml
1 teasp	Cornflour	5 ml
4 fl oz	Carton of single cream or top of milk	120 ml
	Salt and pepper	

Place eggs in a saucepan of cold water. Bring to the boil and simmer for 8 minutes, then drain.

Peel and finely chop onions. Melt butter in a frying pan, add onions, cover and cook until golden over a low heat (about 15 minutes).

Sprinkle with curry powder and cook for 2 minutes, stirring. Pour in the stock and simmer for 10 minutes. Mix cornflour and cream or milk together well, then stir into curry mixture with seasoning. Heat gently but do not boil.

Shell eggs and cut in half lengthways. Remove yolks with a spoon and mash yolks and a little of the curry mixture together with a fork. Spoon back into egg whites. Place eggs in curry sauce and heat through without boiling. Serve with rice or hot buttered toast.

Deep-fried eggs

Overall timing 15 minutes

Freezing Not suitable

To serve 4

	Oil for frying	
8	Eggs	8
	Salt and pepper	
2	Tomatoes	2
	Sprigs of parsley	

Half-fill a shallow frying pan with oil and heat to 370°F (188°C) or until a cube of bread browns in 1 minute. Swirl fat round with a spoon. Break an egg into a cup and carefully slide into the hot oil. Cook for 1–2 minutes, basting with the hot oil all the time and turning the egg once or twice.

Remove from pan with a draining spoon and drain on kitchen paper. Sprinkle with salt and pepper. Keep hot while you fry remaining eggs in the same way. Garnish with tomato wedges and parsley sprigs and serve hot with toast.

Lettuce and egg pipérade

Overall timing 15 minutes

Freezing Not suitable

To serve 4

1	Onion	1
1	Small round lettuce	1
2 oz	Butter	50 g
1 tbsp	Chopped parsley	15 ml
4 oz	Frozen peas	125 g
4	Eggs	4
	Salt and pepper	
8 oz	Hot mashed potatoes	225 g

Peel and finely chop the onion. Wash, trim and shred lettuce.

Melt the butter in a frying pan. Add onion and cook till transparent. Add shredded lettuce, parsley and peas. Cook, stirring, for 5 minutes.

Lightly beat eggs in a bowl and season. Stir into pan, reduce heat and cook, stirring, until egg is lightly scrambled. Remove from heat and arrange on warmed serving dish.

Pipe or spoon mashed potato round the edge of the dish and serve immediately.

Eggs florentine

Overall timing 45 minutes

Freezing Not suitable

To serve 4

2 lb	Spinach	900 g
2 oz	Butter	50 g
	Salt	
¼ teasp	Grated nutmeg	1.25 ml
1½ oz	Plain flour	40 g
¾ pint	Milk	400 ml
3 oz	Cheese	75 g
	Cayenne pepper	
½ teasp	Made mustard	2.5 ml
8	Hard-boiled eggs	8
2 tbsp	Fresh white breadcrumbs	2x15 ml

Preheat the oven to 425°F (220°C) Gas 7.

Wash spinach well in several changes of water. Remove any coarse stalks. Put into saucepan with only the water that still clings to the spinach after washing. Cook for 5–10 minutes till tender. Stir in ½ oz (15 g) of the butter and season with salt and grated nutmeg, then spread over the bottom of a greased ovenproof dish.

Melt remaining butter in a pan. Stir in the flour and cook for 1 minute. Gradually add the milk, bring to the boil, stirring, and cook for 2 minutes.

Grate cheese. Reserve 2 tbsp (2x15 ml) for the topping and stir the rest into the sauce with a pinch each of salt and cayenne and the mustard.

Shell eggs and arrange on top of spinach. Pour sauce over eggs. Mix reserved grated cheese and breadcrumbs and sprinkle over the top. Bake for 10 minutes till cheese is bubbly and golden. Serve immediately.

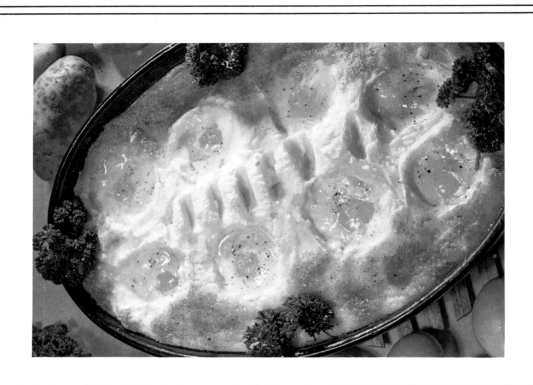

Eggs in a nest

Overall timing 50 minutes

Freezing Not suitable

To serve 4

2 lb	Potatoes	900 g
	Salt and pepper	
½ pint	Milk	300 ml
3 oz	Butter	75 g
8	Eggs	8
2 tbsp	Dried breadcrumbs	2 x 15 ml
	Grated nutmeg	
	Parsley	

Peel the potatoes. Put into a pan of salted water, bring to the boil and cook for 25 minutes. Drain.

Preheat the oven to 425°F (220°C) Gas 7. Grease ovenproof dish.

Add milk to the potatoes and return to low heat. Mash the potatoes and beat in 2 oz (50 g) of the butter until smooth and creamy. Season to taste.

Spread creamed potatoes in ovenproof dish. Using the back of a spoon, hollow out eight "nests" for the eggs. Break an egg into each of the "nests". Sprinkle with breadcrumbs, dot with remaining butter and season with salt, pepper and nutmeg.

Bake for 8–9 minutes or until the eggs are lightly set. Garnish with parsley.

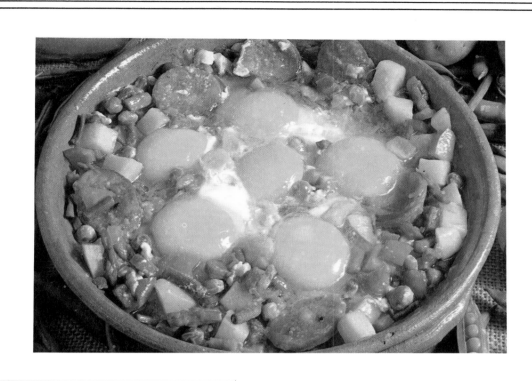

Flamenco eggs

Overall timing 45 minutes

Freezing Not suitable

To serve 4-6

1	Onion	1
4 oz	Back bacon	125 g
2 tbsp	Oil	2x15 ml
8 oz	Can of tomatoes	227 g
2	Potatoes	2
1	Small red pepper	1
2 oz	Runner beans	50 g
2 tbsp	Frozen peas	2x15 ml
2 tbsp	Canned asparagus tips	2x15 ml
6 oz	Chorizo or other spicy sausage	175 g
3 tbsp	Dry sherry	3x15 ml
	Salt and pepper	
6	Eggs	6

Peel and finely chop onion. Derind and dice bacon.

Heat oil in a saucepan or flameproof casserole. Add onion and bacon and cook till golden. Add tomatoes, mashing them into the onion/bacon mixture till well combined.

Peel potatoes and cut into small dice. Wash, deseed and chop pepper. Wash beans. Top and tail them and remove strings. Cut into short lengths. Add potatoes, pepper, beans and peas to pan and cook for 10 minutes.

Add asparagus tips, sliced sausage and sherry. Season and cook for a further 5 minutes.

Break eggs carefully on top of the mixture. Cook for 5 minutes more or until the eggs are lightly set.

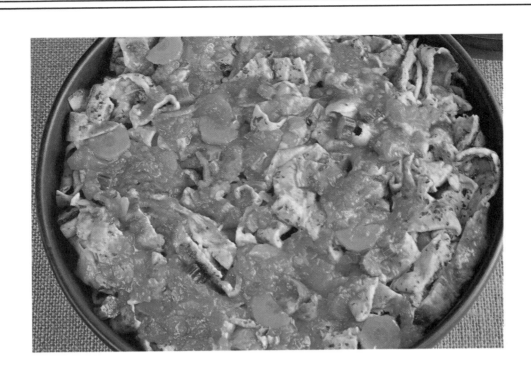

Italian shredded omelette

Overall timing 35 minutes

Freezing Not suitable

To serve 4

1	Small onion	1
1	Garlic clove	1
1	Stalk of celery	1
1	Carrot	1
2 oz	Streaky bacon rashers	50 g
1 tbsp	Oil	15 ml
14 oz	Can of tomatoes	397 g
	Salt and pepper	
9	Eggs	9
1 teasp	Chopped fresh mint	5 ml
3 tbsp	Chopped parsley	3x15 ml
2 oz	Butter	50 g

Peel and finely chop the onion. Peel and crush the garlic. Trim and chop the celery. Scrape and thinly slice the carrot. Derind and finely chop the bacon.

Heat the oil in a saucepan, add the bacon and vegetables and fry gently for 5 minutes. Add the tomatoes and juice, garlic and seasoning, bring to the boil and simmer for 20 minutes, stirring to break up the tomatoes.

Meanwhile, lightly beat the eggs in a bowl with the mint, parsley and seasoning. Melt one-third of the butter in a frying pan. Add one-third of the egg mixture and cook over a moderate heat, drawing the liquid into the centre as the mixture begins to set. When set, slide the omelette on to a board. Make two more omelettes in the same way.

Roll the omelettes loosely and cut into strips about ½ inch (12.5 mm) wide. Add to the tomato sauce and heat through for 3 minutes. Season to taste and pour into a warmed serving dish.

Minted cheese omelette

Overall timing 20 minutes

Freezing Not suitable

To serve 2

10	Fresh mint leaves	10
6	Eggs	6
1 oz	Fresh breadcrumbs	25 g
4 oz	Cheese	125 g
	Salt and pepper	
1 tbsp	Chopped parsley	15 ml
1 oz	Butter	25 g

Wash, dry and roughly chop the mint leaves. Lightly beat the eggs in a bowl with the breadcrumbs, grated cheese and seasoning. Stir in the parsley and mint and leave to stand for 5 minutes.

Melt the butter in a frying pan and pour in the egg mixture (or only half if making two omelettes). Tip the pan so that the bottom is coated and cook over a moderate heat until lightly set.

Using a large fish slice, carefully turn the omelette over and cook for 2 minutes more. Serve with tomato salad and wholemeal rolls.

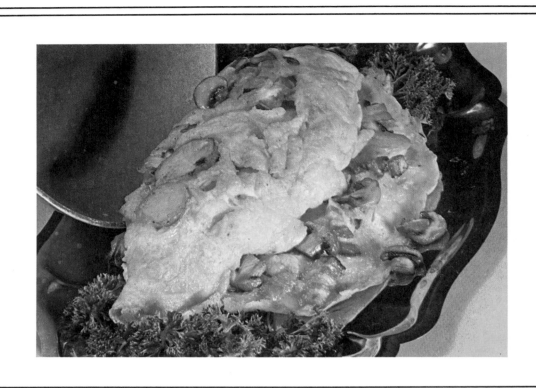

Omelette forestière

Overall timing 25 minutes

Freezing Not suitable

To serve 2

4 oz	Thick streaky bacon rashers	125 g
4 oz	Button mushrooms	125 g
2	Small potatoes	2
2 oz	Butter	50 g
4–6	Eggs	4–6
1 tbsp	Chopped parsley	15 ml
	Salt and pepper	

Derind bacon, then cut into thin strips. Thinly slice mushrooms. Peel and thinly slice potatoes. Melt the butter in a frying pan, add potatoes and bacon and fry till tender and golden all over. Add mushrooms and cook for 5 minutes more.

Meanwhile, lightly beat the eggs in a bowl with parsley and seasoning. Pour over the ingredients in the frying pan. Cook for a few minutes, lifting the edges to ensure the underneath is evenly cooked. Fold over and slide on to warmed serving plate. Serve immediately.

CHEESE DISHES

Anchovy brochettes

Overall timing 30 minutes

Freezing Not suitable

To serve 2

4	Large slices of white bread	4
4 oz	Mozzarella or Gouda cheese	125 g
3 oz	Butter	75 g
	Salt and pepper	
8	Anchovy fillets	8
4 tbsp	Milk	4x15 ml

Preheat the oven to 400°F (200°C) Gas 6.

Cut bread and cheese into small squares. Thread alternately on to four skewers. Arrange in an ovenproof dish so that each end of the skewer is supported by the rim.

Melt half of the butter and brush generously over the brochettes. Season with salt and pepper. Bake for about 15–20 minutes, basting occasionally with butter in dish. The brochettes should be golden brown.

Meanwhile, melt remaining butter in a saucepan. Mash anchovies and add to butter. Gradually add milk and mix well together over gentle heat. Bring to boiling point.

Pour hot anchovy sauce over brochettes and serve immediately.

Welsh rarebit

Overall timing 30 minutes

Freezing Not suitable

To serve 4

8	Slices of bread	8
3 oz	Butter	75 g
12 oz	Cheddar cheese	350 g
½ teasp	Ground mace	2.5 ml
	Pinch of powdered mustard	
5 tbsp	Beer	5x15 ml
	Pepper	

Preheat the oven to 400°F (200°C) Gas 6.

Toast the bread, and butter the slices while still hot. Place on baking tray.

Cut the cheese into small cubes and put in a saucepan with mace, mustard and beer. Cook over a low heat, stirring with a wooden spoon, until cheese melts and is thick and creamy. Spread mixture over toast. Sprinkle generously with pepper and bake for 10 minutes. Serve immediately.

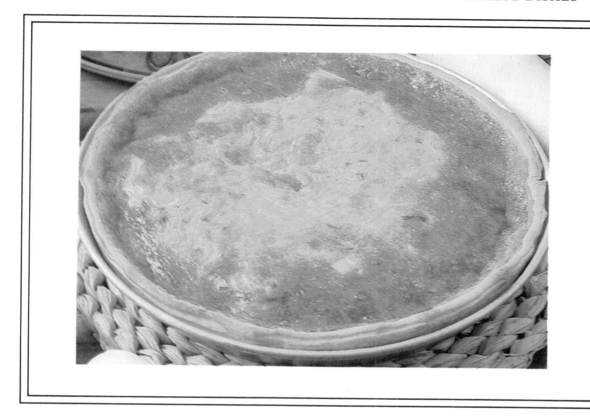

Cheese flan

Overall timing 1½ hours

Freezing Suitable: reheat in 425°F (220°C) Gas 7 oven for 10–15 minutes

To serve 4–6

5 oz	Butter	150 g
¼ pint	Water	150 ml
	Salt and pepper	
8 oz	Self-raising flour	225 g
2	Medium-size onions	2
1 tbsp	Plain flour	15 ml
4 fl oz	Milk	120 ml
3	Eggs	3
¼ teasp	Grated nutmeg	1.25 ml
	Cayenne pepper	
4 oz	Cheddar cheese	125 g
4 oz	Gruyere cheese	125 g

Melt 4 oz (125 g) of the butter. Cool slightly, then stir in 3 tbsp (3x15 ml) of the water and salt. Sift self-raising flour into a bowl. Slowly add butter mixture and mix until smooth. Chill for 30 minutes.

Preheat the oven to 350°F (180°C) Gas 4.

Peel and chop onions. Melt remaining butter in a saucepan and fry onions for 10 minutes until soft. Cool.

Mix plain flour and a little of the milk in a bowl, then add the rest of the milk and the remaining water. Separate the eggs. Mix the yolks into the flour and milk mixture. Season with salt, pepper, nutmeg and a pinch of cayenne. Beat egg whites till stiff, then fold into yolk mixture.

Roll out dough and use to line a greased 9 inch (23 cm) flan tin. Spread onions over bottom of flan, then grate both sorts of cheese on top. Cover with egg and milk mixture.

Bake for 15 minutes. Reduce heat to 325°F (170°C) Gas 3 and bake for a further 45 minutes. Serve hot.

Gnocchi

Overall timing 50 minutes plus cooling

Freezing Suitable: bake from frozen, allowing 1 hour

To serve 4

1½ pints	Milk	850 ml
6 oz	Coarse semolina	175 g
	Salt and pepper	
	Grated nutmeg	
6 oz	Grated Parmesan cheese	175 g
1	Egg yolk	1
2 tbsp	Milk	2 x 15 ml

Heat milk just to boiling in a saucepan, then sprinkle on semolina. Season with salt, pepper and nutmeg. Cook gently, stirring, for 4–5 minutes till mixture becomes solid. Remove pan from heat and beat in 4 oz (125 g) of the cheese. Pour into a greased Swiss roll tin. Leave in a cool place (not the refrigerator) for 45 minutes to 1 hour till cold.

Preheat the oven to 400°F (200°C) Gas 6.

Cut the cooled mixture into about 20 rounds, 2½ inches (6.5 cm) in diameter. Arrange the rounds, overlapping them, in a greased round ovenproof dish. Beat egg yolk and milk and pour over. Sprinkle with the rest of the cheese and bake for 30 minutes till golden brown. Serve immediately.

Gougère

Overall timing 1½ hours

Freezing Not suitable

To serve 6

7 fl oz	Water	200 ml
½ teasp	Salt	2.5 ml
4 oz	Butter	125 g
3½ oz	Plain flour	100 g
4	Eggs	4
8 oz	Gruyère cheese	225 g

Preheat oven to 400°F (200°C) Gas 6.

Put water and salt into a saucepan, with 3 oz (75 g) of the butter, chopped. Bring to the boil, stirring to melt the butter. Remove from heat and quickly add the flour all at once, stirring well. Return pan to heat and beat till the paste is smooth and leaves the sides of the pan cleanly. Remove from heat and allow to cool slightly.

Add three of the eggs, one at a time, beating well between additions. Grate 5 oz (150 g) of the cheese and stir into the paste.

With a large spoon, make a ring of the paste on a greased baking tray. Beat the remaining egg and brush over paste. Dice remaining cheese and place on top of the paste with tiny pieces of the remaining butter.

Bake for 20 minutes, then lower heat to 375°F (190°C) Gas 5, and bake for a further 20–25 minutes. Serve hot.

Deep-fried Mozzarella sandwiches

Overall timing 20 minutes

Freezing Not suitable

To serve 4

8	Slices of bread	8
4	Slices of Mozzarella cheese	4
	Plain flour	
1	Egg	1
	Oil for deep frying	

Remove the crusts from the bread. Make four sandwiches with the cheese and coat all over with flour. Beat the egg in a shallow dish. Dip in the sandwiches so the sides and edges are all coated.

Heat oil in a deep-fryer to 360°F (180°C). Deep fry the sandwiches until they are golden brown. Drain on kitchen paper and serve hot, with salad.

Italian deep-fried cheese

Overall timing 1¼ hours plus chilling

Freezing Not suitable

To serve 2

½	Onion	½
1 oz	Butter	25 g
2 oz	Long grain rice	50 g
4 fl oz	Chicken stock	120 ml
1 teasp	Grated Parmesan cheese	5 ml
	Pinch of grated nutmeg	
	Salt and pepper	
1 oz	Lean cooked ham	25 g
1½ oz	Mozzarella cheese	40 g
1	Egg	1
1 oz	Fine fresh breadcrumbs	25 g
	Oil for deep frying	

Peel and finely chop onion. Melt butter in a saucepan and fry onion till transparent.

Add rice and stir over a low heat for 2 minutes. Stir in stock, cover and bring to the boil. Simmer gently for 15–20 minutes till rice is tender. Remove from heat and stir in Parmesan, nutmeg and seasoning. Leave to cool completely.

Meanwhile, chop ham finely. Cut Mozzarella into four sticks about 1½ inches (4 cm) long and ½ inch (12.5 mm) thick. Break egg on to a plate and beat lightly with a fork. Spread breadcrumbs on another plate.

Beat a little egg and the ham into rice. Put 2 tbsp (2x15 ml) rice mixture in palm of one hand. Place a cheese stick on top and cover with more rice. Pat into a cylinder shape about 2½ inches (6.5 cm) long and 1 inch (2.5 cm) thick. Brush beaten egg over croquette, then coat with breadcrumbs. Shape and coat three more croquettes. Chill for 1 hour.

Heat oil in a deep-fryer to 360°F (180°C). Fry the croquettes for 5–6 minutes till golden. Drain on kitchen paper and serve hot.

Basque cod casserole

Overall timing 1 hour

Freezing Not suitable

To serve 4–6

1 lb	Cod fillets	450 g
	Bouquet garni	
	Salt and pepper	
4	Large potatoes	4
2	Hard-boiled eggs	2
3	Tomatoes	3
3 oz	Butter	75 g
3	Garlic cloves	3
2 oz	Black olives	50 g
2 tbsp	Capers	2x15 ml
1 tbsp	Chopped parsley	15 ml
2 tbsp	Lemon juice	2x15 ml

Place cod in a saucepan and cover with water. Add bouquet garni and seasoning and bring slowly to the boil. Remove pan from heat and leave to cool.

Meanwhile, cook unpeeled potatoes in boiling salted water for 30 minutes. Drain well, then peel and slice potatoes. Shell and slice eggs. Blanch, peel and chop tomatoes.

Melt 1 oz (25 g) butter in a pan and fry tomatoes. Season with salt and pepper.

Preheat the oven to 400°F (200°C) Gas 6.

Arrange egg slices around side of greased soufflé dish and make layers of the potatoes, drained and chopped fish, and the peeled and crushed garlic. Spread tomatoes over top. Dot with remaining butter and bake for 20 minutes.

Garnish with black olives, capers and chopped parsley and sprinkle with lemon juice. Serve hot or cold.

Baked cod with rosemary

Overall timing 45 minutes

Freezing Not suitable

To serve 4–6

2½ lb	End piece of cod	1.1 kg
4 tbsp	Oil	4x15 ml
8	Anchovy fillets	8
	Fresh rosemary	
4	Basil leaves (optional)	4
2 tbsp	Dried breadcrumbs	2x15 ml
	Salt and pepper	

Ask your fishmonger to remove bones from cod, leaving two halves attached at one side. Scale fish, using a descaler or the blunt side of a knife.

Preheat the oven to 350°F (180°C) Gas 4.

Heat half the oil in a flameproof casserole, add the chopped anchovies and heat through. Mash anchovies well, then transfer to a bowl. Put a little of the mashed anchovy mixture inside the fish, together with a few sprigs of fresh rosemary and the basil leaves, if using.

Place fish in the casserole and pour the remaining anchovy mixture and oil over. Add a little more rosemary and sprinkle with breadcrumbs, salt and pepper. Bake for about 30 minutes till the fish is cooked and the top is golden. Serve with boiled potatoes and a green vegetable or salad.

Cod croquettes

Overall timing 45 minutes

Freezing Suitable: bake cooked croquettes from frozen in 375°F (190°C) Gas 5 oven for 30 minutes

To serve 4–6

1 lb	Cooked cod fillets	450 g
1 lb	Mashed potatoes	450 g
	Salt and pepper	
	Grated nutmeg	
1	Egg	1
	Dried breadcrumbs	
	Oil for deep frying	
	Lettuce leaves	
1	Lemon	1

Finely mince cod, then mix with potatoes in a large bowl. Season well with salt, pepper and a pinch of nutmeg. Make small round or oval shapes of the mixture.

Lightly beat egg in a bowl. Dip croquettes in egg, then breadcrumbs.

Heat oil in deep-fryer to 360°F (180°C). Add croquettes and fry for about 5 minutes till golden. Remove croquettes and drain on kitchen paper. Pile them up on a bed of lettuce with pieces of lemon between.

Cod with onions and leeks

Overall timing 35 minutes

Freezing Not suitable

To serve 4-6

1¾ lb	Cod fillets	750 g
3 tbsp	Lemon juice	3x15 ml
	Salt	
2	Large onions	2
2	Leeks	2
3 tbsp	Oil	3x15 ml
¼ pint	Dry cider	150 ml
2 tbsp	Chopped parsley	2x15 ml

Place cod fillets in a bowl with lemon juice and salt.

Peel and chop onions. Trim and chop leeks. Heat oil in a frying pan and cook onions and leeks gently till softened.

Add cod fillets, with any juices, and cider to pan and cook for 15 minutes till fish is cooked through. Sprinkle with parsley before serving with mashed potatoes.

Hake au gratin

Overall timing 30 minutes

Freezing Not suitable

To serve 4

1	Small onion	1
2 tbsp	Chopped parsley	2x15 ml
1¾ lb	Hake steaks	750 g
	Salt and pepper	
	Grated nutmeg	
2 tbsp	Lemon juice	2x15 ml
1 oz	Butter	25 g
4 oz	Cheese	125 g
2 oz	Fresh breadcrumbs	50 g

Preheat oven to 375°F (190°C) Gas 5.

Peel and chop onion and place in a shallow ovenproof dish with half the parsley and the fish steaks. Season with salt and pepper and a pinch of nutmeg. Sprinkle the lemon juice over the fish and dot with butter. Grate the cheese and mix with the breadcrumbs and remaining parsley. Sprinkle over the fish. Bake for about 20 minutes.

Remove from oven and baste with liquid in dish. Bake for another 10 minutes until topping is golden. Serve immediately with jacket-baked potatoes.

Fishermen's herrings

Overall timing 35 minutes plus chilling

Freezing Not suitable

To serve 6

12	Smoked herring fillets	12
1	Onion	1
4	Small gherkins	4
4 oz	Can of herring roes	113 g
1 tbsp	French mustard	15 ml
$\frac{1}{4}$ pint	Oil	150 ml
	Pepper	

Put the herring fillets into a bowl, cover with boiling water and leave for 20 minutes.

Drain herring fillets, rinse and dry on kitchen paper. Peel onion and cut into thin rings. Slice gherkins.

Drain and chop the roes and put into a bowl with the mustard. Beat to a smooth paste with a wooden spoon. Gradually trickle in all but 2 tbsp (2x15 ml) of the oil, beating well after each addition. Add pepper to taste.

Spread roe sauce over bottom of a serving dish and arrange herring fillets on top. Brush with remaining oil and decorate with onion rings and gherkins. Chill for at least 30 minutes, then serve with potato and beetroot salads garnished with snipped chives.

Marinated kipper fillets

Overall timing 15 minutes plus marination

Freezing Not suitable

To serve 6

1	Carrot	1
2	Onions	2
1 lb	Kipper fillets	450 g
	Sprigs of thyme	
4–5	Bay leaves	4–5
4–5	Cloves	4–5
¼ pint	Oil	150 ml
4 tbsp	Wine vinegar or lemon juice	4x15 ml
Garnish		
	Hard-boiled eggs	
	Lemon slices	
	Chopped parsley	
	Capers	

Peel and slice the carrot and onions. Place kipper fillets in a glass or pottery bowl, layered with slices of carrot, onion rings, sprigs of fresh thyme, bay leaves and cloves. Pour oil and wine vinegar or lemon juice over and leave for 24 hours in a cool place.

Drain the kippers and place in a serving dish. Garnish with slices of hard-boiled egg and lemon, chopped parsley and capers. Serve with cold potato and onion salad.

Rollmops

Overall timing 30 minutes plus 48 hours soaking and 4 days standing

Freezing Not suitable

To serve 6

4	Filleted fresh herrings	4
2 pints	Water	1.1 litre
8 oz	Salt	225 g
2 tbsp	Capers	2x15 ml
2	Onions	2
1	Large gherkin	1
4 teasp	Made mustard	4x5 ml
Marinade		
½ pint	Cider vinegar	300 ml
½ pint	Water	300 ml
1	Bay leaf	1
10	Black peppercorns	10
2	Cloves	2
5	Juniper berries	5
1 teasp	Mustard seed	5 ml

Soak herrings in half water and salt for 24 hours. Drain and repeat.

Put all marinade ingredients into a pan. Bring to the boil and boil for 5 minutes. Cool.

Chop capers. Peel onions and cut into rings. Quarter gherkin lengthways. Drain and rinse herrings. Lay skin down and spread with mustard. Sprinkle with capers and onion rings. Add gherkin and roll up. Pour over marinade. Leave 4 days before eating.

Marinated sprats

Overall timing 45 minutes plus overnight marination

Freezing Not suitable

To serve 6

2 lb	Sprats	900 g
	Salt and pepper	
3 oz	Plain flour	75 g
	Oil for frying	
1	Large onion	1
8	Sage leaves	8
6 tbsp	Vinegar	6x15 ml
4 tbsp	Water	4x15 ml

Clean the fish through the gills. Rinse and drain thoroughly. Season the flour and use to coat the fish. Heat 1 inch (2.5 cm) oil in a deep frying pan and fry the floured sprats, a few at a time, for about 4 minutes till crisp and golden. Drain on kitchen paper, then put into a shallow serving dish.

Peel and slice the onion. Heat 2 tbsp (2x15 ml) oil in frying pan, add the onion and fry gently till transparent. Add the sage leaves, vinegar and water and bring to the boil. Boil for 3 minutes, then remove from the heat and season.

Pour the hot marinade over the sprats. Cover and leave to marinate in a cool place overnight. Serve cold with crusty bread and butter.

Scrowled sprats

Overall timing 30 minutes plus salting

Freezing Not suitable

To serve 4

1 lb	Fresh sprats or pilchards	450 g
	Salt	
2	Sprigs of rosemary	2
2 oz	Butter	50 g
	Lemon wedges	

Cover the sprats or pilchards with salt and leave overnight.

The next day, rinse off the salt. Cut off the heads and tails, then slit each fish along the belly and remove the insides, including the backbone. Do this under cold running water. Dry the fish with kitchen paper.

Strip the rosemary leaves from the sprig. Melt the butter. Arrange the fish on the grill rack and sprinkle with the butter and rosemary. Grill until cooked, turning once. Serve with lemon wedges.

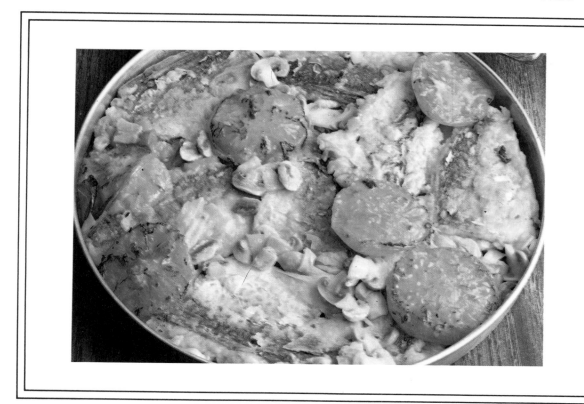

Mackerel in mushroom sauce

Overall timing 40 minutes

Freezing Not suitable

To serve 4

8 oz	Button mushrooms	225 g
2	Onions	2
1	Garlic clove	1
12 oz	Tomatoes	350 g
5 tbsp	Oil	5x15 ml
	Salt and pepper	
2 tbsp	White wine vinegar	2x15 ml
2 lb	Mackerel fillets	900 g
2 tbsp	Plain flour	2x15 ml

Slice mushrooms. Peel and finely chop onions. Peel and crush garlic. Wash tomatoes and cut into ½ inch (12.5 mm) thick slices.

Heat 2 tbsp (2x15 ml) of the oil in a saucepan. Add onions, mushrooms and garlic and fry for 10 minutes, stirring frequently. Season. Stir in the vinegar and boil rapidly till it evaporates.

Coat fillets with seasoned flour. Heat the remaining oil in a large frying pan, add the fillets and fry for 5 minutes on each side. Drain, arrange on a warmed serving dish and keep hot.

Add tomato slices to frying pan and fry for 2 minutes. Spoon mushroom mixture over fillets. Season tomatoes and arrange on top. Serve immediately with minted peas.

Haddock with potatoes and onions

Overall timing 45 minutes

Freezing Not suitable

To serve 4

2	Large onions	2
4	Potatoes	4
4 oz	Butter	125 g
2 lb	Haddock fillets	900 g
2 tbsp	Plain flour	2x15 ml
	Salt and pepper	
1 tbsp	Chopped parsley	15 ml
1 tbsp	Vinegar	15 ml

Peel and thinly slice the onions and potatoes. Melt half the butter in a frying pan, add the onions and cook till transparent.

Add remaining butter and potato slices and fry for 15 minutes, turning occasionally.

Meanwhile, wipe the haddock and pat dry with kitchen paper. Cut into small pieces and coat with seasoned flour. Add to pan and cook for a further 15 minutes, stirring from time to time.

Season with salt and pepper. Add parsley and vinegar and cook over a high heat till vinegar evaporates. Serve immediately with grilled tomatoes.

Barbecued haddock

Overall timing 20 minutes plus marination

Freezing Not suitable

To serve 2

1½ tbsp	Oil	22.5 ml
1½ teasp	Lemon juice	7.5 ml
1 tbsp	Soft brown sugar	15 ml
¼ teasp	Chilli powder	1.25 ml
½ teasp	Worcestershire sauce	2.5 ml
1 teasp	Tomato purée	5 ml
1 lb	Smoked haddock	450 g

Mix together oil, lemon juice, sugar, chilli powder, Worcestershire sauce and tomato purée in a shallow dish. Add the haddock, cover and marinate in the refrigerator for 1 hour, turning fish once or twice.

Preheat the grill.

Remove fish from marinade and place on a large piece of foil on the grill pan. Grill for 5–7 minutes on each side, brushing with marinade from time to time.

Alternatively, place the fish in a fish holder and barbecue over charcoal.

Salmon cakes

Overall timing 25 minutes

Freezing Suitable: fry straight from frozen

To serve 4

1 lb	Boiled potatoes	450 g
2 tbsp	Milk	2x15 ml
1 oz	Butter	25 g
7½ oz	Can of salmon	212 g
2	Lemons	2
	Salt and pepper	
2	Eggs	2
2 tbsp	Plain flour	2x15 ml
4 tbsp	Dried breadcrumbs	4x15 ml
¼ pint	Oil	150 ml
	Lettuce leaves	

Mash the boiled potatoes with the milk and butter. Drain canned salmon and discard skin and bones. Mash flesh and add to potatoes.

Squeeze juice from one of the lemons. Add to salmon with seasoning to taste. Mix well and bind with one of the eggs.

Lightly beat remaining egg. Spread flour and dried breadcrumbs on separate plates. Divide salmon mixture into eight and shape into flat patties. Dip first in flour, then egg, then coat lightly with dried breadcrumbs.

Heat oil in frying pan. Add patties and fry for 5 minutes on each side until crisp and golden. Remove from pan with a draining spoon and arrange on serving plate. Serve immediately, garnished with lettuce leaves and the remaining lemon, cut into wedges.

Indonesian fish curry

Overall timing 40 minutes

Freezing Not suitable

To serve 4

1½ lb	Cod or coley fillets	700 g
	Salt and pepper	
2 tbsp	Plain flour	2x15 ml
1	Onion	1
1	Large cooking apple	1
1 tbsp	Lemon juice	15 ml
2 oz	Butter	50 g
2 tbsp	Oil	2x15 ml
2 tbsp	Curry powder	2x15 ml
1 pint	Stock	560 ml
2 tbsp	Sultanas	2x15 ml
2 tbsp	Cornflour	2x15 ml
2 oz	Split almonds	50 g

Cut fish into pieces, sprinkle with salt and coat with the flour. Peel and slice onion. Peel, core and slice apple and sprinkle with the lemon juice.

Heat the butter and oil in a flameproof casserole. Add curry powder and onion and fry for 5 minutes. Add fish and cook for a few minutes on all sides. Add apple slices and cook for 3 minutes.

Pour stock into casserole and add sultanas. Blend cornflour with a little stock or water and stir in. Bring to the boil and simmer for 10–15 minutes.

Add almonds and cook for a further 2 minutes. Taste and adjust seasoning and serve.

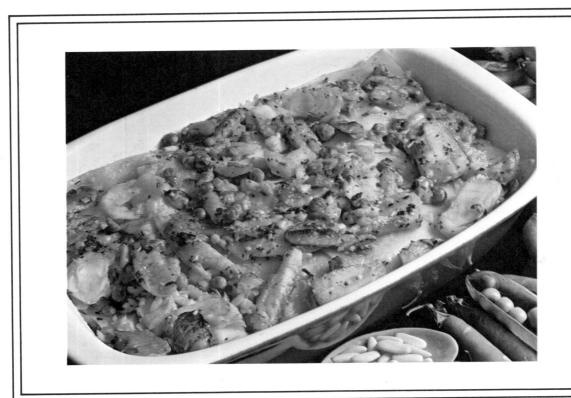

Fish lasagne

Overall timing 1¼ hours

Freezing Suitable: reheat from frozen in 350°F (180°C) Gas 4 oven for 1 hour

To serve 4

1½ lb	Prepared mackerel	700 g
1	Onion	1
3 fl oz	Oil	90 ml
2	Garlic cloves	2
2 tbsp	Tomato purée	2x15 ml
	Salt and pepper	
1 lb	Fresh peas	450 g
4 oz	Mushrooms	125 g
8 oz	Lasagne	225 g
2 tbsp	Grated Parmesan cheese	2x15 ml
2 tbsp	Chopped parsley	2x15 ml

Cut fish into large pieces. Peel and chop onion. Heat 3 tbsp (3x15 ml) of oil in saucepan, add onion and fry until golden. Add fish and cook for 5 minutes, turning once.

Peel and crush garlic. Stir tomato purée into ¼ pint (150 ml) of water and add to pan with half garlic and seasoning. Cover and cook gently for 10 minutes.

Shell peas. Slice mushrooms. Heat 2 tbsp (2x15 ml) of oil in another saucepan, add peas, mushrooms and other half of garlic and cook for 5 minutes. Add 3 fl oz (90 ml) of water and seasoning, cover and cook for 10 minutes.

Meanwhile, cook lasagne in boiling salted water for 10–15 minutes or till tender. Drain thoroughly.

Preheat oven to 350°F (180°C) Gas 4.

Remove fish from pan and cut into pieces, discarding bones. Return to pan with mushroom mixture. Gradually stir in Parmesan and parsley.

Line greased ovenproof dish with one-third of lasagne, cover with one-third of fish mixture and sprinkle with a little oil. Repeat layers, finishing with fish mixture. Sprinkle with oil and bake for 20 minutes.

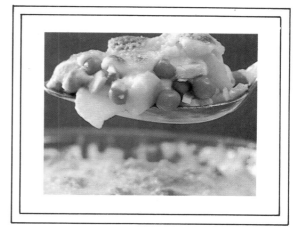

Fish in piquant sauce

Overall timing 1 hour

Freezing Not suitable

To serve 6

4 oz	Streaky bacon rashers	125 g
2 lb	Centre cut steak from large firm-fleshed fish	900 g
4 teasp	Olive oil	4x5 ml
1 oz	Butter	25 g
	Salt and pepper	
½ pint	Fish or chicken stock	300 ml
2 tbsp	Tomato purée	2x15 ml
3 tbsp	Lemon juice	3x15 ml

Derind and stretch the bacon rashers then wrap them round the fish, securing with cocktail sticks.

Heat the oil and butter in a flameproof casserole, add the fish and brown all over. Add salt, pepper, stock, tomato purée and lemon juice. Bring to the boil, cover tightly and simmer gently for 40 minutes, turning fish once.

Remove the fish from the casserole and discard bacon. Cut the fish into thick slices, place on a warmed serving dish and keep hot.

Taste the cooking liquor and adjust seasoning. Thicken if liked with ½ oz (15 g) each of butter and flour mashed together, then pour over the fish.

Tuna and pea casserole

Overall timing 40 minutes

Freezing Not suitable

To serve 4

1 lb	Waxy potatoes	450 g
	Salt and pepper	
8 oz	Frozen peas	225 g
7 oz	Can of tuna	198 g
2 oz	Butter	50 g
1	Onion	1
4 tbsp	Plain flour	4x15 ml
½ pint	Chicken stock	300 ml
½ pint	Milk	300 ml
4 oz	Cheddar cheese	125 g
2 tbsp	Fresh breadcrumbs	2x15 ml

Peel and dice potatoes. Cook in boiling salted water till tender. Add the peas and cook for a further 3 minutes.

Preheat the oven to 400°F (200°C) Gas 6.

Drain the potatoes and peas and put into an ovenproof dish. Drain and flake the tuna and stir into the vegetables.

Melt the butter in a saucepan. Peel and finely chop the onion and fry in the butter till pale golden. Add the flour and cook for 1 minute. Gradually stir in the stock and milk and bring to the boil, stirring. Grate the cheese. Add 3 oz (75 g) of the cheese and seasoning to the pan and stir. Pour over tuna mixture.

Mix the remaining cheese with the breadcrumbs and sprinkle over the top. Bake for 20 minutes.

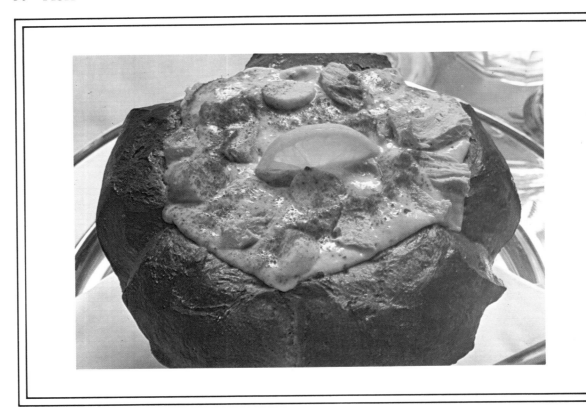

Tuna stuffed loaf

Overall timing 50 minutes

Freezing Not suitable

To serve 4

2	Small round crusty loaves	2
1	Onion	1
4 oz	Button mushrooms	125 g
2 oz	Butter	50 g
2 tbsp	Plain flour	2x15 ml
10½ oz	Can of condensed mushroom soup	298 g
2	Egg yolks	2
2 tbsp	Single cream	2x15 ml
2x7 oz	Cans of tuna	2x198 g
2 tbsp	Lemon juice	2x15 ml
	Salt and pepper	
½ teasp	Paprika	2.5 ml
2	Lemon slices	2

Preheat the oven to 400°F (200°C) Gas 6.

Hollow out each loaf with a sharp knife to leave a thick shell. Place on a baking tray.

Peel and chop the onion. Wipe and thickly slice the mushrooms. Melt the butter in a saucepan, add the onion and fry till transparent. Add the mushrooms and fry for 2 minutes. Stir in the flour and cook for 1 minute. Gradually add the mushroom soup and bring to the boil, stirring constantly. Simmer for 2 minutes, then remove from the heat and allow to cool slightly.

Beat the egg yolks and cream into the mushroom sauce. Drain and flake the tuna and add to the sauce with the lemon juice. Season to taste.

Divide the hot tuna stuffing between the loaves and sprinkle with the paprika. Bake in the centre of the oven for about 25 minutes till bubbling and golden.

Arrange the loaves on a warmed serving dish and garnish each with a slice of lemon. Serve immediately.

Roast pork with oranges

Overall timing 2¼ hours

Freezing Not suitable

To serve 6–8

3 lb	Rolled spare rib of pork	1.4 kg
1 oz	Butter	25 g
	Salt and pepper	
5	Oranges	5
2 tbsp	Lemon juice	2x15 ml
¼ pint	Hot water	150 ml
6	Sugar lumps	6
1 tbsp	Wine vinegar	15 ml
2 teasp	Arrowroot	2x5 ml

Preheat the oven to 450°F (230°C) Gas 8.

Place pork in a roasting tin. Spread butter over lean parts and rub salt and pepper into skin. Roast for 20 minutes.

Meanwhile, squeeze juice from two oranges.

Peel remaining oranges. Cut two into slices and one into segments.

Remove pork from tin and keep warm. Pour off any fat from tin and add orange and lemon juices and water. Stir well, scraping any sediment from bottom of tin. Reduce oven temperature to 400°F (200°C) Gas 6.

Replace meat in tin and roast for a further 1½ hours, basting occasionally.

Meanwhile, put sugar lumps into a saucepan with 1 tbsp (15 ml) water. Stir till dissolved, then boil rapidly, without stirring, till golden. Remove from heat and stir in vinegar. Return to heat and stir till caramel dissolves.

Place pork on a warmed serving dish. Stir cooking liquor from tin into caramel. Blend arrowroot with 2 tbsp (2x15 ml) water and add to caramel. Bring to the boil, stirring. Add the sliced and segmented oranges. Heat through for 1–2 minutes.

Cut pork into thick slices and arrange the pieces of orange around. Serve the sauce separately in a warmed sauceboat.

Cowboy's pork and beans

Overall timing 50 minutes

Freezing Not suitable

To serve 4

1½ lb	Belly of pork rashers	700 g
1	Large onion	1
2 tbsp	Oil	2x15 ml
2	Garlic cloves	2
¼ teasp	Chilli powder	1.25 ml
2 tbsp	Black treacle	2x15 ml
1 tbsp	Vinegar	15 ml
½ teasp	Powdered mustard	2.5 ml
2 tbsp	Tomato ketchup	2x15 ml
½ pint	Chicken stock	300 ml
	Salt and pepper	
2x14 oz	Cans of haricot beans	2x397 g

Preheat the oven to 425°F (220°C) Gas 7.

Cut the pork into ½ inch (12.5 mm) pieces, discarding any bones. Place in roasting tin with no extra fat. Cook in the oven for about 20 minutes till crisp and golden.

Meanwhile, peel and finely chop the onion. Heat the oil in a flameproof casserole and fry the onion till transparent. Peel and crush the garlic and add to the pan with the chilli powder. Fry, stirring, for 2 minutes.

Stir in the treacle, vinegar, mustard, ketchup and chicken stock. Bring to the boil, season and simmer for 5 minutes.

Drain and rinse the canned beans and add to the sauce.

Remove the pork from the oven and reduce the temperature to 350°F (180°C) Gas 4. Add the pork pieces to the beans with 1 tbsp (15 ml) of the fat from the tin. Put the casserole in the oven and cook for about 15 minutes, stirring once, till liquid is reduced by half. Taste and adjust the seasoning, then serve immediately with a tomato and onion salad and crusty bread.

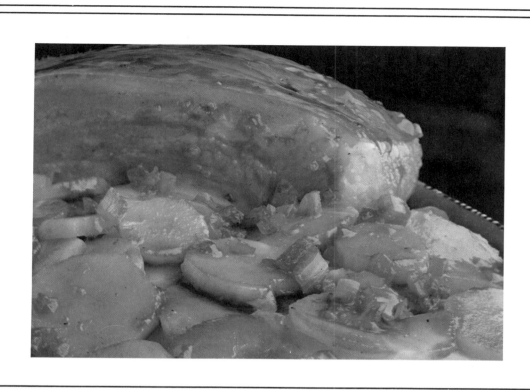

Country pork with parsnips

Overall timing 2¼ hours

Freezing Not suitable

To serve 4–6

2½ lb	Piece of belly pork	1.1 kg
	Salt and pepper	
1 tbsp	Oil	15 ml
2 oz	Butter	50 g
2	Onions	2
2 lb	Parsnips	900 g
½ pint	Stock	300 ml
	Bouquet garni	
1 tbsp	Plain flour	15 ml
¼ pint	Dry white wine	150 ml

Preheat the oven to 400°F (200°C) Gas 6.

Wipe the pork and score the rind with a sharp knife. Rub salt and oil into the rind. Melt the butter in a roasting tin, place the pork in it and roast in the centre of the oven for 1 hour.

Meanwhile, peel and chop the onions. Peel and slice the parsnips.

Remove the roasting tin from the oven and arrange the onions and parsnips around the pork. Pour in the stock (made with cubes if necessary), add the bouquet garni and return to the oven. Roast for a further 45 minutes, basting the parsnips occasionally.

Discard the bouquet garni. Place the pork on a warmed serving dish and arrange the parsnips around it. Keep hot.

Pour all but 2 tbsp (2x15 ml) of the juices from the roasting tin into a jug. Sprinkle the flour into the tin and cook for 1 minute, stirring. Gradually add the reserved cooking liquor and the wine and bring to the boil, stirring constantly. Taste and adjust seasoning and spoon over the parsnips.

Iowa skillet chops

Overall timing 1 hour

Freezing Suitable

To serve 4

8	Pork loin chops	8
	Salt and pepper	
3 tbsp	Oil	3x15 ml
1 lb 12 oz	Can of tomatoes	794 g
1 tbsp	Tomato purée	15 ml
1 tbsp	Worcestershire sauce	15 ml
1	Onion	1
11½ oz	Can of sweetcorn kernels	326 g
1 tbsp	Arrowroot (optional)	15 ml
	Sprigs of parsley	

Sprinkle chops with salt and pepper. Heat oil in a frying pan and cook chops in two batches for 2 minutes on each side. When all chops are cooked, return first batch to pan. Remove from heat.

Purée the tomatoes with juice, tomato purée and Worcestershire sauce in a blender, then pour over chops. Finely chop the onion and add with the drained corn (use some of the corn water if the mixture is too thick). Bring back to the boil and add salt and pepper.

Cover the pan and cook over moderate heat for 25 minutes. Remove lid to reduce sauce a little and cook for a further 10 minutes. Thicken with arrowroot, if you like, blended with a little hot water, and cook till clear. Garnish with parsley and serve straight from the pan.

Barbecued pork chops

Overall timing 20 minutes plus marination

Freezing Not suitable

To serve 4

4	Pork spare rib chops	4
Marinade		
1	Large onion	1
2 tbsp	Lemon juice or vinegar	2x15 ml
2 tbsp	Oil	2x15 ml
½ teasp	Powdered mustard	2.5 ml
2 teasp	Worcestershire sauce	2x5 ml
½ teasp	Salt	2.5 ml
½ teasp	Freshly ground black pepper	2.5 ml
1 teasp	Granulated sugar	5 ml
½ teasp	Paprika	2.5 ml

Place pork chops in bowl. Peel and grate the onion and place in a jug. Add rest of marinade ingredients and mix well, then pour over chops. Leave to marinate for 1 hour in a cool place, turning chops at least twice.

Preheat the grill.

Cook the chops under the grill (or on a barbecue), occasionally brushing them with the reserved marinade. Serve with mixed salad, dressed with vinaigrette flavoured with fresh dill or other herb of choice.

Roast pork with turnips

Overall timing 2¼ hours

Freezing Not suitable

To serve 6

2½ lb	Rolled hindloin of pork	1.1 kg
1	Garlic clove	1
2 oz	Butter	50 g
	Salt and pepper	
2 lb	Small turnips	900 g
2 teasp	Caster sugar	2x5 ml
¾ pint	Light stock	400 ml
1 tbsp	Plain flour	15 ml
1 tbsp	Chopped parsley	15 ml

Preheat the oven to 425°F (220°C) Gas 7.

Peel the garlic clove, cut in half and rub all over the pork. Place the pork in a roasting tin and spread the butter over. Sprinkle with salt and pepper and roast in the centre of the oven for 20 minutes. Reduce the temperature to 375°F (190°C) Gas 5 and cook for a further 40 minutes.

Meanwhile, peel and halve or quarter the turnips according to size. Put into a saucepan, cover with cold salted water and bring to the boil. Drain, then dry on kitchen paper.

Arrange the turnips round the pork. Sprinkle with the sugar and add the stock (made with a cube if necessary). Cover with foil and roast for 30 minutes. Remove the foil, turn the turnips over and cook for a further 15 minutes. Test pork for doneness and cook a little longer if necessary.

Place the pork in a warmed serving dish and carve into thick slices. Arrange the turnips on the dish and keep hot.

Pour off liquid from tin and reserve. Sprinkle the flour into the tin and cook, stirring, for 1 minute. Gradually add the reserved liquid and bring to the boil, stirring constantly. Adjust seasoning. Sprinkle the parsley over the turnips and serve.

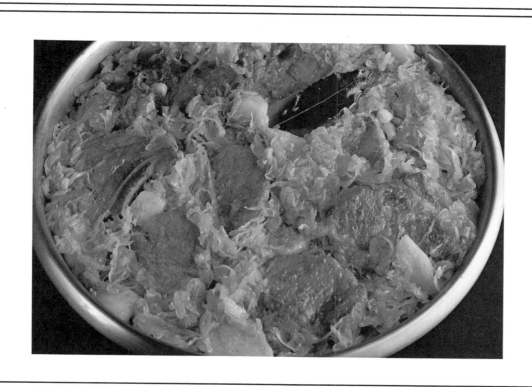

Polish-style pork with sauerkraut

Overall timing 1 hour

Freezing Not suitable

To serve 6

3 tbsp	Oil	3x15 ml
6	Pork loin chops	6
1	Large onion	1
1	Garlic clove	1
	Salt and pepper	
2 lb	Sauerkraut	900 g
1	Bay leaf	1
½ pint	Chicken stock	300 ml
1	Large dessert apple	1
1 teasp	Cumin seeds	5 ml

Heat the oil in flameproof casserole and fry the chops till browned on both sides. Remove from the pan and reserve.

Peel and finely chop the onion; peel and crush the garlic. Add both to the casserole and fry till transparent. Season, and add the drained sauerkraut and bay leaf. Arrange the chops on top. Pour the stock over, bring to the boil and simmer for 15 minutes.

Meanwhile, peel, core and dice the apple. Add to the pan with cumin seeds and stir well, then simmer for a further 15 minutes till the chops are tender.

Taste and adjust the seasoning. Discard the bay leaf. Serve with creamed potatoes, buttered carrots and thin slices of wholemeal bread.

Pork and beans

Overall timing 2¾ hours plus overnight soaking

Freezing Not suitable

To serve 4

1 lb	Dried butter beans	450 g
1	Onion	1
12	Cloves	12
2	Garlic cloves	2
2½ pints	Boiling water	1.5 litres
4 tbsp	Oil	4x15 ml
	Salt and pepper	
1 lb	Piece of smoked streaky bacon or belly of pork	450 g

Put the beans in a large saucepan of cold water and soak overnight.

The next day, bring to the boil and cook beans for 15 minutes. Drain.

Peel onion, spike with the cloves and add to pan with peeled garlic, boiling water, oil, pepper and bacon or belly pork, derinded and cut into thick rashers if easier to handle. Cover and simmer for 1½ hours. Taste and add salt, then cook for a further 30 minutes.

Remove spiked onion and garlic. Remove meat and beans from pan with a draining spoon and place in warmed serving dish. Keep hot.

Reduce cooking liquor to about ¼ pint (150 ml) by boiling fast, uncovered. Pour over beans and serve.

Frankfurter fritters

Overall timing 30 minutes

Freezing Not suitable

To serve 6

5 oz	Plain flour	150 g
	Salt and pepper	
1	Egg	1
1 tbsp	Oil	15 ml
4 fl oz	Beer	120 ml
	Oil for frying	
16	Frankfurters	16
2	Egg whites	2

Sift 4 oz (125 g) of the flour into a bowl with 1½ teasp (7.5 ml) salt and make a well in the centre. Add the whole egg and oil and mix with a wooden spoon. Gradually add the beer and mix to a smooth batter.

Heat the oil in a deep-fryer to 340°F (170°C).

Season the remaining flour. Cut the frankfurters in half and toss in flour. Whisk the egg whites till stiff but not dry and fold into the batter. Dip each frankfurter half into the batter and fry in the oil for about 3 minutes till crisp and golden. Drain on kitchen paper and serve hot.

Pork and sausage stew

Overall timing $1\frac{3}{4}$ hours

Freezing Not suitable

To serve 6

$1\frac{1}{2}$ lb	Onions	700 g
2 oz	Lard	50 g
6	Thin cut pork loin chops	6
1 lb	Coarse pork sausages	450 g
2 tbsp	Plain flour	2x15 ml
$\frac{3}{4}$ pint	Chicken stock	400 ml
3 tbsp	Tomato purée	3x15 ml
	Salt and pepper	

Peel and thinly slice the onions. Heat the lard in a flameproof casserole, add the onions and fry gently for 10 minutes till pale golden.

Meanwhile, wipe the chops and remove the bones and any excess fat. Twist the sausages in half.

Sprinkle flour over the onions and cook for 1 minute. Gradually add the stock (made with a cube if necessary) and bring to the boil, stirring. Stir in the tomato purée.

Add the chops and sausages. Bring to the boil, cover and simmer for $1\frac{1}{4}$ hours, or cook in the centre of the oven preheated to 350°F (180°C) Gas 4 for $1\frac{1}{4}$ hours.

Adjust the seasoning to taste, then serve immediately with buttered pasta and a green salad.

Belgian pork chops

Overall timing 40 minutes

Freezing Not suitable

To serve 4

4	Pork chops	4
	Salt and pepper	
2 tbsp	Plain flour	2x15 ml
3 tbsp	Oil	3x15 ml
4	Onions	4
¼ pint	Beer	150 ml
¼ pint	Chicken stock	150 ml
1½ lb	Brussels sprouts	700 g
1 oz	Butter	25 g
2 teasp	Cornflour	2x5 ml

Coat the chops with seasoned flour. Heat oil in frying pan and cook chops for 3 minutes on each side.

Peel and thinly slice onions. Add to pan and cook for 5 minutes. Pour in beer and stock, season and simmer for 15 minutes.

Meanwhile, trim sprouts and cook in boiling water till just tender. Drain well, toss with butter and keep hot.

Remove chops from pan and place on warmed serving plate. Surround with sprouts. Mix cornflour with a little cold water and add to pan. Bring to the boil and cook for 2 minutes. Pour sauce over chops.

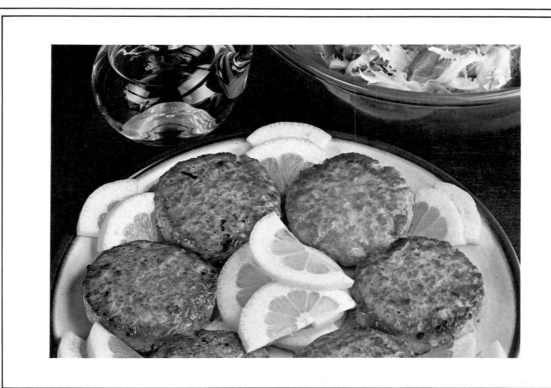

Porkburgers

Overall timing 25 minutes

Freezing Suitable: cook from frozen

To serve 6

1½ lb	Lean pork	700 g
	Salt and pepper	
1	Onion	1
1 teasp	Dried thyme	5 ml
1 tbsp	Oil	15 ml
	Lemon slices	

Mince the pork twice till fine and add plenty of salt and pepper. Peel and finely chop the onion and add to the pork with the dried thyme. Mix well with a wooden spoon.

Divide the meat into six portions and shape into thick burgers about 4 inches (10 cm) in diameter.

Brush a heavy-based frying pan or griddle with oil and heat well. Add the burgers and fry for about 10–15 minutes. Turn burgers carefully with a fish slice and cook for a further 5–10 minutes according to taste.

Garnish with lemon slices and serve with an endive and tomato salad or with chips.

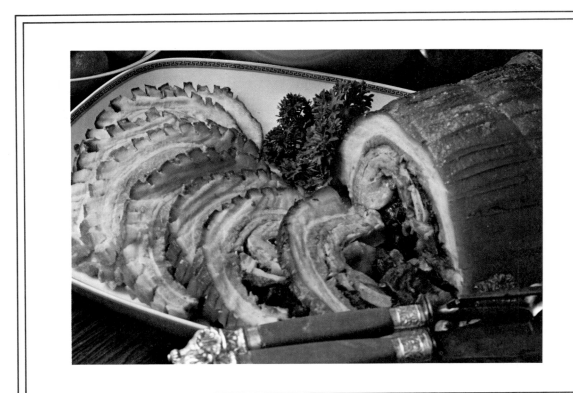

Scandinavian pork

Overall timing 2½ hours plus soaking

Freezing Not suitable

To serve 6–8

8 oz	Plump prunes	225 g
1	Large cooking apple	1
2 tbsp	Lemon juice	2 x 15 ml
3 lb	Piece of belly of pork	1.4 kg
	Salt and pepper	
1 tbsp	Oil	15 ml
½ pint	Stock	300 ml
2 tbsp	Plain flour	2 x 15 ml
	Sprigs of parsley	

Soak prunes in ½ pint (300 ml) hot water for 1 hour.

Preheat the oven to 375°F (190°C) Gas 5.

Drain prunes, reserving soaking water, and remove stones. Peel, core and slice apple. Toss in lemon juice to prevent browning and add to prunes.

Season pork. Place apple and prunes along the centre, then roll up lengthways and tie into a neat shape with fine string. Place in a roasting tin and rub oil into skin. Sprinkle with salt and roast for 45 minutes.

Pour prune soaking liquor and stock over pork. Reduce the temperature to 350°F (180°C) Gas 4 and roast for a further 1¼ hours.

Place the meat on a warmed serving dish, discard the string and keep hot. Drain pan juices into a small saucepan and skim off any fat. Blend flour to a smooth paste with 4 tbsp (4x15 ml) cold water. Add to meat juices and bring to the boil, stirring constantly. Simmer for 4–5 minutes. Carve pork into thick slices and garnish with sprigs of parsley. Serve with gravy.

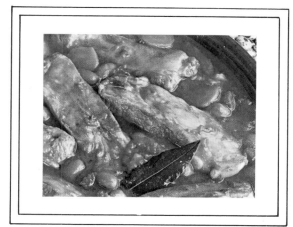

Pork cassoulet

Overall timing 3¼ hours plus soaking

Freezing Not suitable

To serve 6

1 lb	Dried haricot beans	450 g
1	Pig's trotter	1
4 oz	Pork rind	125 g
2	Garlic cloves	2
2	Carrots	2
2	Onions	2
	Bouquet garni	
8 oz	Italian salami	225 g
	Salt and pepper	
2 tbsp	Oil	2x15 ml
14 oz	Can of tomatoes	397 g
1 oz	Fresh breadcrumbs	25 g

Soak beans overnight.

Quarter trotter lengthways. Chop pork rind. Add to beans with peeled garlic, carrots, one onion and bouquet garni. Cover with water, cover and simmer for 1¼ hours.

Peel salami, prick and add to pan with seasoning. Cook for 15 minutes.

Chop remaining onion. Heat oil in a saucepan and fry onion till transparent. Add 1 pint (560 ml) water, tomatoes and seasoning. Simmer for 10 minutes.

Preheat the oven to 350°F (180°C) Gas 4.

Drain beans, reserving pork rind. Add sausage and trotter to other pan. Line deep ovenproof dish with pork rind. Add layers of beans and meat mixture; top with crumbs. Bake for 30 minutes.

Rib and bean stew

Overall timing 1½ hours plus soaking

Freezing Not suitable

To serve 4–6

8 oz	Dried borlotti beans	225 g
2	Carrots	2
2	Stalks of celery	2
2	Bay leaves	2
2 lb	Pork spare ribs	900 g
2	Large onions	2
4 tbsp	Oil	4x15 ml
14 oz	Can of tomatoes	397 g
4 tbsp	Tomato purée	4x15 ml
1 tbsp	Sugar	15 ml
¾ pint	Chicken stock	400 ml
	Salt and pepper	

Soak beans overnight, then drain and cover with fresh water. Slice carrots and celery and add to beans with bay leaves. Simmer for 1 hour.

Separate ribs. Peel and finely chop onions. Heat oil in saucepan and fry onions till transparent. Add ribs and brown all over. Add tomatoes, tomato purée, sugar and stock and bring to the boil.

Drain beans and add to meat. Season and simmer for 15 minutes till meat is tender and cooking liquor is thick.

Baked pork chops

Overall timing 40 minutes

Freezing Not suitable

To serve 4

4	Pork chops	4
	Salt and pepper	
2 tbsp	Oil	2x15 ml
1 lb	Cooking apples	450 g
1 oz	Butter	25 g
1 tbsp	Chopped fresh rosemary	15 ml
$\frac{1}{4}$ pint	Stock	150 ml

Preheat the oven to 400°F (200°C) Gas 6.

Season chops with salt and pepper. Heat oil in a flameproof casserole and brown the chops for 2 minutes on each side.

Peel, core and slice apples. Arrange in casserole round the chops and dot with the butter. Sprinkle with rosemary, add stock (made with $\frac{1}{2}$ stock cube if liked) and cover casserole.

Bake in the centre of the oven for about 30 minutes, removing lid for last 10 minutes of cooking time. Serve with creamed potatoes and salad.

Pork chops with bananas

Overall timing 30 minutes

Freezing Not suitable

To serve 4

1 oz	Butter	25 g
4	Pork chops	4
3	Small, firm bananas	3
	Salt and pepper	
	Pinch of cayenne pepper	
1	Lemon	1
	Sprigs of parsley	
1 teasp	Plain flour	5 ml
¼ pint	Stock	150 ml

Melt the butter in a frying pan over medium heat. Add the chops and cook for 10–12 minutes on each side depending on thickness.

Five minutes before the chops are cooked, peel bananas and cut in half lengthways. Add to the frying pan and sprinkle with salt, pepper and cayenne.

Lift out the pork chops and bananas and arrange on a warmed serving dish. Garnish with lemon and parsley.

Stir the flour into the pan juices and add the stock gradually. Simmer for 2–3 minutes, then pour this gravy into a small serving jug.

Serve with plain boiled rice which will provide a contrast to the sweeter meat and bananas.

Pot roast pork with apples

Overall timing 1½ hours

Freezing Not suitable

To serve 4–6

2 oz	Butter	50 g
3¼ lb	Rolled pork	1.5 kg
	Salt and pepper	
2 tbsp	Cinnamon	2x15 ml
8	Granny Smith apples	8

Preheat oven to 400°F (200°C) Gas 6.

Melt 1 oz (25 g) butter in a flameproof casserole. Roll pork joint in a mixture of salt, pepper and half the cinnamon, then brown on all sides. Cover casserole and cook on the middle shelf of the oven for about 1 hour, turning joint over halfway through.

Peel and core apples and cut into quarters. Put into a saucepan with remaining butter and cinnamon. Cover and cook for about 10 minutes over a low heat, shaking the pan to prevent sticking.

Arrange the apples around the roast 15 minutes before the end of cooking time.

·Remove pork from casserole; slice and place on warmed serving plate. Surround with apples. Make gravy from cooking juices and serve separately.

Braised pork with plum sauce

Overall timing 1¾ hours

Freezing Not suitable

To serve 6

2 oz	Lard	50 g
	Salt and pepper	
2½ lb	Boned and rolled loin of pork	1.1 kg
½ pint	Light stock	300 ml
3	Sage leaves	3
2 lb	Small potatoes	900 g
1½ lb	Red plums	700 g
2 oz	Sugar	50 g
1 tbsp	Chopped parsley	15 ml

Preheat the oven to 400°F (200°C) Gas 6.

Melt lard in a roasting tin. Season pork and fry quickly over a high heat till browned on all sides. Pour off the fat and reserve. Add the stock and sage leaves, cover the tin with foil and braise in the oven for 45 minutes.

Meanwhile, peel potatoes. Put into a saucepan, cover with cold salted water and bring to the boil. Drain.

Remove meat from oven and strain stock into a saucepan. Add reserved fat to roasting tin with the potatoes, return to the oven and cook uncovered for a further 50 minutes, basting the meat and potatoes occasionally.

Meanwhile, wash plums. Halve 1 lb (450 g) of them and discard stones. Add to the stock with the sugar. Bring to the boil, then cover and simmer for 10–15 minutes, stirring occasionally. Poach the rest of the plums whole in a little water till tender.

Remove meat from tin, carve into thick slices and arrange on a warmed serving plate. Arrange the potatoes and whole poached plums around the meat. Sprinkle with parsley. Lightly mash remaining plums and pour into a warmed sauceboat.

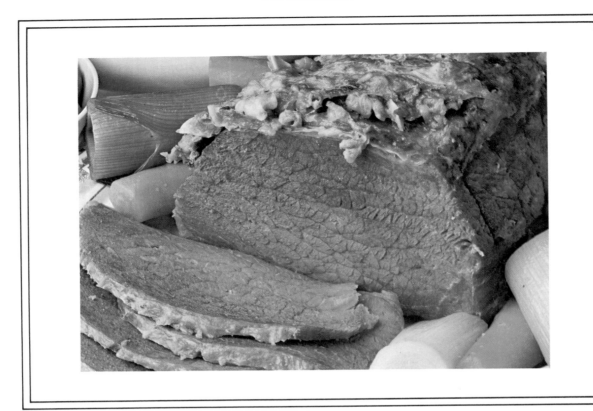

Salt beef

Overall timing 3½ hours plus 2 weeks salting

Freezing Not suitable

To serve 8–10

2 lb	Coarse salt	900 g
4 oz	Sugar	125 g
1 tbsp	Saltpetre	15 ml
1 oz	Pickling spice	25 g
4	Bay leaves	4
1	Sprig of thyme	1
5 lb	Silverside or brisket of beef	2.3 kg
3	Large onions	3
5	Cloves	5
1	Stalk of celery	1
1 teasp	Black peppercorns	5 ml
1 lb	Medium carrots	450 g
2	Medium turnips	2
1 lb	Leeks	450 g

Put salt, sugar and saltpetre into a large saucepan with pickling spices tied in muslin. Add bay leaves, thyme and 8 pints (4.5 litres) water and heat gently, stirring, till sugar and salt have dissolved. Bring to the boil, then pour into bowl and cool.

Add meat to bowl, making sure that salt solution covers it. Cover with clean tea-towel and leave to soak in cold place for up to 2 weeks. Turn meat occasionally.

To cook, remove from pickle and wash under cold running water. Put into a large saucepan with one onion, peeled and spiked with cloves. Chop celery and add to pan with peppercorns. Cover with cold water and bring to the boil slowly. Skim, reduce heat, cover and simmer for 2½ hours.

Meanwhile, peel and chop carrots and turnips. Peel remaining onions and slice thickly. Chop leeks. Add vegetables to pan, bring back to the boil and simmer for 30 minutes. Use strained cooking liquor to make a sauce.

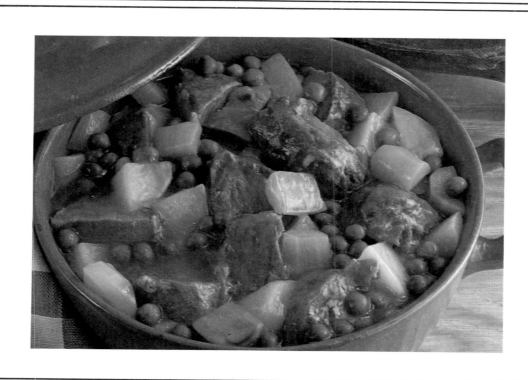

Beef and vegetable stew

Overall timing 2 hours

Freezing Suitable: simmer for 30 minutes only; add vegetables after reheating in 350°F (180°C) Gas 4 oven for 45 minutes

To serve 6–8

2 lb	Stewing steak	900 g
	Salt and pepper	
4 tbsp	Plain flour	4 x 15 ml
1 lb	Onions	450 g
3 tbsp	Oil	3 x 15 ml
1¼ pints	Beef stock	700 g
2 tbsp	Tomato purée	2 x 15 ml
	Bay leaf	
1 lb	Carrots	450 g
1 lb	Potatoes	450 g
1 lb	Parsnips	450 g
8 oz	Frozen peas	225 g

Wipe and trim the meat and cut into 1½ inch (4 cm) cubes. Season the flour and toss the pieces of meat in it till evenly coated. Peel and slice the onions.

Heat the oil in a heavy-based saucepan and fry the onions till transparent. Add the meat and fry till browned all over, then add any remaining flour. Gradually add the stock (made with cubes if necessary) and bring to the boil, stirring constantly. Add the tomato purée, bay leaf and seasoning, cover and simmer for 1 hour.

Scrape the carrots and peel the potatoes and parsnips. Cut all into chunks and add to the meat. Cover and simmer for a further 30 minutes. Taste and adjust seasoning.

Stir in the peas and simmer for 10 minutes, then serve.

Boeuf en croûte

Overall timing 1½ hours plus cooling and chilling

Freezing Not suitable

To serve 6

1 lb	Frozen puff pastry	454 g
3 lb	Fillet of beef	1.4 kg
1	Garlic clove	1
1 oz	Softened butter	25 g
	Salt and pepper	
1 teasp	Dried thyme	5 ml
4 oz	Smooth liver pâté	125 g
1	Egg	1

Thaw pastry. Preheat the oven to 425°F (220°C) Gas 7.

Trim meat of all fat, then tie into a neat shape with fine string. Make tiny slits in meat with tip of a sharp knife and insert slivers of peeled garlic. Spread butter over beef, season and sprinkle with half the thyme. Place in roasting tin and roast for 10 minutes. Take meat out of tin, place on a wire rack and leave to cool completely.

Remove string from meat. Roll out dough to a large rectangle just over twice the size of the meat. Place meat on one half of dough rectangle and brush dough edges with water. Spread pâté over top of meat and sprinkle with remaining thyme. Fold dough over to enclose meat and seal edges. Trim round three sides and, if liked, make a hole in the top. Make a funnel from foil and place in hole if liked. Place on dampened baking tray.

Cut decorative shapes out of dough trimmings, dip them into beaten egg and arrange on dough. Glaze all over with egg and chill for 1 hour.

Preheat oven to 425°F (220°C) Gas 7. Bake for 35 minutes till pastry is well risen and golden. Place on a warmed serving dish, garnish with watercress and serve, cut into thick slices.

Bohemian goulash

Overall timing 2¼ hours

Freezing Suitable: add cream after reheating

To serve 4

8 oz	Boned shoulder of lamb	225 g
8 oz	Belly pork	225 g
8 oz	Chuck steak	225 g
2 oz	Butter	50 g
2	Onions	2
3	Garlic cloves	3
2 teasp	Paprika	2x5 ml
	Bouquet garni	
1 tbsp	Tomato purée	15 ml
	Salt and pepper	
¼ pint	Carton of soured cream	150 ml

Cut meats into chunks. Melt the butter in a flameproof casserole and brown the meats on all sides.

Peel and slice the onions. Peel and crush the garlic. Add both to the casserole and cook gently till golden brown. Stir in the paprika and cook for 2 minutes.

Add bouquet garni, tomato purée and seasoning. Cover with water and bring to the boil. Cover and simmer for 1½–2 hours.

Discard bouquet garni; adjust seasoning. Stir in soured cream and serve with boiled new potatoes and a crisp green salad.

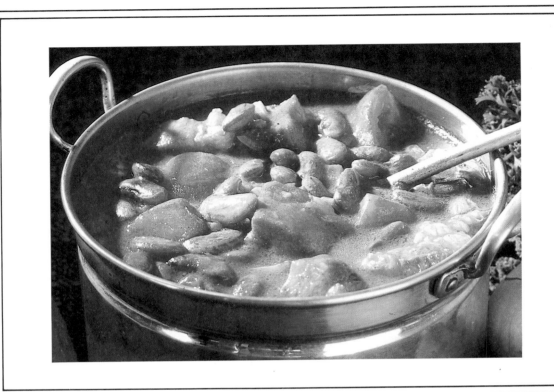

Chilli con carne

Overall timing 3¼ hours plus overnight soaking

Freezing Suitable

To serve 4–6

8 oz	Dried brown or red beans	225 g
1¾ pints	Water	1 litre
2 lb	Braising steak	900 g
1	Onion	1
1 tbsp	Pork dripping or olive oil	15 ml
1 oz	Butter	25 g
	Salt and pepper	
1 teasp	Chilli powder	5 ml
1 tbsp	Sweet paprika	15 ml
8 oz	Canned tomatoes	225 g
2 teasp	Cornflour (optional)	2x5 ml

Soak beans in water overnight. The next day, place water and beans in saucepan, cover and cook gently for 1½ hours.

Cut the beef into 1 inch (2.5 cm) cubes. Peel and chop onion. Heat the dripping or oil and butter in frying pan. Add the beef. Cook till brown, then add the onion and cook till transparent.

Mix the meat and onion in with the cooked beans and season with salt, pepper, chilli powder and paprika. Cover and cook gently for 1 hour.

Add the drained tomatoes, cover and cook for 30 minutes more. Adjust seasoning. If you wish to thicken the sauce, blend the cornflour with a little water and add it to the mixture. Cook for a few minutes, then serve from the cooking pot with plain boiled rice or chunks of wholemeal bread and a crisp green salad.

Corned beef hash

Overall timing 1 hour

Freezing Not suitable

To serve 4

2	Medium-size onions	2
6 tbsp	Oil *or*	6x15 ml
2 oz	Dripping	50 g
1	Stalk of celery	1
1	Large carrot	1
1 lb	Corned beef	450 g
	Salt and pepper	
½ teasp	Powdered mustard	2.5 ml
1 lb	Potatoes	450 g
1 pint	Beef stock	560 ml

Peel and thinly slice onions. Heat oil or dripping in saucepan. Add the onions and cook gently till transparent.

Finely chop celery. Peel and grate or dice carrot. Cut corned beef into 1 inch (2.5 cm) cubes. Add all of these to onions and cook for a few minutes, then season with salt, pepper and mustard (add more if a stronger taste is preferred). Cook gently for 5 minutes.

Meanwhile, peel potatoes and cut into chunks. Add to pan with boiling stock and cook for 20 minutes. Serve in warm bowls topped with fried or poached eggs, and with lots of fresh bread to mop up the juices.

Corned beef patties

Overall timing 30 minutes

Freezing Suitable: cook from frozen

To serve 4

12 tbsp	Fresh breadcrumbs	12x15 ml
3 tbsp	Warm milk	3x15 ml
1 lb	Corned beef	450 g
2	Eggs	2
2 tbsp	Grated Parmesan cheese	2x15 ml
	Grated rind of ½ lemon	
	Plain flour	
2 oz	Butter	50 g
1 tbsp	Oil	15 ml
	Lemon wedges	
	Sprigs of parsley	

Soak 4 tbsp (4x15 ml) breadcrumbs in the milk. Cut off any excess fat from the edge of the corned beef and discard. Mash beef in a bowl with a fork, then add squeezed-out breadcrumbs, 1 egg, the cheese and lemon rind. Mix well.

With well floured hands, make patties from the mixture, then coat with flour. Lightly beat remaining egg. Using two forks, dip the patties first into beaten egg, then into remaining breadcrumbs.

Heat butter and oil in a large frying pan. Add the patties and cook over a moderate heat till brown on both sides. Remove from pan and drain on kitchen paper. Garnish with lemon wedges and parsley.

Danish meatballs

Overall timing 40 minutes

Freezing Suitable: fry meatballs after thawing, or fry from frozen, allowing 25 minutes

To serve 4

4 oz	Fresh breadcrumbs	125 g
¼ pint	Milk	150 ml
1	Small onion	1
8 oz	Minced beef	225 g
8 oz	Minced pork	225 g
	Salt and pepper	
½ teasp	Ground allspice	2.5 ml
1	Egg	1
2 tbsp	Plain flour	2x15 ml
2 oz	Butter	50 g
3 tbsp	Oil	3x15 ml
8	Lettuce leaves	8
2	Pickled beetroot	2
4 tbsp	Pickled red cabbage	4x15 ml

Put fresh breadcrumbs into a bowl with the milk and soak for 10 minutes.

Peel onion and grate into a large bowl. Add the beef and pork, squeezed out breadcrumbs, salt, pepper and allspice. Mix well and bind together with the beaten egg. Shape mixture into eight balls and coat lightly with flour.

Heat butter and oil in a frying pan. Add meatballs and fry gently for 15 minutes till brown all over and cooked through.

Meanwhile, wash and dry lettuce leaves and arrange in a shallow basket or serving dish. Drain and dice pickled beetroot.

Remove meatballs from pan with a draining spoon and drain on kitchen paper. Put one meatball on each lettuce leaf and spoon a little drained pickled cabbage and beetroot around. Serve with a lettuce, tomato and olive salad.

Flemish hotpot

Overall timing $3\frac{3}{4}$ hours

Freezing Not suitable

To serve 6

2	Pig's trotters	2
1 lb	Piece of belly of pork	450 g
1 lb	Beef flank	450 g
5 pints	Water	2.8 litres
1 tbsp	Salt	15 ml
2	Bay leaves	2
12	Peppercorns	12
3	Onions	3
4	Cloves	4
$1\frac{1}{2}$ lb	Potatoes	700 g
1 lb	Carrots	450 g
1 lb	Cabbage *or*	450 g
12 oz	Spinach	350 g

Split trotters lengthways, then halve each half. Cut belly of pork into 3x2 inch (7.5x5 cm) strips. Roll up beef and tie with string. Put water into a large pan and add meats with salt, bay leaves and peppercorns. Peel onions and spike one with cloves. Add it to pan and bring to the boil. Skim and simmer for 2 hours.

Remove meats from pan. Strain stock and return to pan with meats.

Peel and chop potatoes. Scrape and thickly slice carrots. Chop cabbage or spinach. Quarter remaining onions. Bring stock to the boil and add vegetables. Simmer for 20–25 minutes till vegetables are tender.

Lift meats out of stock. Remove string from beef and carve into thick slices. Strain off 1 pint (560 ml) of the stock and reserve.

Taste the soup and adjust the seasoning. Pour into a warmed tureen and serve immediately. Serve the meats after the soup with reserved stock thickened and made into gravy.

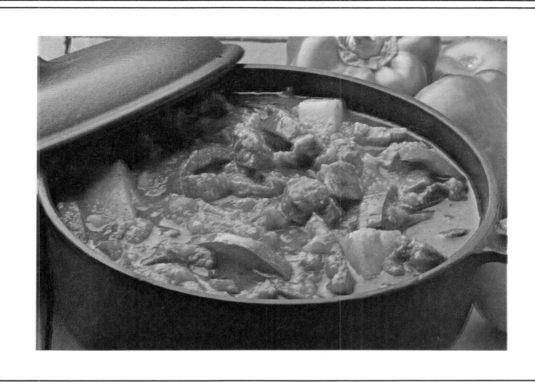

Goulash

Overall timing 2¼ hours

Freezing Suitable

To serve 6

2 lb	Stewing beef	900 g
2 oz	Pork dripping	50 g
8 oz	Onions	225 g
2	Garlic cloves	2
1 tbsp	Plain flour	15 ml
1	Beef stock cube	1
1 pint	Boiling water	560 ml
	Salt and pepper	
½ teasp	Dried marjoram	2.5 ml
½ teasp	Caraway seed	2.5 ml
	Brown sugar	
½ teasp	Paprika	2.5 ml
8 oz	Potatoes	225 g
2	Green peppers	2
5	Tomatoes	5
¼ pint	Red wine	150 ml
¼ pint	Carton of soured cream (optional)	150 ml

Cube beef. Heat dripping in a large saucepan. Add beef and fry till meat is brown on all sides. Peel and chop onions and garlic. Add to meat and cook till transparent.

Sprinkle in flour and stir into mixture. Mix stock cube into boiling water and pour over meat. Season with salt, pepper, marjoram, caraway seed, a pinch of sugar and paprika. Cover tightly and cook gently for 1¼ hours.

Peel and roughly chop the potatoes. Deseed and slice peppers. Blanch, peel and chop tomatoes. Add all to pan, cover and cook for a further 25 minutes.

Add wine and check seasoning. Bring to simmering point and stir in soured cream, if using, or serve it separately.

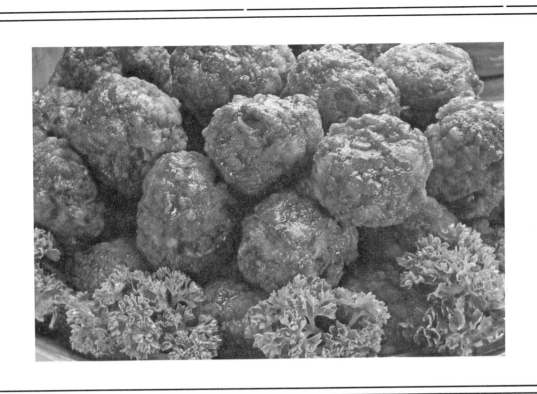

Spicy meatballs

Overall timing 30 minutes

Freezing Not suitable

To serve 4–6

1	Small onion	1
1	Garlic clove	1
1½ lb	Lean minced beef	700 g
1	Egg	1
1 oz	Fresh white breadcrumbs	25 g
	Salt and pepper	
½ teasp	Ground allspice	2.5 ml
	Oil for frying	

Peel and finely chop the onion; peel and crush the garlic. Put with rest of ingredients (except for the oil) into a bowl and mix well together. Shape mixture into walnut-sized balls.

Fry the meatballs in shallow oil for about 15 minutes, turning once. Arrange on a warmed serving plate and serve with rice or pasta, and a tomato sauce or gravy.

Beef and carrot fry-up

Overall timing 45 minutes

Freezing Suitable

To serve 4

1 lb	Carrots	450 g
2	Leeks	2
2 oz	Butter	50 g
9 fl oz	White wine or beef stock	250 ml
	Salt and pepper	
1 lb	Minced beef	450 g
½ teasp	Worcestershire sauce	2.5 ml

Scrape carrots and chop into 1 inch (2.5 cm) pieces. Trim, wash and chop leeks into ½ inch (1.25 cm) slices. Melt half the butter in a frying pan or saucepan and fry chopped carrots for 3 minutes. Pour in white wine or stock, cover and cook over a low heat for 20 minutes.

Add the leeks, season with salt and pepper and cook for a further 15 minutes, or until tender.

Meanwhile, put mince in bowl and mix in salt and pepper with a fork. Roughly shape mince into 1 inch (2.5 cm) pieces. Melt remaining butter in another frying pan and fry meat for about 15 minutes until lightly browned and no longer pink in the middle. Stir from time to time.

Reduce any excess liquid in vegetable pan by boiling rapidly for a minute or two. Add meat and sprinkle with Worcestershire sauce. Serve from the pan, with creamy mashed potatoes and a green vegetable.

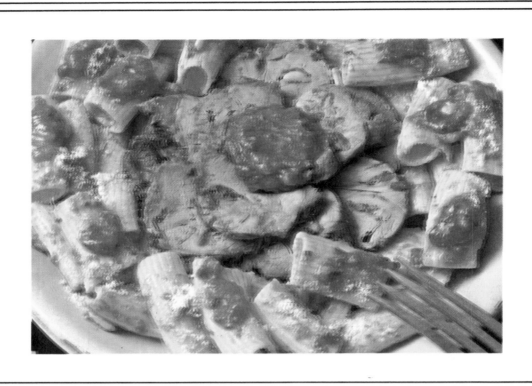

Neapolitan beef

Overall timing 2½ hours

Freezing Not suitable

To serve 4

2 oz	Back bacon	50 g
2 oz	Belly pork fat	50 g
1 tbsp	Chopped parsley	15 ml
1 tbsp	Seedless raisins	15 ml
	Salt and pepper	
1 lb	Top rump of beef	450 g
1	Onion	1
1	Garlic clove	1
2 tbsp	Oil	2x15 ml
14 oz	Can of tomatoes	397 g
½ pint	Beef stock	300 ml
12 oz	Rigatoni	350 g
2 tbsp	Grated Parmesan cheese	2x15 ml

Chop or finely mince bacon and pork fat and mix with parsley to form a smooth paste. Work in raisins and seasoning. With a larding needle, make several deep holes in meat and firmly stuff paste into them. Tie meat into a neat roll with string.

Peel and finely chop onion. Peel and crush garlic. Heat oil in flameproof casserole, add onion and garlic and fry till transparent. Add the meat roll and fry, turning frequently, to seal. Press tomatoes and their juice through a sieve and add to casserole with the stock and seasoning. Mix well, cover and simmer for 1½ hours or till tender.

Meanwhile, cook rigatoni in boiling salted water till tender. Drain and keep hot.

Lift meat out of casserole, remove string and slice. Arrange on a warmed serving dish and arrange rigatoni round meat. Taste sauce and adjust seasoning. Spoon sauce over meat and rigatoni. Sprinkle with Parmesan. Serve immediately.

Pot roast beef with milk

Overall timing 3 hours plus overnight marination

Freezing Not suitable

To serve 6–8

3 lb	Silverside of beef	1.4 kg
1	Large onion	1
1	Large carrot	1
4	Stalks of celery	4
4	Fresh basil leaves	4
	Salt and pepper	
¾ pint	Milk	400 ml
2 tbsp	Brandy (optional)	2x15 ml
14 oz	Can of tomatoes	397 g
2 tbsp	Tomato purée	2x15 ml
8 oz	Pickling onions	225 g
1 oz	Butter	25 g

Tie the meat into a neat shape. Put into a flame-proof casserole. Peel and chop the onion and carrot. Wash, trim and chop the celery. Add to the meat with the basil leaves, salt, pepper, milk and brandy (if used), cover and marinate in a cool place overnight.

The next day, preheat the oven to 325°F (170°C) Gas 3. Stir the tomatoes with juice and tomato purée into the casserole. Cover and cook in oven for 2 hours.

Meanwhile, peel the small onions and blanch in boiling water for 5 minutes. Melt butter in a frying pan and fry onions till golden. Add to casserole and cook for further 30 minutes.

Remove the meat from the casserole and discard the string. Place the meat on a warmed serving dish and keep hot.

Purée the cooking liquor in a blender or rub through a sieve, setting aside the button onions. Put purée and onions into saucepan and reheat. Meanwhile, cut the meat into slices. Taste and adjust the seasoning of the sauce and pour around the meat.

Hungarian beef

Overall timing 2½ hours

Freezing Suitable: reheat in 325°F (170°C) Gas 3 oven for 20 minutes, then add vegetables

To serve 4

1½ lb	Braising steak	700 g
2 oz	Lard	50 g
2	Onions	2
1 tbsp	Paprika	15 ml
½ teasp	Caraway seeds	2.5 ml
¾ pint	Beef stock	400 ml
	Salt and pepper	
2	Green peppers	2
8 oz	Tomatoes	225 g
1 lb	Potatoes	450 g

Preheat the oven to 325°F (170°C) Gas 3.

Cut steak into four equal-size pieces. Melt half the lard in a flameproof casserole, add the steaks and brown quickly on both sides. Remove from casserole and reserve.

Peel and chop the onions. Add remaining lard to casserole and fry onions gently for about 10 minutes till golden, stirring frequently. Remove casserole from the heat and stir in the paprika, mixing well. Add the caraway seeds, one-third of the stock, the steak and seasoning. Cover and cook in the oven for 1½ hours.

Meanwhile, deseed and slice peppers. Blanch, peel and chop tomatoes. Peel and thinly slice potatoes. Remove casserole from oven and stir in remaining stock, peppers, tomatoes and potatoes. Cover and cook for a further 30 minutes till potatoes are tender. Taste and adjust seasoning.

Lift out meat and place in individual deep serving plates. Spoon vegetables and sauce over.

Steamed steak and kidney pudding

Overall timing 5¾ hours

Freezing Suitable: steam from frozen for 2½–3 hours

To serve 6

1½ lb	Chuck or blade steak	700 g
8 oz	Ox kidney	225 g
1	Large onion	1
	Salt and pepper	
3 tbsp	Plain flour	3x15 ml
12 oz	Self-raising flour	350 g
6 oz	Shredded suet	175 g
½ pint	Cold beef stock	300 ml

Cut the meat into 1½ inch (4 cm) cubes. Trim the kidney, removing any core, and cut into 1 inch (2.5 cm) cubes. Peel and thinly slice the onion. Season plain flour and use to coat the steak, kidney and onion.

Sift the self-raising flour and 1½ teasp (7.5 ml) salt into a bowl and stir in the suet and enough cold water to mix to a soft but not sticky dough. Knead lightly till smooth.

Roll out on a floured surface to a round, big enough to line a 3 pint (1.7 litre) pudding basin (about 14 inches/35 cm in diameter). Cut out one-quarter of the dough round and reserve. Lift the large piece and place it in the basin, curving it so it fits neatly, and sealing the edges together. Place the meat mixture in the basin and add the cold stock to come half-way up the meat.

Roll out the reserved dough to a round slightly larger than the top of the basin. Brush the top edge of the dough lining with water and cover with the dough lid. Seal the edges well.

Cover with greased, pleated greaseproof paper and pleated foil, or a pudding cloth and secure with string. Steam for 5 hours, topping up with boiling water as required.

Tripe and onions French style

Overall timing 1 hour 50 minutes

Freezing Not suitable

To serve 4

1	Large carrot	1
1½ lb	Onions	700 g
2	Stalks of celery	2
3 pints	Cold water	1.7 litres
	Bay leaf	
6	Peppercorns	6
1 tbsp	Lemon juice	15 ml
1½ lb	Dressed tripe	700 g
3 oz	Butter	75 g
	Salt and pepper	
2 tbsp	Chopped parsley	2x15 ml
2 tbsp	White wine vinegar	2x15 ml

Peel and chop carrot and one of the onions. Trim and chop celery. Put into a saucepan with water, bay leaf, peppercorns and lemon juice. Bring to the boil and simmer for 30 minutes. Strain and return to pan.

Cut tripe into pieces. Place in pan with stock and bring to the boil. Skim off any scum, cover and simmer for 1½ hours till tender.

Peel and slice remaining onions. Melt butter in a frying pan, add the onions and fry gently till golden.

Drain the tripe thoroughly, discarding the stock, and cut into thin strips. Add to the onions with plenty of seasoning and fry over a moderate heat for 10 minutes, stirring frequently. Add the parsley and vinegar and mix lightly. Season to taste and pour into a warmed serving dish. Serve immediately with crusty bread.

LAMB

New Zealand roast lamb

Overall timing 3–3½ hours

Freezing Not suitable

To serve 4–6

4 lb	Leg of lamb	1.8 kg
2 tbsp	Oil	2x15 ml
	Fresh rosemary *or*	
2 teasp	Dried rosemary	2x5 ml
	Salt and pepper	
¼ pint	Water	150 ml
2 lb	Potatoes	900 g

Preheat oven to 350°F (180°C) Gas 4.

Place lamb in roasting tin, then rub the oil into the skin. Either make small slits in the meat and insert fresh rosemary leaves, or sprinkle surface with dried rosemary, then season well. Add water to the tin and cook for 3–3½ hours – the meat should almost be falling off the bone.

Meanwhile, peel, parboil and dry the potatoes. Add them to the roasting tin 1½ hours before end of cooking time and turn them till coated in fat. Turn again once during roasting.

Beanpot with lamb

Overall timing 2 hours 50 minutes plus overnight soaking

Freezing Not suitable

To serve 4

8 oz	Dried haricot beans	225 g
½ teasp	Salt	2.5 ml
1 oz	Dripping	25 g
1 lb	Chump lamb chops	450 g
1	Onion	1
4 tbsp	Tomato purée	4x15 ml
½ teasp	Ground cumin	2.5 ml
1	Bay leaf	1
½ teasp	Dried rosemary	2.5 ml
½ teasp	Garlic salt	2.5 ml
	Brown sugar	
½ teasp	Vinegar	2.5 ml
1 tbsp	Chopped chives	15 ml

Soak beans in 2½ pints (1.5 litres) water overnight. Next day, transfer beans and water to a saucepan, add salt and cook for 1 hour.

Melt dripping in a flameproof casserole and brown chops well on all sides. Peel and chop onion and add to casserole. Cook till transparent. Add beans and water, tomato purée, cumin, bay leaf, rosemary and garlic salt. Cover and cook for 1 hour.

Uncover and cook for a further 20 minutes till meat is tender.

Just before serving, stir in a pinch of sugar and the vinegar and sprinkle with chopped chives.

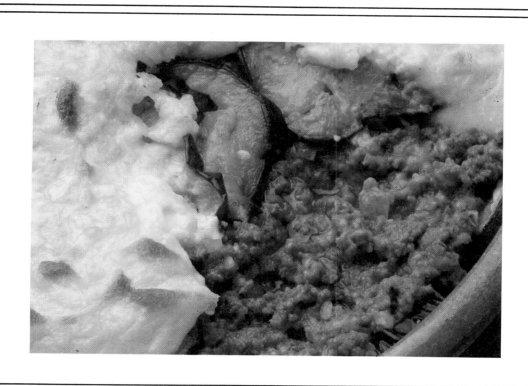

Moussaka

Overall timing 2¼ hours

Freezing Suitable: bake from frozen in 375°F (190°C) Gas 5 oven for 1½ hours; add cheese sauce and bake 30 minutes more

To serve 6

1 lb	Onions	450 g
4	Garlic cloves	4
¼ pint	Oil	150 ml
1 tbsp	Chopped parsley	15 ml
2 lb	Minced lamb	900 g
4	Tomatoes	4
2 tbsp	Tomato purée	2x15 ml
	Salt and pepper	
¼ pint	Stock	150 ml
2 oz	Fresh breadcrumbs	50 g
2 lb	Aubergines	900 g
1 oz	Plain flour	25 g
2	Egg yolks	2
¾ pint	Thick white sauce	400 ml
4 oz	Strong cheese	125 g

Peel and chop onions; peel and crush garlic. Heat 1 tbsp (15 ml) oil in saucepan and fry onions, parsley, garlic and lamb till browned. Peel and quarter tomatoes and add to pan with tomato purée, seasoning and stock. Cover and simmer for 45 minutes. Remove from heat and stir in breadcrumbs.

Preheat oven to 350°F (180°C) Gas 4.

Thinly slice aubergines. Dust lightly with flour. Heat remaining oil in frying pan and brown aubergines. Drain on kitchen paper.

Arrange two-thirds of aubergines to cover bottom and sides of greased casserole. Add meat mixture, then top with remaining aubergines. Stir beaten egg yolks into sauce with half cheese, grated. Pour sauce over aubergines. Cover with rest of grated cheese. Put casserole in a roasting tin containing a little water. Bake for 1 hour.

Lamb kebabs with prunes

Overall timing 50 minutes

Freezing Not suitable

To serve 4

12	Prunes	12
¼ pint	Red wine	150 ml
1 lb	Lean lamb cut from the leg	450 g
3 tbsp	Oil	3x15 ml
	Salt and pepper	
½ teasp	Dried thyme	2.5 ml
2	Firm tomatoes	2
1	Medium onion	1
3	Thick rashers of streaky bacon	3

Put the prunes into a saucepan, add the red wine and bring to the boil. Remove from the heat and leave to soak for 30 minutes.

Cut lamb into 12 large cubes. Place in bowl with oil, seasoning and thyme. Cover and leave for 30 minutes.

Meanwhile, quarter the tomatoes. Peel the onion and cut through the root into eight wedges. Derind bacon and cut each rasher into four. Preheat the grill.

Drain the prunes, reserving the wine. Make a slit in each prune and remove the stone. Thread the lamb, prunes, tomatoes, bacon and onion on to four skewers. Brush the kebabs with the lamb marinade and the wine from the prunes, then sprinkle with salt and pepper. Grill for about 15 minutes, turning occasionally, till the lamb is tender. Arrange on a warmed serving dish and serve with boiled rice.

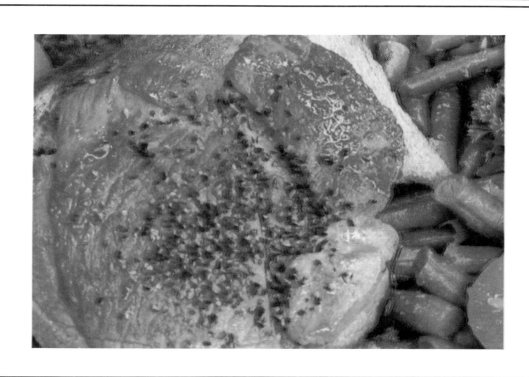

Lamb steaks with beans

Overall timing 45 minutes

Freezing Not suitable

To serve 4

1½ lb	Green beans	700 g
2 oz	Butter	50 g
	Salt and pepper	
4 fl oz	Meat stock	120 ml
5 tbsp	Oil	5x15 ml
2	Slices of white bread	2
¼ teasp	Garlic salt	1.25 ml
4	Lamb steaks	4
1 teasp	Mustard seed	5 ml
2 tbsp	Chopped parsley	2x15 ml
2	Tomatoes	2
	Sprigs of parsley	

Top and tail beans and remove strings. Break or cut into short lengths. Melt the butter in a saucepan. Add the beans and cook for a few minutes. Season with salt and pour in the stock. Cook for 10–15 minutes till just tender.

Meanwhile, heat half the oil in a frying pan. Halve the slices of bread and lightly brown them on both sides in the oil. Remove from pan and keep warm.

Add rest of oil to pan and heat. Sprinkle garlic salt over the lamb steaks. Cook the steaks for 5 minutes on each side. Sprinkle with salt, then with pepper mixed with ground mustard seed.

Mix chopped parsley into beans and spread over bottom of warmed serving dish. Put the lamb steaks on the bread and place on top of the beans. Garnish with tomatoes, cut into eighths, and a few parsley sprigs.

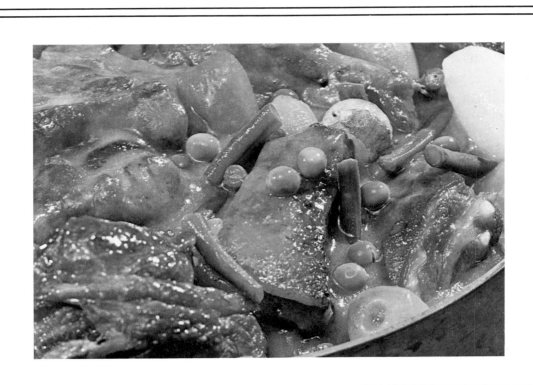

Summer casserole of lamb

Overall timing 1 hour

Freezing Suitable: add potatoes, beans and peas after reheating

To serve 6

8 oz	Button onions	225 g
1 oz	Butter	25 g
1 tbsp	Oil	15 ml
2½ lb	Middle neck lamb chops	1.1 kg
6	New carrots	6
2	Garlic cloves	2
1 tbsp	Plain flour	15 ml
4	Tomatoes	4
2 tbsp	Tomato purée	2x15 ml
¾ pint	Stock	400 ml
	Bouquet garni	
	Salt and pepper	
1 lb	New potatoes	450 g
2 oz	Green beans	50 g
2 oz	Peas	50 g

Peel button onions. Heat butter and oil in flameproof casserole and fry onions for 5 minutes. Remove from pan and reserve. Add chops and brown on all sides over a high heat.

Scrape carrots and halve if liked. Add to pan with peeled and crushed garlic and cook for 5 minutes. Sprinkle flour over and cook, stirring, for 3 minutes.

Blanch, peel and chop tomatoes. Add to the pan with tomato purée, stock, bouquet garni and seasoning. Cover and simmer for 30 minutes.

Scrape potatoes and add to the casserole. Cook for a further 10 minutes. Top and tail beans and cut into short lengths. Add to pan with peas and reserved onions. Cover and cook for a further 10 minutes. Taste and adjust seasoning if necessary. Discard bouquet garni and serve.

Dolma kara

Overall timing 1¾ hours

Freezing Not suitable

To serve 6

2 tbsp	Oil	2x15 ml
2	Onions	2
1 lb	Boned lamb	450 g
4 oz	Canned chickpeas	125 g
½ pint	Stock	300 ml
	Salt and pepper	
2 tbsp	Tomato purée	2x15 ml
8 oz	Minced cooked lamb	225 g
2 oz	Cooked rice	50 g
1	Egg	1
1 teasp	Lemon juice	5 ml
2 tbsp	Chopped parsley	2x15 ml
	Ground cinnamon	
1 lb	Courgettes	450 g

Heat oil in a saucepan. Peel and chop one of the onions and fry till tender. Cut the lamb into small pieces and add to the pan. Cook for 5–10 minutes.

Add the drained chickpeas, stock, salt, pepper and tomato purée. Cover and simmer for 30 minutes.

Preheat the oven to 375°F (190°C) Gas 5.

Mix the cooked lamb with the cooked rice, remaining onion, peeled and finely chopped, egg, lemon juice, half the parsley, seasoning and a pinch of cinnamon.

Trim courgettes, then cut them in half lengthways. Scoop out the seeds with a teaspoon. Blanch courgettes in boiling salted water for 5 minutes. Drain, then stuff the courgettes with the rice and lamb mixture.

Put the lamb and chickpea stew in an oven-proof dish and place stuffed courgettes on top. Cover with foil and bake for 40 minutes. Serve hot sprinkled with remaining parsley.

Lamb with broad beans and potatoes

Overall timing 1½ hours

Freezing Not suitable

To serve 6

4	Tomatoes	4
4 oz	Streaky bacon rashers	125 g
2	Onions	2
2	Garlic cloves	2
2 tbsp	Oil	2x15 ml
6	Lamb blade chops	6
½ pint	Stock	300 ml
1 tbsp	Lemon juice	15 ml
½ teasp	Dried thyme	2.5 ml
	Salt and pepper	
1½ lb	Shelled broad beans	700 g
1½ lb	Potatoes	700 g

Blanch, peel and chop tomatoes. Derind and chop bacon. Peel and slice onions. Peel and crush garlic. Heat oil in a flameproof casserole and fry onion and garlic till transparent. Add the chops and bacon and brown on all sides.

Add tomatoes, stock, lemon juice, thyme and seasoning. Cover and simmer for 30 minutes.

Blanch beans in boiling water for 5 minutes, then drain. Peel and slice the potatoes. Add potatoes to casserole and cook for 10 minutes. Add beans and cook for a further 15 minutes. Serve immediately.

Italian-style roast lamb

Overall timing 1½ hours

Freezing Not suitable

To serve 4

2 lb	Chump end of loin of lamb	900 g
	Sprigs of rosemary	
2 lb	Potatoes	900 g
2 tbsp	Oil	2x15 ml
3 oz	Butter	75 g
1	Garlic clove	1
	Salt and pepper	

Preheat the oven to 350°F (180°C) Gas 4.

Slash through the chops, leaving the loin joined at the bottom. Place sprigs of rosemary in the slashes. Peel potatoes and cut into chunks.

Heat oil and butter in roasting tin. Add the meat and arrange potatoes around it. Peel and crush garlic and add to the lamb and potatoes with salt and pepper. Roast for 45 minutes–1 hour, basting occasionally and turning potatoes halfway through cooking. Serve with a mixed salad or a seasonal green vegetable and gravy.

Sweet sour lamb riblets

Overall timing 1¼ hours plus overnight marination

Freezing Not suitable

To serve 4

1	Onion	1
2	Garlic cloves	2
2 tbsp	Honey	2x15 ml
1 tbsp	Oil	15 ml
4 tbsp	Soy sauce	4x15 ml
¼ pint	Dry sherry	150 ml
1 teasp	Ground ginger	5 ml
2 oz	Caster sugar	50 g
1 teasp	Ground allspice	5 ml
2½ lb	Breast of lamb riblets	1.1 kg

Peel and slice onion. Peel and crush garlic. Put into a bowl with the honey, oil, soy sauce, sherry, ginger, sugar and allspice. Add the breast riblets, cover and marinate overnight in the refrigerator, turning occasionally.

The next day, preheat the oven to 375°F (190°C) Gas 5.

Put the meat into a roasting tin and spoon the marinade over. Bake for 1 hour, basting frequently with the marinade. Serve with plain boiled rice.

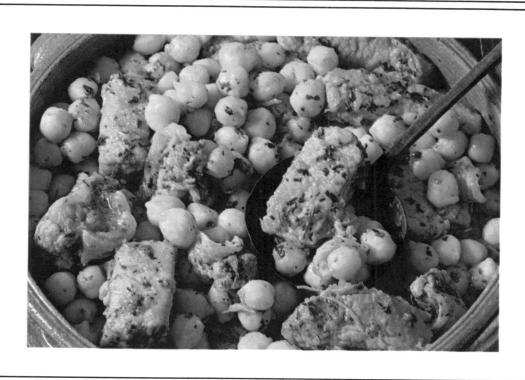

Turkish lamb stew

Overall timing 2¾ hours plus overnight soaking

Freezing Not suitable

To serve 6

12 oz	Dried chickpeas	350 g
	Bouquet garni	
2 lb	Boned shoulder of lamb	900 g
1	Onion	1
1	Garlic clove	1
2 oz	Butter	50 g
3 tbsp	Oil	3x15 ml
1 teasp	Ground cumin	5 ml
1 teasp	Ground cinnamon	5 ml
	Sprig of rosemary	
1	Bay leaf	1
	Salt and pepper	
14 oz	Can of tomatoes	397 g
2 tbsp	Lemon juice	2x15 ml
1 tbsp	Chopped parsley	15 ml

Soak chickpeas in water to cover overnight. The next day, drain chickpeas and put into saucepan. Cover with boiling water and add bouquet garni. Cover and simmer for 1 hour.

Cut the lamb into large pieces. Peel and chop the onion. Peel and crush garlic. Heat the butter and oil in flameproof casserole and fry the onion, garlic, cumin and cinnamon for 5 minutes. Add meat pieces to pan and brown on all sides.

Drain chickpeas and add to casserole with the rosemary, bay leaf, seasoning and tomatoes. Cover and cook gently for 1½ hours. Adjust seasoning and sprinkle with lemon juice and parsley just before serving.

Lamb with cauliflower

Overall timing 1½ hours

Freezing Not suitable

To serve 6

1	Small cauliflower	1
½ pint	Water	300 ml
	Salt and pepper	
8 oz	Tomatoes	225 g
1	Large onion	1
2	Garlic cloves	2
2 tbsp	Oil	2x15 ml
2 lb	Breast of lamb riblets	900 g
¼ pint	Tomato juice	150 ml

Trim cauliflower and divide into florets. Bring water and ½ teasp (2.5 ml) salt to the boil in a saucepan, add cauliflower and cook for 5 minutes. Drain, reserving cooking liquor.

Blanch, peel and chop tomatoes. Peel and chop onion. Peel and crush garlic. Heat the oil and garlic in a saucepan, add onion and cook till transparent. Season meat, add to pan and brown quickly on all sides over a high heat, turning frequently to prevent the riblets burning.

Add tomatoes to pan with reserved cooking liquor and tomato juice. Bring to the boil. Add pepper and cook, covered, for 1 hour.

Add cauliflower and cook for a further 15 minutes. Adjust seasoning, then serve with boiled potatoes.

French lamb hot-pot

Overall timing 1¾ hours

Freezing Not suitable

To serve 4

4 oz	Streaky bacon	125 g
2	Onions	2
1 oz	Butter	25 g
2 tbsp	Oil	2x15 ml
2½ lb	Neck of lamb chops	1.1 kg
1 tbsp	Plain flour	15 ml
¾ pint	Light stock	400 ml
1 lb	Turnips	450 g
1 lb	Potatoes	450 g
2	Garlic cloves	2
1 teasp	Caster sugar	5 ml
	Bouquet garni	
	Salt and pepper	
4	Large tomatoes	4

Derind the bacon and cut into strips. Peel onions and slice into thin rings. Heat the butter and oil in a saucepan and fry the bacon and onions. Add lamb and fry over a high heat till browned on both sides. Sprinkle in the flour and cook, stirring, till it browns. Gradually add the stock and bring to the boil.

Peel the turnips and potatoes and cut into quarters. Add to the pan with the peeled and crushed garlic, sugar, bouquet garni and seasoning. Cover and simmer for 1¼ hours.

Remove bouquet garni. Add the tomatoes and cook for a further 15 minutes. Taste and adjust the seasoning. Arrange the meat and vegetables on a warmed serving dish and spoon the cooking liquor over. Serve immediately.

Shepherds' pie

Overall timing 1 hour

Freezing Not suitable

To serve 4

2 lb	Potatoes	900 g
	Salt and pepper	
1	Large onion	1
3 tbsp	Oil	3x15 ml
1	Garlic clove	1
1 lb	Minced cooked lamb	450 g
2 oz	Butter	50 g
¼ pint	Milk	150 ml
3 oz	Cheese	75 g

Peel and halve potatoes. Cook in boiling salted water for 25–30 minutes.

Peel and finely chop onion. Heat oil in a frying pan, add onion and cook for about 10 minutes. Peel and crush garlic. Add garlic and meat to pan and cook for about 5 minutes, stirring.

Preheat the oven to 425°F (220°C) Gas 7.

Drain potatoes and mash with half the butter and the milk. Season to taste. Cover bottom of ovenproof dish with half of the mashed potato, cover with the meat, then spread or pipe the remaining potato on top.

Grate cheese. Sprinkle over potato, dot with remaining butter and bake for about 15 minutes till the top is browned. Serve with green salad.

Lamb stew

Overall timing 2 hours

Freezing Suitable: add potatoes after reheating

To serve 4

2 oz	Butter	50 g
1 tbsp	Oil	15 ml
2½ lb	Middle neck lamb chops	1.1 kg
2 tbsp	Plain flour	2x15 ml
½ pint	Stock or water	300 ml
8 oz	Turnips	225 g
2	Onions	2
8 ŏz	Carrots	225 g
1	Stalk of celery	1
	Bouquet garni	
	Salt and pepper	
1 lb	Potatoes	450 g

Heat the butter and oil in a flameproof casserole, add the chops and brown well on all sides. Sprinkle flour over and cook, stirring, for 3 minutes. Gradually stir in stock or water.

Peel and chop turnips and onions. Peel carrots and cut into pieces lengthways. Add to casserole with celery stalk, bouquet garni and seasoning. Cover and cook for 1½ hours over low heat.

Peel potatoes and cut into large chunks. Add to casserole and cook, covered, for a further 20 minutes. Discard bouquet garni before serving.

Russian lamb burgers

Overall timing 30 minutes

Freezing Suitable: coat with flour and fry after thawing

To serve 2

1 oz	Fresh breadcrumbs	25 g
2 tbsp	Milk	2x15 ml
8 oz	Minced shoulder of lamb	225 g
1 oz	Gruyère cheese	25 g
1	Small egg	1
	Salt and pepper	
1 tbsp	Plain flour	15 ml
1 oz	Butter	25 g
8 oz	Can of tomatoes	226 g

Put breadcrumbs in a large bowl with the milk and soak for a few minutes. Add the lamb, grated cheese, egg and seasoning and mix well. Divide the mixture into four and shape into patties. Coat lightly with flour.

Melt butter in a frying pan and fry for 5 minutes on each side. Remove from pan with a spatula and place on a warmed serving dish. Keep hot.

Heat tomatoes in a saucepan. Drain and arrange on serving dish with the burgers. Serve a hot tomato sauce separately, if liked, and mashed potatoes topped with crisp fried breadcrumbs and bacon bits.

Shoulder of lamb with turnips

Overall timing 2 hours

Freezing Not suitable

To serve 6

3 lb	Boned shoulder of lamb	1.4 kg
	Salt and pepper	
1	Carrot	1
1	Onion	1
3 oz	Butter	75 g
	Bouquet garni	
¼ pint	Stock	150 ml
2 lb	Turnips	900 g
8 oz	Buttons onions	225 g

Preheat the oven to 350°F (180°C) Gas 4.

Season the lamb inside and out. Roll up and tie firmly with string into a neat shape. Peel and thinly slice carrot and onion.

Melt the butter in flameproof casserole, add onion and carrot and fry till golden. Add lamb and brown on all sides. Season and add bouquet garni and stock. Cover and cook in centre of oven for 1 hour.

Peel turnips and button onions. Place in a saucepan of cold salted water and bring to the boil. Drain and dry on kitchen paper. Arrange turnips and onions around the meat and adjust seasoning. Return to oven and cook for a further 45 minutes.

Remove bouquet garni and string. Transfer lamb to warmed serving plate and surround with turnips and onions.

Stuffed breast of lamb

Overall timing 2½ hours

Freezing Not suitable

To serve 8

1 or 2	Boned breasts of lamb	1 or 2
2 lb	Potatoes	900 g
1½ lb	Small carrots	700 g
4	Turnips	4
2	Stalks of celery	2
4	Leeks	4
1	Onion	1
4	Cloves	4
2 oz	Butter	50 g
1 pint	Stock	560 ml
	Bouquet garni	
Stuffing		
3	Lambs' kidneys	3
8 oz	Streaky bacon	225 g
8 oz	Sausagemeat	225 g
½ teasp	Ground allspice	2.5 ml
3 tbsp	Chopped parsley	3x15 ml
1 teasp	Dried marjoram	5 ml
1	Egg	1
	Salt and pepper	

Preheat the oven to 325°F (170°C) Gas 3.

Prepare and finely chop kidneys. Derind and chop bacon. Mix all stuffing ingredients.

Cut a deep pocket in lamb and fill with stuffing. Sew up opening. If using two breasts, place together with skin side out and sew around sides.

Peel potatoes and carrots. Peel and halve turnips. Chop celery and leeks. Peel onion and spike with cloves. Melt butter in flameproof casserole, add meat and brown all over. Remove. Add vegetables and fry for 2 minutes. Return meat and add stock, bouquet garni and salt. Cover and cook in oven for 2 hours.

Slice meat. Arrange vegetables around meat, discarding onion. Boil stock till reduced by half. Strain over vegetables.

Lamb with vegetables

Overall timing 2 hours

Freezing Not suitable

To serve 6

1½ lb	Best end of neck of lamb	700 g
2 pints	Water	1.1 litres
1 lb	Small swedes	450 g
8 oz	Carrots	225 g
2	Large leeks	2
	Salt and pepper	
1 lb	Waxy potatoes	450 g
1 tbsp	Chopped parsley	15 ml
2 tbsp	Plain flour	2x15 ml

Wipe and trim the lamb, removing the skin. Put into a large saucepan with the water and bring slowly to the boil.

Meanwhile, peel the swedes thickly and cut into quarters. Scrape and thickly slice the carrots. Wash and trim the leeks; slice the white parts and reserve the green.

Add the prepared vegetables to the pan with salt and pepper and bring back to the boil. Cover and simmer for 1 hour.

Peel the potatoes and cut into quarters. Add to the pan and simmer for 20 minutes.

Shred the green part of the leeks and add to the pan with the parsley. Simmer for 5 minutes.

Remove the meat from the pan and keep hot. Blend the flour to a smooth paste with 5 tbsp (5x15 ml) water. Add to the cooking liquor and bring to the boil, stirring constantly. Simmer for 3 minutes. Taste and adjust the seasoning, then pour into a warmed serving dish. Arrange the meat on top and serve.

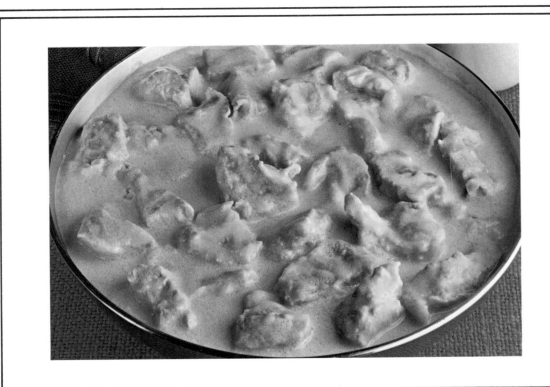

Lamb fricassee

Overall timing 1¼ hours

Freezing Not suitable

To serve 4

1½ lb	Boned shoulder of lamb	700 g
1	Onion	1
1	Stalk of celery	1
2 oz	Butter	50 g
1 tbsp	Plain flour	15 ml
¼ pint	Milk	150 ml
¼ pint	Stock	150 ml
1	Carrot	1
2	Sprigs of parsley	2
2	Sprigs of basil	2
2	Sprigs of sage	2
	Salt and pepper	
2	Egg yolks	2
1 tbsp	Lemon juice	15 ml

Cut the lamb into neat pieces. Peel and chop the onion. Trim and chop the celery. Melt half the butter in a flameproof casserole. Add onion and celery and fry over low heat for 5 minutes without browning.

Stir in the flour and fry until golden. Gradually add milk and stock, stirring constantly. Bring to the boil, then remove from heat.

Scrape and chop carrot. Tie in a piece of muslin with parsley, basil and sage. Add to casserole with remaining butter, the lamb and seasoning. Stir well. Cover and cook gently for 1 hour, stirring occasionally. Remove muslin bag.

Beat the egg yolks in a bowl and blend with the lemon juice. Stir gently into the fricassee until blended; do not boil. Taste and adjust seasoning, then serve with creamed potatoes and minted peas.

Kidneys in their jackets

Overall timing 45 minutes

Freezing Not suitable

To serve 4

8	Lamb kidneys in their suet	8
4	Slices of bread	4
	Salt and pepper	
1	Tomato	1
	Sprigs of parsley	

Preheat the oven to 400°F (200°C) Gas 6.

Place kidneys in their suet in a roasting tin. Bake for about 35 minutes till the fat is crisp and golden.

Pour a little of the melted fat from the roasting tin into a frying pan and fry the bread till golden on both sides. Arrange slices in warmed individual dishes.

Cut a deep cross in the top of the kidneys and open out like petals. Season inside and place on top of fried bread. Wash tomatoes and cut into wedges. Arrange with parsley sprigs on top of kidneys. Serve with sauté or mashed potatoes.

Ham roasted in stout

Overall timing 2½ hours plus cooling

Freezing Suitable: slice meat and cover with sauce; reheat from frozen in moderate oven

To serve 6

3 lb	Lightly salted ham or bacon (collar, slipper, or gammon)	1.4 kg
2	Onions	2
½ pint	Stout	300 ml
1 oz	Butter	25 g
1 oz	Plain flour	25 g
¼ teasp	Crushed caraway seed	1.25 ml
	Pepper	

Preheat the oven to 400°F (200°C) Gas 4.

If using bacon joint, remove rind. Place ham or bacon in an ovenproof dish. Peel onions and slice into rings. Cover ham with onion rings. Pour stout over. Roast for 2 hours, turning meat once during cooking.

Remove meat from dish and place on warmed serving dish. Keep hot. Sieve cooking liquor, cool quickly and skim fat from surface. Place liquor in measuring jug and make up to ½ pint (300 ml) with water if necessary.

Melt butter in saucepan. Stir in flour and allow to brown lightly. Gradually add cooking liquor and simmer, stirring, till thickened. Season with crushed caraway seed and black pepper. Cook for 5 minutes, then pour over the roast and serve.

Bacon with lentils

Overall timing 2½ hours plus 3 hours soaking

Freezing Not suitable

To serve 6

2¼ lb	Middle cut bacon hock	1 kg
1	Carrot	1
2	Onions	2
1	Garlic clove	1
	Bouquet garni	
8	Peppercorns	8
1 lb	Continental lentils	450 g
	Salt and pepper	

Put bacon joint in a large saucepan and cover with cold water. Soak for 3 hours, changing the water several times.

Drain the bacon joint and cover with fresh water. Peel and slice the carrot; peel and quarter the onions; peel and halve the garlic. Add to the bacon with the bouquet garni and peppercorns. Bring to the boil, cover and simmer for 45 minutes.

Remove bouquet garni. Wash and pick over lentils. Add to bacon, cover and cook for a further hour till lentils are tender. Adjust seasoning, then arrange on warmed dish and serve with mustard.

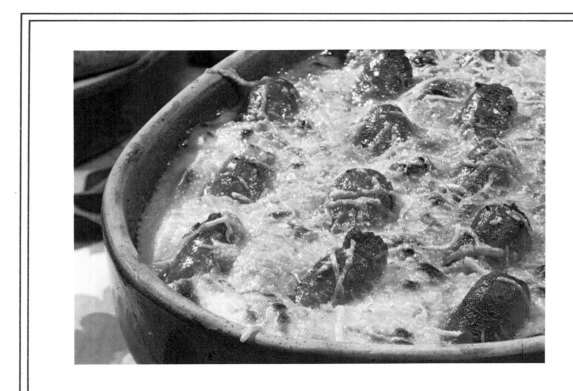

Sausage surprise

Overall timing 35 minutes

Freezing Not suitable

To serve 4–6

2 lb	Potatoes	900 g
	Salt and pepper	
1 lb	Chipolatas	450 g
½ pint	Milk	300 ml
2 oz	Butter	50 g
6 oz	Cheese	175 g
½ teasp	Grated nutmeg	2.5 ml

Preheat the grill. Peel the potatoes and cut into quarters. Cook in boiling salted water for about 10 minutes till tender.

Meanwhile, grill the chipolatas for about 15 minutes, turning occasionally till well browned.

Drain the potatoes in a colander. Add the milk to the pan and bring just to the boil. Return the potatoes to the pan with the butter and mash till smooth.

Grate cheese and beat 4 oz (125 g) into potatoes with nutmeg and seasoning. Spread the mixture in a flameproof dish and push the chipolatas diagonally into the potato so that the tops are just showing.

Sprinkle the remaining cheese over and grill for about 5 minutes till golden.

Sausage and vegetable stew

Overall timing 3¼ hours

Freezing Not suitable

To serve 6

1	White cabbage	1
3	Carrots	3
1	Leek	1
1	Bacon knuckle	1
1	Pig's knuckle	1
3½ pints	Water	2 litres
	Salt and pepper	
2	Large potatoes	2
8 oz	Sausages	225 g

Shred cabbage. Peel and chop carrots. Trim and slice leek. Put vegetables into a pan with the knuckles, water and seasoning. Bring to the boil, then cover and cook for 2½ hours.

Remove knuckles from pan and cut meat from bones. Peel potatoes and cut into large chunks. Cut sausages in half. Add meat, potatoes and sausages to pan and cook for a further 30 minutes. Taste and adjust seasoning before serving.

Poule-au-pot

Overall timing 4 hours

Freezing Not suitable

To serve 6

2 oz	Streaky bacon	50 g
4 oz	Pork sausagemeat	125 g
2 oz	Fresh breadcrumbs	50 g
2 tbsp	Chopped parsley	2 x 15 ml
	Salt and pepper	
2	Eggs	2
3½ lb	Boiling chicken	1.6 kg
4	Medium-size onions	4
4	Small turnips	4
6	Large carrots	6
2	Leeks	2
4	Stalks of celery	4
2 oz	Dripping	50 g
	Bouquet garni	
12 oz	Long grain rice	350 g

Derind bacon, reserving rinds, and chop finely. Mix sausagemeat, bacon, breadcrumbs, parsley and seasoning and bind with eggs. Spoon into chicken and truss.

Peel onions, turnips and carrots. Trim leeks and celery. Heat dripping in a large pan and brown chicken all over. Add one of the onions, turnips, leeks and celery stalks and two carrots and fry for 3 minutes. Pour off excess fat.

Add bouquet garni, bacon rinds, giblets and cold water to cover the chicken and bring to the boil. Skim off any scum. Cover and simmer for about 2¼ hours.

Discard vegetables, bacon rinds and bouquet garni. Add remaining vegetables and seasoning. Cover and simmer for a further 45 minutes. Remove from heat. Strain 2¼ pints (1.3 litres) of stock into another saucepan. Keep chicken hot.

Add rice to stock with salt and cover tightly. Bring to boil and simmer for 15–20 minutes till rice is tender.

Fluff rice and arrange on a serving dish. Place chicken on rice and discard trussing strings. Arrange vegetables around chicken and serve.

Chicken supreme

Overall timing 2 hours

Freezing Not suitable

To serve 4

2	Carrots	2
2	Onions	2
2	Leeks	2
1	Stalk of celery	1
	Salt	
2½ pints	Water or stock	1.5 litres
3 lb	Ovenready chicken	1.4 kg
½	Lemon	½
8 oz	Rice	225 g
Sauce		
2 oz	Butter	50 g
1 tbsp	Plain flour	15 ml
2	Egg yolks	2
2 tbsp	Single cream	2x15 ml
	Salt and pepper	

Peel carrots and onions. Chop leeks and celery. Bring salted water or stock to the boil in a flameproof casserole, add prepared vegetables and cook for 15 minutes.

Rub chicken with the lemon. Add to casserole, cover and simmer gently for 1 hour. (If you prefer, chicken joints can be used instead of a whole chicken – they need only to be cooked for 45 minutes.)

Measure out 1 pint (560 ml) stock from casserole and place in a saucepan. Continue cooking chicken for a further 15 minutes. Bring stock in saucepan to the boil, add rice and cook for 15 minutes.

Meanwhile, prepare sauce. Melt butter in a saucepan and stir in flour. Measure out another 1 pint (560 ml) stock from casserole and gradually stir into pan. Cook, stirring till thickened. Remove from heat and stir in egg yolks and then cream. Season.

Drain rice and place on warmed serving dish. Remove chicken from casserole, cut into portions and arrange on top of rice. Pour sauce over and serve.

Chicken with pineapple

Overall timing 45 minutes

Freezing Not suitable

To serve 2

1½ lb	Chicken joints	675 g
2 teasp	Potato flour or cornflour	2x5 ml
3 tbsp	Oil	3x15 ml
1 tbsp	Soy sauce	15 ml
1½ teasp	Dry sherry	7.5 ml
	Salt and pepper	
4 oz	Canned pineapple rings or chunks	125 g

Remove meat from chicken joints and cut it into chunky pieces.

Mix together potato flour or cornflour, half the oil, the soy sauce, sherry and seasoning in a bowl. Add the chicken pieces and coat well. Leave to marinate for 15 minutes.

Heat the rest of the oil in a heavy-based saucepan. Drain the chicken, saving the marinade, and add to the pan. Cook over a fairly high heat for 5 minutes, stirring constantly.

Drain the pineapple, reserving 4 tbsp (4x15 ml) of the syrup. Cut the rings into sections or halve the chunks. Add the reserved marinade from the chicken and the pineapple pieces to the pan and cook for a further 12 minutes, continually turning the chicken over.

When the chicken is golden brown, add the reserved pineapple syrup, adjust seasoning and cook for a further 5 minutes. Serve with saffron rice.

Cheesy chicken rolls

Overall timing 45 minutes

Freezing Not suitable

To serve 6

6	Large chicken breasts	6
	Salt and pepper	
2 teasp	Made mustard	2x5 ml
6	Thin slices of Derby cheese	6
6	Thin streaky bacon rashers	6
	Plain flour	
2 oz	Butter	50 g
2 tbsp	Oil	2x15 ml
½ pint	Light ale	300 ml
12	Stoned green olives	12

Remove skin and bones from chicken breasts. Season underside of chicken breasts and spread with mustard, then place a slice of cheese on each. Roll up and wrap a rasher of bacon around. Tie rolls firmly with string and coat lightly in flour.

Heat butter and oil in flameproof casserole. Lightly brown chicken rolls all over. Add beer, taking care that it does not fill more than half the casserole. Add more seasoning if required. Cover and simmer for 10 minutes.

Meanwhile, scald olives in boiling water. Drain well and add to casserole. Cover and simmer for 10 minutes more. Carefully remove string from chicken rolls and serve with rice or potatoes.

Chicken with turnips

Overall timing 1 hour

Freezing Not suitable

To serve 6

8 oz	Button onions	225 g
6	Saffron strands	6
3 lb	Ovenready chicken	1.4 kg
1½ lb	Small turnips	700 g
8 oz	Courgettes	225 g
2 oz	Butter	50 g
2 tbsp	Oil	2x15 ml
½ pint	Chicken stock	300 ml
4	Bay leaves	4
	Salt and pepper	

Blanch and peel onions. Soak saffron in 2 tbsp (2x15 ml) warm water. Cut chicken into 12 portions. Peel and chop turnips. Slice courgettes.

Heat butter and oil in frying pan and brown chicken pieces all over. Remove from pan with a draining spoon. Add onions and turnips and fry for 3 minutes, then add courgettes and fry for a further 2 minutes till browned.

Return chicken to pan with saffron and soaking water, stock, bay leaves and seasoning. Cover and simmer for 20 minutes till chicken is tender.

Lombardy chicken

Overall timing 2¼ hours

Freezing Not suitable

To serve 4

2 oz	Breadcrumbs	50 g
¼ pint	Milk	150 ml
4 oz	Cooked ham	125 g
3 lb	Chicken with giblets	1.4 kg
4 oz	Sausagemeat	125 g
2 tbsp	Chopped parsley	2x15 ml
1	Egg	1
2 oz	Grated Parmesan cheese	50 g
2 tbsp	Dry vermouth	2x15 ml
	Salt and pepper	
1	Stalk of celery	1
1	Carrot	1
1	Onion	1
2 teasp	Arrowroot	2x5 ml

Soak breadcrumbs in milk. Mince or finely chop ham, and liver and heart from giblets. Place in a bowl with the sausagemeat, parsley, egg, Parmesan, vermouth, salt and pepper. Squeeze liquid out of the breadcrumbs and add them to the mixture. Mix well together.

Wipe chicken and stuff with the mixture, leaving a little space for expansion. Close opening with a small skewer or by sewing with thick thread.

Half fill a large saucepan with lightly salted water and bring to the boil. Chop celery and carrot. Peel and quarter onion. Add them all to the pan and bring back to the boil.

Add the chicken and the rest of the giblets. Cover and simmer for 1¾ hours or until chicken is tender.

Lift chicken out of the stock and keep warm on serving dish. Dissolve the arrowroot in a little of the strained stock, then add a further ½ pint (300 ml) stock. Cook, stirring, until thick and clear.

Chicken baked in salt

Overall timing 1¾ hours

Freezing Not suitable

To serve 4-6

3½ lb	Ovenready chicken	1.6kg
1	Sprig of fresh tarragon	1
	Black pepper	
6 lb	Coarse sea-salt	2.6kg

Preheat the oven to 450°F (230°C) Gas 8.

Wipe the chicken, put the tarragon inside and sprinkle inside and out with pepper. Truss with string.

Line a casserole with a large sheet of foil and spread with one-third of the salt. Place chicken breast-bone down on salt. Cover completely with remaining salt. Fold the foil over the top of the chicken and join together at top, sealing well. Bake, covered, near the top of the oven for 1½ hours.

Take the chicken out of the oven, unwrap and remove the crust of salt. Brush off any salt that clings, then carve the chicken in the usual way.

Pastry-wrapped stuffed chicken

Overall timing 2¼ hours

Freezing Not suitable

To serve 4

3 lb	Ovenready chicken	1.4 kg
	Salt	
1 oz	Butter	25 g
12 oz	Shortcrust pastry	350 g
1	Egg	1
Stuffing		
8 oz	Mushrooms	225 g
1 oz	Butter	25 g
2 tbsp	Sherry	2 x 15 ml
	Salt and pepper	
6 oz	Chicken livers	175 g
1	Small onion	1
2 oz	Dried breadcrumbs	50 g

First make stuffing. Slice mushrooms. Melt butter in a pan and fry mushrooms for 3 minutes. Add sherry and cook for 3 minutes. Season with salt and pepper.

Finely chop chicken livers. Peel and finely chop onion. Add both to pan with breadcrumbs and mix well. Heat gently for 5 minutes.

Season chicken inside and out with salt. Stuff with liver mixture and close the opening. Melt butter in a roasting tin and brown chicken on all sides for 20 minutes.

Preheat the oven to 400°F (200°C) Gas 6.

Roll out dough on a lightly floured surface till about ¼ inch (6 mm) thick and large enough to wrap round chicken. Remove chicken from roasting tin. Drain and allow to cool slightly, then place, breast side down, on dough. Moisten edges and wrap dough round chicken. Press edges together well.

Place chicken on greased baking tray with seam underneath. Use dough trimmings to decorate top. Brush with beaten egg and bake for 1½–1¾ hours. If pastry shows signs of overbrowning, cover with foil.

Chicken in soured cream

Overall timing 1 hour

Freezing Not suitable

To serve 4

3 lb	Chicken portions	1.4 kg
2 tbsp	Plain flour	2x15 ml
4 oz	Button mushrooms	125 g
1	Onion	1
2 oz	Butter	50 g
2 tbsp	Oil	2x15 ml
	Salt and pepper	
2 tbsp	Brandy	2x15 ml
¼ pint	Carton of soured cream	150 ml

Wash chicken portions and dry on kitchen paper. Coat lightly with the flour. Wipe and slice mushrooms. Peel and slice onion.

Heat butter and oil in a frying pan and fry onion till golden. Add floured chicken portions and brown on all sides. Season with salt and pepper. Cover and cook for 40 minutes.

Pour brandy over the chicken and heat for a few minutes, then set alight. When the flames have died down, add the sliced mushrooms and cook over a gentle heat for 5 minutes.

Add soured cream to pan. Heat through, stirring, for 2 minutes. Do not allow to boil. Serve at once with noodles and a mixed salad.

Poached chicken

Overall timing 2 hours

Freezing Not suitable

To serve 4

8	Chicken legs and wings	8
12 oz	Carrots	350 g
8 oz	Button onions	225 g
2	Stalks of celery	2
	Salt	
1 lb	Potatoes	450 g

Put chicken joints in a large saucepan and cover with cold water. Peel and chop carrots; peel onions; chop celery. Add a few pieces of carrot, four onions, all the celery and salt to chicken. Bring slowly to the boil, then reduce the heat until just simmering, cover and cook for about 1½ hours.

Meanwhile, cook remaining carrots and onions in boiling salted water for 5 minutes. Peel and chop potatoes and add to pan. Simmer for a further 20 minutes. Drain and keep hot.

Drain chicken (keep the cooking liquor and vegetables for soup) and serve on a warmed plate with the separately cooked carrots, onions and potatoes.

Chicken Kiev

Overall timing 1½ hours

Freezing Suitable: egg, crumb and fry after thawing

To serve 4

4 oz	Softened butter	125 g
2 tbsp	Lemon juice	2x15 ml
1	Garlic clove	1
1 tbsp	Chopped parsley	15 ml
	Salt and pepper	
4	Boneless chicken breasts	4
	Oil for frying	
3 tbsp	Plain flour	3x15 ml
1	Egg	1
3 tbsp	Fresh white breadcrumbs	3x15 ml

Work together the butter and lemon juice until smooth. Peel and crush the garlic and add to the butter with the parsley and seasoning. Mix well. Shape into a cylinder, wrap in foil and place in freezer for 1 hour to firm.

Place the chicken breasts between two sheets of dampened greaseproof paper on a flat surface and beat flat with a heavy knife or wooden mallet until thin.

Heat the oil in a deep-fryer to 350°F (170°C).

Place a piece of butter on each chicken breast. Roll chicken round butter and secure with a cocktail stick. Coat each piece of chicken all over with the flour, then dip in the beaten egg to cover and finally in the breadcrumbs, pressing them on well. Fry for 12–15 minutes until golden brown. Drain on kitchen paper, remove cocktail sticks and serve immediately with lemon wedges and a green salad.

Soufflé-topped chicken

Overall timing 1¼ hours

Freezing Not suitable

To serve 4-6

2 tbsp	Oil	2x15 ml
3 lb	Chicken portions	1.4 kg
	Salt and pepper	
1 lb	Can of sweetcorn kernels	450 g
2 tbsp	Fresh breadcrumbs	2x15 ml
Sauce		
3 oz	Butter	75 g
2 oz	Plain flour	50 g
¼ pint	Milk	150 ml
2	Eggs	2
¼ pint	Carton of single cream	150 ml
	Salt and pepper	
	Grated nutmeg	

Preheat the oven to 400°F (200°C) Gas 6.

Heat oil in flameproof casserole. Add chicken and cook for about 10 minutes until pieces are browned on all sides. Season with salt and pepper.

Drain corn and add to the casserole with 4 tbsp (4x15 ml) of the liquid.

To make the sauce, melt 2 oz (50 g) of the butter in a saucepan, sprinkle with the flour and cook till browned, stirring all the time. Gradually add milk and cook, stirring, for 5 minutes. Remove from heat.

Separate eggs. Mix cream, egg yolks, salt, pepper and a pinch of nutmeg in a bowl. Stir into the sauce and heat through but do not boil. Remove from heat and set aside.

Beat egg whites in a bowl until they hold stiff peaks. Fold into sauce with a metal spoon and pour over corn and chicken mixture. Sprinkle with breadcrumbs, dot with remaining butter and bake in the centre of the oven for 45 minutes. Serve with broccoli garnished with chopped hard-boiled eggs.

Crisp lemon chicken

Overall timing 30 minutes plus marination

Freezing Not suitable

To serve 4

8	Chicken portions	8
3 tbsp	Lemon juice	3x15 ml
2 tbsp	Oil	2x15 ml
2 oz	Plain flour	50 g
	Salt and pepper	
½ teasp	Paprika	2.5 ml
	Lemon wedges	

Wash and dry chicken portions. Mix together lemon juice and oil and rub into the chicken. Cover and leave to marinate for 2–3 hours.

Preheat the grill. Mix together the flour, seasoning and paprika.

Arrange chicken portions skin-side down on grill rack. Sift half the seasoned flour over the chicken and grill for 7–10 minutes.

Turn chicken portions over. Sprinkle with remaining sifted flour and grill for a further 7–10 minutes until crisp and golden, and juices run clear when a skewer is inserted. Arrange on a warmed serving dish and garnish with lemon wedges. Serve with a bean, cucumber and tomato salad.

Chicken Maryland

Overall timing 1¾ hours

Freezing Not suitable

To serve 8

8	Boned chicken breasts	8
	Salt	
	Cayenne pepper	
2 oz	Plain flour	50 g
2	Eggs	2
4 oz	Fresh breadcrumbs	125 g
	Oil for frying	
4	Bananas	4
12	Bacon rashers	12
Corn fritters		
4 oz	Plain flour	125 g
1	Whole egg	1
¼ pint	Milk	150 ml
11½ oz	Sweetcorn kernels	325 g
1	Egg white	1

To make the fritter batter, sift flour and pinch of salt into a bowl and make a well in the centre. Add the whole egg and gradually beat in the milk. Drain corn and add. Leave batter to stand.

Cut each chicken breast in half. Season with salt and cayenne pepper. Dip into the flour, then into beaten eggs, then into breadcrumbs.

Heat the oil in a deep-fryer until hot enough to brown a cube of bread in 30 seconds. Fry the chicken pieces a few at a time for about 10–15 minutes, depending on thickness. Remove from pan, drain on kitchen paper and keep hot. Skim surface of oil.

Peel bananas and cut into three, then halve each piece lengthways. Derind and stretch bacon rashers and cut in half. Wrap a piece of bacon round each piece of banana and secure with a wooden cocktail stick. Fry in hot oil, then drain and keep hot.

Whisk egg white till stiff and fold into fritter batter. Drop in spoonfuls into hot oil and fry till puffed and golden brown. Drain. Arrange fritters, chicken and bacon-wrapped bananas on plate and serve.

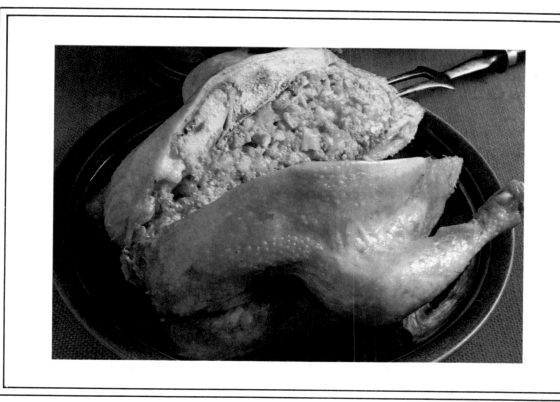

Tunisian chicken

Overall timing 2¼ hours

Freezing Not suitable

To serve 4

3 lb	Ovenready chicken with giblets	1.4 kg
	Salt and pepper	
5 oz	Sweetcorn kernels	150 g
3	Carrots	3
3	Medium potatoes	3
4	Tomatoes	4
4 oz	Cheddar cheese	125 g
1	Egg	1
2 tbsp	Breadcrumbs	2x15 ml
1	Hard-boiled egg	1
1	Stalk of celery	1
1	Sprig of parsley	1
2 oz	Butter	50 g
4 tbsp	Oil	4x15 ml

Season chicken inside and out. Chop heart, liver and gizzard. Drain sweetcorn. Peel carrots and potatoes. Blanch, peel and quarter tomatoes.

Dice the cheese and mix with the sweetcorn, giblets, egg and breadcrumbs. Mash the hard-boiled egg with a fork and add to the mixture with seasoning. Mix well. Stuff the chicken with the mixture, then close opening.

Put carrots, potatoes and tomatoes into a flameproof casserole with celery and parsley. Cover with 2½ pints (1.5 litres) water and bring to the boil. Lower heat and add chicken with half the butter. Cover and simmer for 1½ hours.

Remove chicken and drain on kitchen paper. Strain cooking liquor and return to casserole. Purée vegetables and add to casserole. Heat soup through.

Heat remaining butter and oil in a frying pan. Put in whole chicken and brown evenly, turning it over with two spoons. Bring chicken and soup to table in separate dishes.

Welsh chicken and mace pie

Overall timing 1 hour

Freezing Not suitable

To serve 6

1½ lb	Cooked chicken	700 g
4 oz	Cooked tongue	125 g
1	Onion	1
4	Leeks	4
3	Stalks of celery	3
2 oz	Butter	50 g
1 teasp	Ground mace	5 ml
1 tbsp	Chopped parsley	15 ml
½ pint	Chicken stock	300 ml
	Salt and pepper	
12 oz	Shortcrust pastry	350 g
1	Egg	1

Preheat oven to 400°F (200°C) Gas 6.

Chop chicken into medium-size pieces. Cut the tongue into strips. Peel and thinly slice onion. Trim leeks, then cut into thin slices. Trim and finely chop the celery. Melt butter.

Put chicken, tongue and prepared vegetables in a bowl with mace, parsley and butter and mix well. Place in a large pie dish and add stock and seasoning.

Roll out dough and place on dish. Press edge to dish to seal. Lightly beat the egg and brush over the dough. Bake for 40 minutes, or until the pastry is golden. Serve immediately with mashed potatoes.

Chicken pieces with nutty sauce

Overall timing 1 hour plus marination

Freezing Not suitable

To serve 4

5	Onions	5
1	Garlic clove	1
2 oz	Walnuts	50 g
	Salt	
3 tbsp	Lemon juice	3x15 ml
4	Boned chicken breasts	4
2 tbsp	Groundnut oil	2x15 ml
	Pinch of chilli powder	
2 oz	Roasted peanuts	50 g
2 teasp	Soy sauce	2x5 ml
½ pint	Water	300 ml

Peel and finely chop two onions. Peel and crush garlic. Place both in a mortar or blender with walnuts and salt. Crush or blend to a paste, gradually adding 2 tbsp (2x15 ml) lemon juice to give a creamy mixture. Cut chicken into bite-size pieces. Place in a shallow dish and pour walnut mixture over. Leave to marinate for 1 hour, turning occasionally.

Meanwhile, peel and finely chop two onions. Heat half oil in a frying pan and fry onions till crisp and golden. Remove from pan and drain. Preheat the grill.

Peel and finely chop remaining onion and purée in mortar or blender with chilli powder, salt and peanuts till smooth. Heat remaining oil in pan and fry peanut mixture for 3 minutes, stirring constantly. Stir in soy sauce, water and remaining lemon juice. Cook over low heat for 5 minutes.

Thread chicken pieces on to four oiled skewers. Grill for 10 minutes, turning frequently and brushing with walnut mixture. Add any remaining walnut mixture and fried onions to peanut sauce and heat through.

Chicken parcels

Overall timing 45 minutes

Freezing Suitable: bake from frozen, allowing 35–45 minutes

To serve 6

13 oz	Frozen puff pastry	375 g
1	Medium-size onion	1
1 oz	Butter	25 g
10 oz	Cooked boneless chicken	275 g
3 tbsp	Chopped parsley	3x15 ml
4 tbsp	Double cream	4x15 ml
	Salt and pepper	
3	Slices of cooked ham	3
1	Egg yolk	1
6	Lettuce leaves	6

Thaw pastry. Preheat oven to 400°F (200°C) Gas 6.

Peel and chop onion and fry in the butter till transparent.

Set aside six fairly large pieces of chicken and finely chop the rest. Put chopped chicken into a bowl with the parsley and fried onion. Lightly beat the cream, then stir into the chicken with seasoning.

Roll out the dough on a lightly floured surface. Cut out six 5 inch (12.5 cm) squares. Cut ham slices in half and place one piece in centre of each dough square. Top with a piece of chicken, then cover with chopped chicken mixture. Dampen dough edges with cold water. Fold corners to centre to cover the filling, pinching the edges together, but leaving a small hole in the top. Place parcels on a greased baking tray.

Beat the egg yolk with a pinch of salt and brush over parcels. Bake for 25 minutes or until well risen and golden brown. Serve the parcels on lettuce leaves.

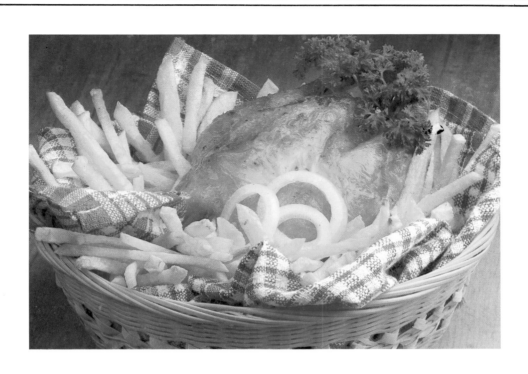

Chicken in a basket

Overall timing 40 minutes

Freezing Not suitable

To serve 2

2x1lb	Ovenready poussins	2x450g
2 tbsp	Oil	2x15ml
	Salt and pepper	
1 lb	Potatoes	450g
	Oil for frying	
	Fresh parsley	
1	Small onion	1

Preheat the oven to 400°F (200°C) Gas 6.

Place the poussins in roasting tin. Brush with oil and season well. Roast for 30 minutes, or until juices from the legs run clear when pierced with a skewer.

Meanwhile, peel potatoes and cut into thin, matchstick chips. Heat oil in a deep-fryer to 340°F (170°C). Fry chips for 3–5 minutes till golden. Drain well.

Arrange napkins in two small baskets. Place chips in folds of cloth. Place poussins in baskets. Garnish with parsley sprigs and onion rings. Eat with your fingers or a knife and fork if preferred.

Variation

To make barbecue-style poussins, mix together 2 tbsp (2x15 ml) tomato purée, 1 tbsp (15 ml) Worcestershire sauce, 1 tbsp (15 ml) oil, 1 peeled and crushed garlic clove and seasoning. Spread over poussins, cover with foil and roast for 40 minutes. Serve as above.

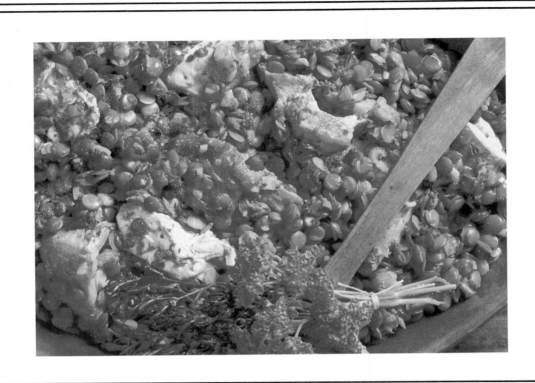

Chicken with lentils

Overall timing 1¼ hours

Freezing Not suitable

To serve 6

12 oz	Continental lentils	350 g
1	Onion	1
1	Carrot	1
	Bouquet garni	
	Salt and pepper	
1 lb	Boned chicken	450 g
1 tbsp	Oil	15 ml
3 oz	Butter	75 g
1 tbsp	Chopped parsley	15 ml

Wash and pick over lentils. Place in a saucepan and add enough cold water just to cover. Peel and finely chop onion. Peel and halve carrot. Add to lentils with bouquet garni and seasoning. Bring to boil, cover and simmer for 35 minutes.

Meanwhile, cut chicken into neat pieces. Heat oil and half the butter in a frying pan, add chicken pieces and fry for 5 minutes, turning once. Add chicken to lentils, cover and simmer for a further 30 minutes.

Discard bouquet garni and carrot. Stir the remaining butter into lentils. Taste and adjust seasoning. Arrange chicken and lentils on a warmed serving dish and sprinkle with parsley. Serve immediately with a mixed salad.

Turkey fries

Overall timing 40 minutes plus marination

Freezing Not suitable

To serve 8

4 tbsp	Oil	4x15 ml
3 tbsp	Lemon juice	3x15 ml
	Salt	
8x4 oz	Slices of turkey breast	8x125 g
4 teasp	Dijon mustard	4x5 ml
2	Eggs	2
8 oz	Fresh breadcrumbs	225 g
2 oz	Butter	50 g
	Chopped parsley	
	Lemon wedges	

Mix 2 tbsp (2x15 ml) of the oil with the lemon juice and a pinch of salt in a shallow dish. Add the turkey, mix well and leave to marinate for 1 hour.

Drain the turkey and pat dry on kitchen paper. Spread thinly with the mustard. Beat the eggs lightly on a plate and use to coat turkey. Dip turkey slices into the breadcrumbs, pressing them on gently.

Melt the butter and remaining oil in a frying pan and gently fry the turkey for about 10 minutes on each side, till tender and golden.

Drain on kitchen paper and arrange on a warmed dish. Garnish with chopped parsley and lemon wedges and serve immediately with a tomato and onion salad dressed with vinaigrette.

Turkey with lemon sauce

Overall timing 30 minutes

Freezing Not suitable

To serve 6

6	Slices of turkey breast	6
	Salt and pepper	
2 tbsp	Plain flour	2x15 ml
2	Thick rashers of back bacon	2
3 oz	Butter	75 g
¼ pint	Chicken stock	150 ml
2 tbsp	Lemon juice	2x15 ml
2 tbsp	Chopped parsley	2x15 ml
	Lemon slices	
	Sprigs of parsley	

Place each slice of turkey between two sheets of damp greaseproof paper and flatten with a rolling pin. Season the flour and use to coat the turkey. Derind bacon and cut into strips.

Melt the butter in a frying pan and cook the bacon for 5 minutes. Add turkey pieces and fry for 3–5 minutes on each side. Remove turkey and bacon from pan and arrange on a warmed serving plate. Keep hot.

Add any remaining seasoned flour to pan and stir well with a wooden spoon, scraping the sediment from the bottom of the pan. Gradually add the stock (made with a cube if necessary) and bring to the boil. Simmer gently for 5 minutes.

Remove pan from heat and stir in the lemon juice and chopped parsley. Taste and adjust seasoning. Pour over the turkey breasts and garnish with lemon slices and parsley sprigs. Serve immediately with a mixed salad.

Oven-fried rabbit

Overall timing 1¼ hours

Freezing Not suitable

To serve 4–6

2 lb	Young rabbit	900 g
	Salt and pepper	
3 tbsp	Plain flour	3x15 ml
½ teasp	Paprika	2.5 ml
2	Eggs	2
2 tbsp	Milk	2x15 ml
2 oz	Dried breadcrumbs	50 g
1 oz	Butter	25 g
4 tbsp	Oil	4x15 ml
4 tbsp	Thick mayonnaise	4x15 ml
2 tbsp	Horseradish sauce	2x15 ml
2 tbsp	Single cream	2x15 ml
1 teasp	Lemon juice	5 ml

Preheat the oven to 350°F (180°C) Gas 4.

Cut rabbit into small pieces, removing small bones. Season flour, add paprika and coat rabbit pieces.

Beat eggs with milk. Dip rabbit into egg mixture then into breadcrumbs.

Heat butter and oil in a frying pan and brown rabbit pieces on both sides. Place on baking tray and bake for about 40 minutes till tender.

Meanwhile, mix mayonnaise, horseradish sauce, cream, lemon juice and seasoning. Serve with rabbit.

Stuffed drumsticks

Overall timing 2 hours

Freezing Not suitable

To serve 4

2x1 lb	Turkey drumsticks	2x450 g
	Salt and pepper	
4 oz	Smoked back bacon	125 g
	Rosemary leaves	
2 oz	Butter	50 g
2 teasp	Plain flour	2x5 ml
¼ pint	Chicken stock	150 ml
4 tbsp	Dry vermouth	4x15 ml

Preheat the oven to 375°F (190°C) Gas 5.

Remove bone from drumsticks. Return drumsticks to their original shape, then season. Derind and chop bacon and stuff into cavities in the drumsticks. Close openings with skewers. Pierce the skin in several places and insert the rosemary leaves. Rub butter over drumsticks and place in a flameproof casserole. Cover and bake for about 1¼ hours.

Lift out the drumsticks and remove the skewers. Cut into thick slices, arrange on a serving dish and keep hot.

Add the flour to the casserole and stir over a low heat for 1 minute. Gradually add the stock and vermouth and bring to the boil, stirring. Simmer for 2 minutes then adjust the seasoning to taste.

Pour sauce over the turkey.

Rabbit carbonnade

Overall timing 2½ hours

Freezing Not suitable

To serve 4–6

2½ lb	Ovenready rabbit	1.1 kg
3 tbsp	Plain flour	3x15 ml
2	Carrots	2
1	Onion	1
4 oz	Streaky bacon rashers	125 g
2 oz	Butter	50 g
	Bouquet garni	
1	Garlic clove	1
	Salt and pepper	
1 pint	Pale ale	560 ml

Preheat the oven to 350°F (180°C) Gas 4.

Cut the rabbit into neat pieces. Toss in the flour till lightly coated.

Peel and thinly slice the carrots. Peel and chop the onion. Derind the bacon and cut into strips. Melt the butter in a flameproof casserole and fry the carrots, onion and bacon for 5 minutes. Add the rabbit pieces and fry till browned.

Add the bouquet garni, peeled and crushed garlic and seasoning. Pour the ale over, cover tightly and cook in the oven for 1¾–2 hours till the rabbit is tender. Serve with boiled potatoes.

Duck with apples and cream

Overall timing 1 hour 20 minutes

Freezing Not suitable

To serve 4

3½ lb	Ovenready duck	1.6 kg
	Salt and pepper	
6	Granny Smith apples	6
1 oz	Butter	25 g
½ pint	Carton of single cream	284 ml

Preheat the oven to 400°F (200°C) Gas 6.

Sprinkle duck inside and out with salt and pepper. Prick all over with a fork and place on wire rack in roasting tin. Roast for 20 minutes, then reduce heat to 350°F (180°C) Gas 4.

Peel and core the apples. Cut two of them into quarters and leave the rest whole. Arrange around the duck, dot with butter and continue roasting for 1 hour or till tender.

Remove duck and apples from the tin. Place duck on serving plate. Keep hot. Pour off excess fat from pan juices, then stir in the cream. Replace apples in tin and baste thoroughly with the sauce. Cook for a further 5 minutes.

Arrange apples round duck. Spoon some sauce over. Serve rest separately.

Chicken liver brochettes

Overall timing 25 minutes

Freezing Not suitable

To serve 4

8 oz	Carton of chicken livers	225 g
2 oz	Piece of smoked streaky bacon	50 g
4 oz	Mushrooms	125 g
	Salt and pepper	
2 oz	Butter	50 g

Wash the chicken livers and dry on kitchen paper. Chop bacon into bite-size pieces. Wipe mushrooms.

Thread livers, bacon and mushrooms alternately on to skewers. Season with salt and pepper.

Melt the butter in a frying pan and cook brochettes for about 8 minutes, turning them from time to time. Alternatively, brush brochettes with oil and cook under a hot grill.

Serve hot with tomato sauce, rice and a mixed salad for lunch, or with crusty bread and butter for supper.

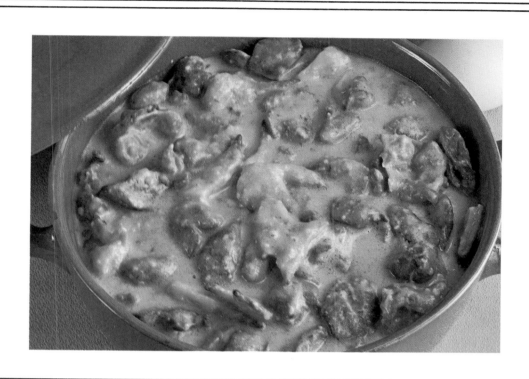

Giblet fricassee

Overall timing 1½ hours

Freezing Not suitable

To serve 4

1¼ lb	Poultry giblets	600 g
1	Onion	1
3 tbsp	Oil	3x15 ml
¾ pint	Chicken stock	400 ml
1 teasp	Ground cumin	5 ml
	Salt and pepper	
1 tbsp	Plain flour	15 ml
2	Egg yolks	2
2 tbsp	Lemon juice	2x15 ml

Chop giblets. Peel and chop onion. Heat the oil in a saucepan and fry onion till transparent. Add giblets and brown on all sides. Pour in the stock and add cumin and seasoning. Bring to the boil, cover and simmer for about 1 hour or until giblets are tender.

Blend the flour with the egg yolks and mix in the lemon juice. Stir into fricassee and cook for a further 5 minutes, stirring. Serve with creamed potatoes and a mixed salad.

Rich leek flan

Overall timing 1 hour

Freezing Suitable : reheat from frozen, covered, in 375°F (190°C) Gas 5 oven for 35 minutes

To serve 6–8

13 oz	Frozen puff pastry	375 g
2 lb	Leeks	900 g
2 oz	Butter	50 g
1 tbsp	Plain flour	15 ml
½ pint	Light stock	300 ml
	Salt and pepper	
1	Egg	1
1	Egg yolk	1
½ pint	Carton of single cream	284 ml

Thaw pastry. Preheat the oven to 425°F (220°C) Gas 7.

Trim leeks. Cut into 1 inch (2.5 cm) lengths. Blanch in boiling water for 5 minutes, then drain thoroughly.

Melt butter in a frying pan and fry the leeks for 5 minutes. Sprinkle with flour and cook until lightly browned. Gradually stir in the stock and bring to the boil. Season and cook gently for 10 minutes.

Meanwhile, roll out dough and use to line a 9 inch (23 cm) flan dish. Prick bottom several times with a fork.

Beat the whole egg, yolk and cream together in a bowl. Remove leeks from heat and add cream mixture. Pour into flan dish and spread evenly. Bake for 30 minutes till lightly set and golden. Serve hot.

Quiche lorraine

Overall timing 1½ hours

Freezing Suitable: reheat in hot oven

To serve 4–6

8 oz	Plain flour	225 g
	Salt and pepper	
5 oz	Butter	150 g
2 tbsp	Water	2x15 ml
2	Throughcut bacon rashers	2
3 oz	Cheddar cheese	75 g
2	Eggs	2
½ pint	Milk or single cream	300 ml

Sift the flour, salt and pepper into a bowl. Rub in 4 oz (125 g) of the butter till mixture resembles breadcrumbs. Gradually add the water and knead to a dough. Roll out and use to line a greased 8 inch (20 cm) pie plate or flan dish. Leave to stand for 30 minutes.

Preheat the oven to 400°F (200°C) Gas 6.

Derind and dice the bacon. Fry lightly in the remaining butter. Grate or thinly slice the cheese. Sprinkle bacon and cheese over the bottom of the flan case. Beat together the eggs, milk or cream and seasoning in a bowl. Pour mixture into flan. Do not overfill.

Bake for 15 minutes, then reduce heat to 325°F (170°C) Gas 3 and bake for further 25–30 minutes. Serve hot or cold with salad and potatoes.

Onion quiche

Overall timing 1½ hours

Freezing Suitable: reheat from frozen, covered, in 350°F (180°C) Gas 4 oven for 20 minutes

To serve 4

1 lb	Medium-size onions	450 g
2 oz	Lard	50 g
4 oz	Smoked streaky bacon	125 g
6 oz	Rich shortcrust pastry	175 g
3	Eggs	3
¼ pint	Milk	150 ml
¼ pint	Carton of single cream	150 ml
	Salt and pepper	

Preheat the oven to 400°F (200°C) Gas 6.

Peel and thinly slice the onions. Melt the lard in a frying pan and fry the onions over a moderate heat till pale golden.

Derind and dice the bacon and add to the pan. Fry for a further 4–5 minutes till the onions and bacon are golden brown.

Roll out the dough and use to line an 8½ inch (22 cm) flan dish. Prick the bottom and bake blind for 15 minutes.

Remove foil and baking beans and spread the onion and bacon mixture over the pastry base. Mix the eggs with the milk and cream and season to taste. Pour over the onions.

Bake for a further 25 minutes till lightly set and golden. Serve hot with mixed salads.

Welsh parsley flan

Overall timing 1 hour

Freezing Suitable: reheat from frozen in 350°F (180°C) Gas 4 oven for 25 minutes

To serve 4–6

8 oz	Shortcrust pastry	225 g
4 oz	Streaky bacon	125 g
1 oz	Butter	25 g
3	Eggs	3
½ pint	Milk	300 ml
3 tbsp	Chopped parsley	3x15 ml
	Salt and pepper	

Preheat the oven to 400°F (200°C) Gas 6.

Roll out the dough and use to line a 9 inch (23 cm) flan tin. Prick the bottom with a fork and bake blind for 15 minutes.

Meanwhile, derind and chop the bacon. Melt the butter in a frying pan and fry the bacon till golden. Arrange the bacon in the flan case. Reduce oven temperature to 350°F (180°C) Gas 4.

Beat the eggs, milk and parsley together, season to taste and pour over the bacon. Bake for a further 20–25 minutes till set. Serve hot or cold.

Onion flan

Overall timing 2¼ hours

Freezing Suitable: reheat from frozen in 350°F (180°C) Gas 4 oven for 20 minutes

To serve 4–6

1 teasp	Dried yeast	5 ml
	Pinch of sugar	
4 fl oz	Lukewarm water	120 ml
8 oz	Plain flour	225 g
1 teasp	Salt	5 ml
1	Egg	1
Filling		
5 oz	Bacon rashers	150 g
6 oz	Onions	175 g
1 oz	Butter	25 g
5 oz	Cheddar cheese	150 g

Mix yeast and sugar with most of the water and leave in a warm place for 15 minutes till frothy.

Sift flour and salt into bowl, make a well in the centre and add yeast mixture, any remaining water and egg. Mix well to a dough, then turn on to floured surface and knead for 5 minutes until smooth and elastic. Place dough in a clean bowl, cover with a damp cloth and leave to rise in a warm place for 45 minutes–1 hour, until doubled in size.

Preheat oven to 400°F (200°C) Gas 6.

Roll out dough on a floured surface and use to line a greased 10 inch (25 cm) loose-bottomed flan tin. Prove for 15 minutes.

Derind and chop bacon. Peel onions and cut into rings. Melt butter in a pan and fry onions for 5 minutes till golden. Slice the cheese.

Cover flan base with onions and bacon and arrange cheese slices on top. Bake for 30–35 minutes. Remove from tin and serve hot.

Asparagus quiche

Overall timing 1¼ hours

Freezing Suitable: thaw and refresh in hot oven for 10 minutes

To serve 4

8 oz	Shortcrust pastry	225 g
2 tbsp	Butter	2x15 ml
4 tbsp	Plain flour	4x15 ml
¾ pint	Milk	400 ml
	Salt and pepper	
	Pinch of grated nutmeg	
2	Eggs	2
4 oz	Mature cheese	125 g
12 oz	Can of asparagus	340 g

Preheat the oven to 425°F (220°C) Gas 7.

Roll out the dough to ¼ inch (6 mm) thick and use to line greased 10 inch (25 cm) flan ring or dish. Prick with fork. Bake blind for 5 minutes.

Melt the butter in a small saucepan. Stir in flour. Gradually stir in ½ pint (300 ml) of the milk. Season with salt, pepper and nutmeg. Bring to the boil, stirring constantly. Cook for 2 minutes. Remove pan from heat. Separate the eggs and stir one yolk into sauce. Grate the cheese and add to the sauce.

Pour the sauce into the flan case. Return to the oven and bake for 15 minutes.

Remove quiche from oven. Reduce heat to 375°F (190°C) Gas 5. Drain asparagus, cut into small lengths and arrange evenly over surface. Mix together the rest of the milk, the remaining egg yolk and 2 egg whites and pour this over top. Bake for 30 minutes more.

Olive and caper pizza

Overall timing 1¾ hours

Freezing Not suitable

To serve 2

6 oz	Potatoes	175 g
	Salt and pepper	
8 oz	Self-raising flour	225 g
2 oz	Butter	50 g
12 oz	Tomatoes	350 g
4	Anchovy fillets	4
1 tbsp	Capers	15 ml
4 oz	Black olives	125 g
4 tbsp	Milk	4x15 ml
2 teasp	Dried oregano	2x5 ml
1 tbsp	Olive oil	15 ml

Preheat the oven to 425°F (220°C) Gas 7.

Peel potatoes and cut into small chunks. Cook in boiling salted water till tender.

Meanwhile, sift the flour into a bowl and rub in the butter till the mixture resembles fine breadcrumbs. Blanch, peel and chop tomatoes. Chop anchovy fillets. Drain capers. Stone olives.

Drain potatoes and mash well. Stir into rubbed-in mixture. Add milk and mix to form a soft dough. Knead lightly till smooth. Roll out dough and use to line a greased 9 inch (23 cm) pizza pan or flan tin.

Arrange tomatoes, anchovies, capers and olives on top. Sprinkle with salt, pepper and oregano. Sprinkle olive oil over and bake for about 55 minutes till well risen and golden. Cut into wedges to serve.

Spring vegetable pie

Overall timing 2 hours

Freezing Not suitable

To serve 6

1 lb	Spring greens	450 g
2	Small globe artichokes	2
1½ lb	Fresh peas	700 g
	Salt and pepper	
1	Large onion	1
3 oz	Butter	75 g
8 oz	Shortcrust pastry	225 g
4	Eggs	4
4 tbsp	Grated Parmesan cheese	4x15 ml
1 tbsp	Chopped parsley	15 ml

Pick over the spring greens, discarding any damaged parts, and chop coarsely. Remove stems and tough outer leaves from artichokes and cut artichokes into quarters, discarding the hairy chokes. Shell peas. Bring a pan of lightly salted water to the boil, add the artichokes and peas and simmer for 10 minutes.

Peel and chop onion. Melt butter in large saucepan, add onion and fry till golden.

Drain artichokes and peas and add to the onion with the spring greens and seasoning. Mix well, cover tightly and simmer for 10 minutes, shaking the pan occasionally. Cool.

Preheat oven to 400°F (200°C) Gas 6.

Roll out two-thirds of dough and use to line an 8 inch (20cm) springform tin. Spread vegetables in tin. Beat three of the eggs lightly with cheese and parsley, then pour over vegetables. Roll out remaining dough and cover filling. Beat remaining egg and brush over pie. Place tin on a baking tray and bake for 30 minutes.

Remove sides of tin. Brush sides of pie with egg and bake for a further 10–15 minutes till golden.

Sicilian fish pie

Overall timing 2 hours

Freezing Not suitable

To serve 8

12 oz	Rich shortcrust pastry	350 g
2 tbsp	Caster sugar	2x15 ml
½ teasp	Grated lemon rind	2.5 ml
12 oz	White fish steaks	350 g
1	Large stalk of celery	1
3 oz	Stoned green olives	75 g
1	Large onion	1
3 tbsp	Olive oil	3x15 ml
1 tbsp	Drained capers	15 ml
2 tbsp	Tomato purée	2x15 ml
	Salt and pepper	
3	Courgettes	3
1	Egg	1
3 tbsp	Plain flour	3x15 ml
	Oil for deep frying	
1	Egg yolk	1

Make pastry, adding sugar and lemon rind with 3 egg yolks. Cube fish; chop celery; slice olives. Peel and thinly slice onion. Heat oil in a saucepan, add onion and fry till golden. Add celery, olives, capers, tomato purée, fish, ¼ pint (150 ml) water and seasoning. Simmer for 15 minutes.

Preheat oven to 350°F (180°C) Gas 4.

Cut courgettes into thin fingers. Beat egg; season flour. Dip courgettes into egg, then into flour. Deep fry till golden. Drain.

Divide dough into thirds. Roll out one and use to line a greased and floured 8 inch (20 cm) springform tin. Roll out remaining dough to two 8 inch (20 cm) rounds.

Layer fish mixture, courgettes and dough rounds in tin. Brush with beaten egg yolk and bake for 50 minutes. Remove from tin and serve hot.

Pork and apple pie

Overall timing 1½ hours

Freezing Not suitable

To serve 6

Pastry		
10 oz	Plain flour	275 g
2 teasp	Salt	2x5 ml
¼ teasp	Powdered mustard	1.25 ml
5 oz	Lard	150 g
Filling		
4 oz	Streaky bacon rashers	125 g
2	Medium-size onions	2
1½ lb	Lean minced pork	700 g
¼ teasp	Dried sage	1.25 ml
¼ pint	Chicken stock	150 ml
	Salt and pepper	
3	Dessert apples	3
4 tbsp	Demerara sugar	4x15 ml
¼ teasp	Grated nutmeg	1.25 ml

Preheat the oven to 400°F (200°C) Gas 6.

Sift the flour, salt and mustard into a bowl and rub in the lard. Add enough cold water to mix to a soft but not sticky dough and knead till smooth. Roll out two-thirds of the dough and use to line an 8½ inch (22 cm) round pie dish.

Derind and dice the bacon. Peel and finely chop the onions. Mix the pork with the bacon, onions, sage, stock and plenty of seasoning.

Peel, quarter, core and slice the apples. Put into a bowl with the sugar and nutmeg and toss gently till mixed.

Spread one-third of the pork in the pie dish and arrange half the apple mixture on top. Repeat the layers, finishing with the pork mixture.

Roll out the remaining dough to a round and use to cover the pie. Crimp the edges to seal. Place the pie on a baking tray. Bake just above the centre of the oven for 1 hour, covering the top of the pie lightly with foil after the first 30 minutes.

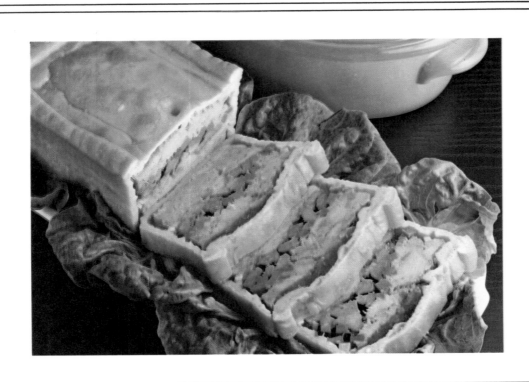

Ham, veal and pork pie

Overall timing 2½ hours plus overnight marination and chilling

Freezing Suitable

To serve 6–8

12 oz	Pie veal	350 g
2	Bay leaves	2
1 tbsp	Brandy	15 ml
	Salt and pepper	
8 oz	Cooked ham	225 g
12 oz	Belly of pork	350 g
4 oz	Streaky bacon	125 g
1 lb	Plain flour	450 g
5 oz	Butter	150 g
6 fl oz	Water	175 ml
2	Egg yolks	2

Cut veal into thin strips and place in a bowl with bay leaves, brandy and a pinch of salt.

Leave to marinate overnight. Cut ham into thin strips, add to veal and leave to marinate for another 2 hours.

Preheat the oven to 375°F (190°C) Gas 5.

Pass pork and bacon through a mincer twice. Mix with a little of the marinade and seasoning.

Sift flour and 1 teasp (5 ml) salt into a large bowl and make a well in the centre. Melt butter in water and bring to the boil. Pour quickly into the flour and mix well. Add one egg yolk and knead to a smooth dough.

Working quickly, roll out two-thirds of dough and use to line a greased 2 lb (900 g) loaf tin. Spread half the pork mixture on bottom, cover with ham and veal mixture and spread remaining pork mixture on top. Roll out remaining dough to fit pie. Seal edges. Put strips from leftover dough on sides of rectangle, moistening first to secure.

Lightly beat remaining egg yolk with a pinch of salt and brush over dough. Bake for 1 hour, then reduce heat to 170°F (325°C) Gas 3, cover with foil to prevent over-browning and bake for another hour.

Australian-style lamb pie

Overall timing 1¼ hours

Freezing Suitable: cover with pastry after thawing, then bake

To serve 4

1½ lb	Boned shoulder of lamb	700 g
	Salt and pepper	
2 tbsp	Plain flour	2x15 ml
1	Onion	1
8 oz	Carrots	225 g
4 oz	Mushrooms	125 g
1 oz	Butter	25 g
2 tbsp	Oil	2x15 ml
¾ pint	Stock	400 ml
2 tbsp	Chopped parsley	2x15 ml
6 oz	Shortcrust pastry	175 g
1	Egg	1

Wipe meat and cut into thin slices. Coat in seasoned flour. Peel and chop onion. Scrape and grate carrots. Wipe and slice mushrooms.

Heat butter and oil in frying pan and brown meat on all sides. Add onion, carrots and mushrooms and cook for 5 minutes. Stir in stock (made from cubes if necessary) and add seasoning. Cover and simmer gently for 10 minutes.

Preheat oven to 400°F (200°C) Gas 6.

Transfer meat mixture to pie dish and sprinkle with parsley. Roll out pastry and cover pie dish. Brush surface with lightly beaten egg and bake for 40–45 minutes until golden brown. Serve hot with jacket potatoes and minted peas.

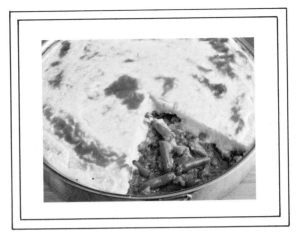

Suet and bacon tart

Overall timing 45 minutes plus resting

Freezing Not suitable

To serve 8

8 oz	Streaky bacon rashers	225 g
4 oz	Cracklings from rendered suet	125 g
12 oz	Self-raising flour	350 g
2 oz	Chopped suet	50 g
2	Eggs	2
1 tbsp	Tomato purée	15 ml
¼ teasp	Chilli sauce	1.25 ml
	Salt and pepper	

Derind the bacon, then grill till crisp. Allow to cool, then break into pieces and mix with the suet cracklings.

Grease an 8 inch (20 cm) loose-bottomed cake tin.

Sift flour into bowl and add half the crackling mixture, the suet, eggs, tomato purée, chilli sauce, salt and pepper. Mix to a soft but not sticky dough. Knead lightly, then press into cake tin. Leave to rest for 20 minutes.

Preheat oven to 400°F (200°C) Gas 6.

Sprinkle rest of crackling mixture over dough and press in lightly. Bake for about 30 minutes till well risen and golden.

Cottage pie

Overall timing 1¼ hours

Freezing: Suitable: reheat in 425°F (220°C) Gas 7 oven for 1 hour

To serve 6

2 lb	Floury potatoes	900 g
	Salt and pepper	
2	Large onions	2
1 oz	Beef dripping	25 g
2 lb	Minced beef	900 g
2 tbsp	Plain flour	2x15 ml
½ pint	Strong beef stock	300 ml
14 oz	Can of tomatoes	397 g
8 oz	Frozen vegetables	225 g
¼ pint	Milk	150 ml
2 oz	Butter	50 g

Peel and quarter the potatoes; cook in boiling salted water till tender.

Preheat the oven to 375°F (190°C) Gas 5.

Peel and thinly slice onions. Heat dripping in a flameproof casserole and fry onions till transparent. Add beef and fry till browned.

Sprinkle in the flour and cook, stirring for 1 minute. Gradually add stock and bring to the boil, stirring. Add tomatoes and juice, seasoning and frozen vegetables and simmer for 5 minutes.

Drain potatoes. Add milk and butter and mash well. Spread potato over beef mixture. Bake for 30 minutes.

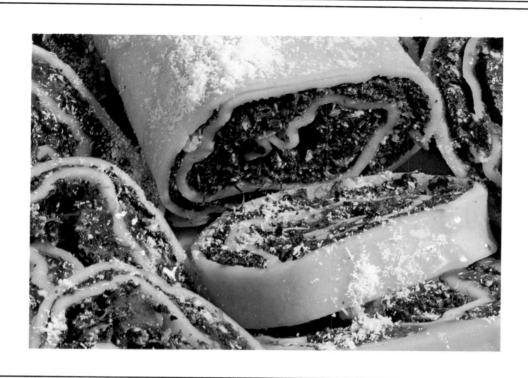

Cottage spinach roll

Overall timing 1¾ hours

Freezing Not suitable

To serve 4–6

8 oz	Plain flour	225 g
	Salt and pepper	
2	Eggs	2
2 lb	Spinach	900 g
3 oz	Butter	75 g
8 oz	Cottage cheese	225 g
¼ teasp	Grated nutmeg	1.25 ml
6 tbsp	Grated Parmesan cheese	6x15 ml

Sift the flour and ½ teasp (2.5 ml) salt into a bowl. Beat the eggs lightly in a bowl, pour half into the flour and mix with a palette knife. Add enough of the remaining egg to make a stiff dough. Knead till smooth, then chill for 30 minutes.

Meanwhile, wash and pick over the spinach. Put into a saucepan with only the water that clings to it. Cover and cook gently for 5 minutes. Drain thoroughly, then shred.

Melt 1 oz (25 g) of the butter in a frying pan, add the spinach and cook for 5 minutes, stirring occasionally. Pour into a bowl and add the cottage cheese, nutmeg, half the Parmesan and seasoning. Mix well. Leave to cool.

Roll out the dough on a floured surface to a rectangle about 15x12 inches (38x30 cm). With a long side nearest you, spread the filling over the dough, leaving a 1 inch (2.5 cm) border. Fold the bottom border over the filling and roll up. Pinch the ends together to seal.

Wrap the roll in a double thickness of muslin, tying the ends with string. Place in a large pan of boiling salted water, cover and simmer for 25 minutes.

Drain and unwrap the roll and place on a warmed serving dish. Melt the remaining butter. Cut the roll into thick slices, pour the butter over and sprinkle with the remaining Parmesan. Serve immediately.

Brazilian meat pasties

Overall timing 50 minutes

Freezing Suitable: omit hard-boiled eggs and bake from frozen in 425°F (220°C) Gas 7 oven for 30 minutes

To serve 4

13 oz	Frozen puff pastry	375 g
1	Onion	1
4 oz	Belly pork rashers	125 g
1 oz	Butter	25 g
8 oz	Minced beef	225 g
3 tbsp	Seedless raisins	3x15 ml
	Pinch of ground cloves	
	Salt and pepper	
¼ teasp	Paprika	1.25 ml
2	Hard-boiled eggs	2
8	Stoned green olives	8
1	Egg	1

Thaw the pastry. Roll out to a rectangle 8x16 inches (20x40 cm). Cut into eight 4 inch (10 cm) squares.

Preheat oven to 400°F (200°C) Gas 6.

Peel and finely chop the onion. Derind and mince the belly pork rashers. Melt the butter in a frying pan and fry the onion and pork till golden. Add the minced beef and fry briskly, stirring frequently, till brown.

Remove from heat and add the raisins, cloves, salt, pepper and paprika. Mix well. Shell and coarsely chop the hard-boiled eggs. Chop the olives, add to the pan with the eggs and mix well.

Place one eighth of the meat mixture on half of each dough square. Brush the edges with a little of the beaten egg and fold dough over. Crimp edges to seal.

Arrange on a dampened baking tray and brush tops with beaten egg. Bake for about 25 minutes till well risen and golden.

Leek pie

Overall timing 1 hour

Freezing Suitable: reheat in 350°F (180°C) Gas 4 oven for 30 minutes

To serve 4

1½ lb	Leeks	700 g
2	Onions	2
2 oz	Butter	50 g
	Salt and pepper	
8 oz	Streaky bacon rashers	225 g
12 oz	Shortcrust pastry	350 g
1 tbsp	Cornflour	15 ml
¼ pint	Carton of single cream	150 ml
1	Egg	1

Preheat the oven to 400°F (200°C) Gas 6.

Wash, trim and slice leeks. Peel and slice onions. Melt butter in a frying pan and fry onions till golden. Add sliced leeks, salt and pepper and cook gently for 5 minutes.

Meanwhile, derind and lightly fry bacon rashers in another pan.

Roll out two-thirds of the dough and use to line a shallow pie dish. Cover with leek mixture and arrange bacon rashers on top. Mix cornflour with the cream and pour over.

Roll out remaining dough and cover filling. Seal and crimp edges, using any trimmings to decorate top. Glaze with beaten egg. Bake for 45 minutes until golden brown.

Ham pie

Overall timing 1 hour

Freezing Not suitable

To serve 4

8 oz	Shortcrust pastry	225 g
1 lb	Can of ham	453 g
1	Egg	1

Preheat the oven to 425°F (220°C) Gas 7.

Roll out the dough to ¼ inch (6 mm) thickness. Place ham in centre. Dampen the dough edges and fold around the ham. Seal well. Place in ovenproof dish and decorate with trimmings, if liked.

Lightly beat the egg and brush all over the dough. Bake for 40 minutes till golden.

SNACKS

Ham and vegetable bake

Overall timing 1 hour 10 minutes

Freezing Suitable: top with egg after reheating in 350°F (180°C) Gas 4 oven for 1¼ hours

To serve 4

8 oz	Frozen spinach	225 g
1 lb	Celeriac	450 g
2 lb	Potatoes	900 g
	Salt and pepper	
2½ oz	Butter	65 g
3 tbsp	Single cream	3x15 ml
3 fl oz	Hot milk	90 ml
1	Small stalk of celery	1
8 oz	Sliced ham	225 g
4 oz	Cheddar cheese	125 g
2	Eggs	2

Place spinach in a sieve to thaw. Peel celeriac and potatoes and cut into small chunks. Put prepared vegetable chunks into a saucepan of cold salted water and bring to the boil. Cook for 20 minutes till tender. Drain well and mash or purée with 2 oz (50 g) of the butter, the cream and enough milk to give a creamy purée. Season to taste.

Preheat oven to 400°F (200°C) Gas 6.

Wash and top and tail celery. Blanch in boiling water for 5 minutes. Drain well and cut into pieces.

Grease ovenproof dish with remaining butter. Spread the well-drained spinach over, arrange the chopped celery on top and cover with ham slices. Grate the cheese. Sprinkle over half the cheese and cover with the celeriac and potato purée. Bake on centre shelf of oven for 15 minutes.

In a bowl, lightly beat the eggs with salt and pepper. Pour over the purée, top with remaining cheese and return to oven. Bake for another 15 minutes till golden. Serve immediately.

Club sandwiches

Overall timing 30 minutes

Freezing Not suitable

To serve 4

12	Slices of bread	12
	Mayonnaise	
4	Slices of cooked chicken or turkey	4
4	Lettuce leaves	4
4–8	Back bacon rashers	4–8
5	Tomatoes	5

Preheat the grill.

Grill the bacon until crisp. Toast four slices of bread on both sides, but toast the remaining slices of bread on one side only. Slice the tomatoes.

To assemble the sandwiches, spread the untoasted sides of bread with mayonnaise. Place four pieces, toasted side down, on a board and top with the chicken or turkey slices. Cover with the completely toasted bread. Add the lettuce, bacon, tomato slices (reserving some for the garnish) and remaining bread, mayonnaise side down. Press lightly together, then halve the sandwiches diagonally. Garnish with the reserved tomato slices.

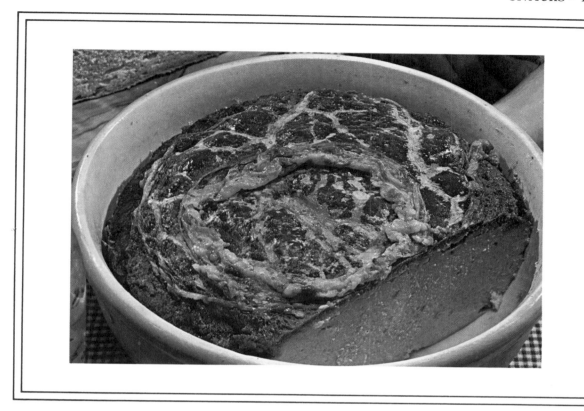

Country-style liver pâté

Overall timing 3 hours plus maturing

Freezing Suitable

To serve 12

1½ lb	Pig's liver	700 g
1 lb	Back bacon	450 g
8 oz	Lard	225 g
1	Egg	1
1 tbsp	Plain flour	15 ml
	Salt and pepper	
½ teasp	Ground allspice	2.5 ml
1	Pig's caul (optional)	1

Preheat the oven to 350°F (180°C) Gas 4.

Chop the liver. Derind and dice bacon. Put liver and bacon through a fine mincer. Melt the lard in a saucepan and gradually beat into minced liver and bacon in bowl. Beat egg and add with flour, seasoning and allspice. Mix well.

Line greased ovenproof dish with caul, if using, leaving edges hanging over sides. Add liver mixture and smooth top. Wrap caul edges over. Cover dish with lid or foil and place in a roasting tin containing 1 inch (2.5 cm) water. Bake for 1¾ hours.

Allow to cool, then leave in the refrigerator for 2–3 days to mature. Serve with crusty bread.

Crusty mushroom bread

Overall timing 1 hour

Freezing Suitable: cook after thawing

To serve 6–8

1	Round loaf of bread	1
4 oz	Butter	125 g
1 lb	Mushrooms	450 g
	Salt and pepper	
3 tbsp	Lemon juice	3x15 ml
½ pint	White sauce	300 ml
2	Eggs	2

Preheat the oven to 350°F (180°C) Gas 4.

Slice the top off the bread and scoop out most of the crumbs, leaving a ½ inch (12.5 mm) thick shell. Spread the inside with half the butter, place on a baking tray and bake for 10 minutes.

Meanwhile, finely chop the mushrooms. Melt the remaining butter in a saucepan and fry the mushrooms for 5 minutes, stirring frequently. Add salt, pepper and lemon juice. Stir the mushrooms into the white sauce.

Separate the eggs and beat the egg yolks, one at a time, into the sauce. Return to the heat and heat through gently. Whisk the egg whites till stiff but not dry. Gently fold into the mushroom mixture.

Pour the mixture into the bread shell and sprinkle the top with a few of the scooped out breadcrumbs, grated. Bake for 30 minutes till well risen and crisp. Serve hot.

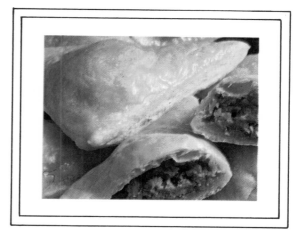

Broccoli toasts

Overall timing 40 minutes

Freezing Not suitable

To serve 4

1 lb	Calabrese broccoli	450 g
½ pint	Beef stock	300 ml
8	Slices of bread	8
½ pint	Thick white sauce	300 ml
	Salt and pepper	
	Grated nutmeg	
½ teasp	Mixed herbs	2.5 ml
2	Hard-boiled eggs	2
1	Tomato	1
	Sprigs of parsley	
½	Red pepper	½

Trim broccoli and chop into large pieces. Bring stock to boil, add broccoli and cook for 7–10 minutes.

Toast bread and place on baking tray. Drain broccoli well, then divide it between toast.

Preheat oven to 375°F (190°C) Gas 5.

Heat sauce, then add seasoning, pinch of nutmeg and herbs. Finely chop one of the hard-boiled eggs and add to the sauce. Pour sauce over broccoli. Bake for 15 minutes.

Serve hot, garnished with remaining egg, sliced tomato, parsley and strips of pepper.

Pirozski

Overall timing 1 hour

Freezing Suitable: refresh in 350°F (180°C) Gas 4 oven for 10 minutes

To serve 6

7½ oz	Frozen puff pastry	212 g
8 oz	Liver pâté	225 g
1	Egg	1

Thaw pastry. Preheat the oven to 400°F (200°C) Gas 6.

Roll out dough very thinly on a floured surface and cut into 3 inch (7.5 cm) squares. Cut in half diagonally to make triangles. Put about 1 teasp (5 ml) liver pâté on half of the triangles. Moisten dough edges and cover with remaining triangles. Press edges together to seal.

Arrange triangles on greased baking tray and brush with beaten egg. Bake for 10–15 minutes till well risen and golden. Serve hot.

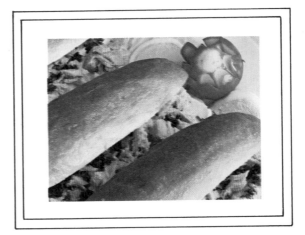

Hot frankfurter salad

Overall timing 45 minutes

Freezing Not suitable

To serve 4

1 lb	Waxy potatoes	450 g
	Salt and pepper	
4	Frankfurters	4
2	Onions	2
4	Anchovy fillets	4
2 oz	Chopped gherkins	50 g
2 tbsp	Oil	2x15 ml
2 tbsp	White wine vinegar	2x15 ml

Peel and slice potatoes, then cook in boiling salted water for about 7 minutes till tender.

Heat frankfurters in boiling water for 5 minutes, then drain and slice. Peel and slice onions into rings. Finely chop anchovies and gherkins. Drain potatoes and mix with frankfurters and onions.

Beat together oil and vinegar, season and pour over the warm salad. Mix well and leave for 10 minutes. Add anchovies and gherkins and serve.

Tuna rolls

Overall timing 15 minutes

Freezing Not suitable

To serve 4

4	Long rolls	4
	Butter	
	Mayonnaise	
1x7 oz	Can of tuna fish	1x200 g
	Chopped parsley	
2	Hard-boiled eggs	2
	Radish roses	

Halve the rolls, not cutting all the way through, and butter the cut surfaces. Spread a thick layer of mayonnaise over the bottom cut surface.

Drain the tuna and flake it. Divide between the rolls and sprinkle with parsley. Arrange the sandwiches on a serving plate.

Shell and slice the eggs and use to garnish the sandwiches with radish roses.

Ham and potato cake

Overall timing 1¼ hours

Freezing Not suitable

To serve 4

1½ lb	Medium-size potatoes	700 g
	Salt and pepper	
8 oz	Sliced cooked ham	225 g
8 oz	Cheese	225 g
3 oz	Butter	75 g
3 tbsp	Fresh breadcrumbs	3 x 15 ml
¼ pint	Milk	150 ml

Cook potatoes in boiling salted water for 20 minutes.

Meanwhile, chop the ham and grate cheese. Grease a 7 inch (18 cm) springform tin with a little of the butter and sprinkle breadcrumbs over the bottom and sides, shaking off any excess. Preheat oven to 350°F (180°C) Gas 4.

Drain and peel the potatoes, then cut into ¼ inch (6 mm) thick slices. Arrange a few of the slices, slightly overlapping, in the bottom of the tin. Melt the remaining butter and brush a little over the potatoes. Scatter some of the ham, then some of the cheese over and season. Continue layering, reserving a little of the butter, and finishing with a layer of potato topped with cheese. Pour the milk over and brush with remaining butter.

Bake for about 30 minutes till potatoes are tender and cheese has melted. Turn cake out of tin to serve.

RICE

Pilau rice

Overall timing 45 minutes plus soaking

Freezing Not suitable

To serve 4–6

1 lb	Patna rice	450 g
1	Large onion	1
1	Garlic clove	1
6	Whole allspice	6
8	Cardamom pods	8
4 oz	Butter or ghee	125 g
2 inch	Cinnamon stick	5 cm
8	Cloves	8
1 teasp	Ground turmeric	5 ml
	Salt	
2 oz	Flaked almonds	50 g
4 oz	Sultanas	125 g

Soak rice in cold water for 1 hour, then drain thoroughly.

Peel and finely chop the onion. Peel and crush garlic. Lightly crush allspice and cardamom pods. Melt 3 oz (75 g) of the fat in a saucepan. Add onion, garlic and spices and fry till onion is transparent but not browned.

Add rice and cook over a low heat, stirring, for 3–4 minutes. Add salt to taste and enough boiling water to come 1 inch (2.5 cm) above the rice. Cover pan tightly and simmer over a very low heat for about 20 minutes till water is absorbed and rice is tender.

Melt remaining fat in frying pan and fry almonds and sultanas for 3–5 minutes. Mix lightly into rice and serve immediately.

Lentil risotto

Overall timing 1 hour

Freezing Not suitable

To serve 6

8 oz	Continental lentils	225 g
1	Onion	1
4 oz	Butter	125 g
	Salt and pepper	
12 oz	Long grain rice	350 g
2 pints	Stock	1.1 litres
2 oz	Grated Parmesan cheese	50 g

Wash and pick over lentils. Peel and finely chop the onion. Melt the butter in a large saucepan, add the onion and cook till transparent. Add the lentils and enough water to cover. Season and bring to the boil. Reduce heat, cover and simmer for 1 hour.

Add the rice and stock. Bring back to the boil, reduce heat, cover and simmer for a further 15–18 minutes or until rice is just tender.

Stir in the Parmesan, and taste and adjust seasoning. Serve hot.

Arabian pilaf

Overall timing 30 minutes

Freezing Not suitable

To serve 4

1 oz	Butter	25 g
2 oz	Capelli d'angelo (angels' hair pasta)	50 g
1¼ pints	Chicken stock	700 ml
8 oz	Long grain rice	225 g
2 tbsp	Grated Parmesan cheese	2x15 ml
	Salt and pepper	

Melt the butter in a saucepan. Break up the pasta, add to the pan and fry, stirring, over a moderate heat till golden. Remove from pan and reserve.

Add the stock to the pan and bring to the boil. Stir in the rice, bring back to the boil and simmer gently for 15 minutes till the rice is just tender.

Stir in the fried pasta and cook for 2–3 minutes till pasta and rice are tender and all the liquid has been absorbed. Stir in Parmesan and seasoning with a fork. Transfer to a warmed serving dish and serve immediately.

Seafood spaghetti

Overall timing 20 minutes

Freezing Not suitable

To serve 4

12 oz	Spaghetti	350 g
	Salt and pepper	
1	Garlic clove	1
3 tbsp	Oil	3x15 ml
8 oz	Large shelled prawns	225 g
10 oz	Can of baby clams or mussels	280 g
8 oz	Can of tomatoes	227 g
1 tbsp	Chopped parsley	15 ml

Cook spaghetti in boiling salted water till tender.

Meanwhile, peel and crush garlic. Heat oil in a large saucepan, add garlic and fry for 1 minute. Add prawns and fry, stirring, for 2–3 minutes.

Drain clams or mussels and add to pan with tomatoes and their juice and seasoning. Cook for about 3 minutes, stirring to break up tomatoes.

Drain spaghetti thoroughly. Add to seafood sauce with parsley and toss lightly over a low heat till well coated. Serve immediately.

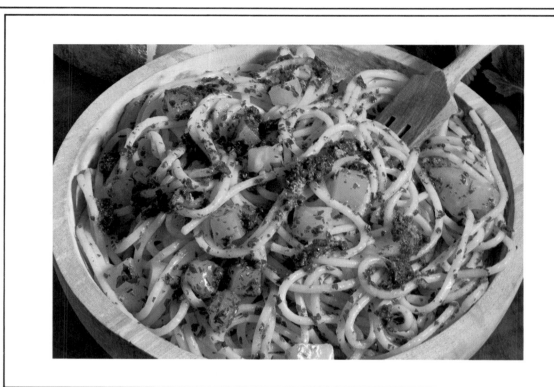

Spaghetti with goat's cheese

Overall timing 35 minutes

Freezing Not suitable

To serve 2

1	Garlic clove	1
2	Anchovy fillets	2
2 tbsp	Olive oil	2x15 ml
1 tbsp	Chopped parsley	15 ml
	Salt and pepper	
8 oz	Spaghetti	225 g
4 oz	Firm goat's cheese	125 g
1 oz	Butter	25 g

Peel and crush the garlic into a bowl. Add the anchovy fillets and pound to a paste with a wooden spoon. Beat in the oil, parsley and seasoning. Leave to stand for 15 minutes.

Meanwhile, cook the spaghetti in boiling salted water till tender. Derind the cheese and cut into small cubes.

Drain the spaghetti in a colander. Melt the butter in the spaghetti pan and add the cheese. Cook, stirring, over a low heat for 2 minutes.

Return spaghetti to the pan and toss lightly till coated with butter. Arrange in a warmed serving dish, pour the anchovy dressing over and toss lightly before serving with crusty bread.

Crisp-topped macaroni with tuna

Overall timing 35 minutes

Freezing Not suitable

To serve 4

1	Onion	1
3 oz	Butter	75 g
¼ pint	Chicken stock	150 ml
	Salt and pepper	
1	Medium cauliflower	1
8 oz	Short ·cut macaroni	225 g
6	Anchovy fillets	6
1 oz	Fresh breadcrumbs	25 g
7 oz	Can of tuna	198 g
4 tbsp	Grated Parmesan cheese	4x15 ml

Peel and chop the onion. Melt 1 oz (25 g) of the butter in a large saucepan and fry the onion till golden. Add the chicken stock and seasoning. Bring to the boil and simmer for 5 minutes.

Divide cauliflower into florets and cook in boiling salted water for 4 minutes. Remove with a draining spoon and reserve. Add macaroni to boiling water and cook till tender.

Meanwhile, melt remaining butter in a frying pan and fry cauliflower till golden. Roughly chop anchovies and add to pan with breadcrumbs. Fry till crisp. Remove from heat.

Preheat the grill.

Drain the macaroni and add to the stock mixture. Drain and flake tuna and stir carefully into the macaroni with half the Parmesan. Taste and adjust seasoning and heat through gently.

Pour the macaroni mixture into a flameproof dish and scatter cauliflower and breadcrumb mixture over it. Sprinkle with remaining cheese, then grill for 5 minutes till golden.

Spaghetti with chicken sauce

Overall timing 1 hour

Freezing Suitable: cook spaghetti and almonds after reheating sauce

To serve 4

2	Thick rashers of streaky bacon	2
12 oz	Boned chicken breasts	350 g
2 oz	Butter	50 g
2 tbsp	Oil	2x15 ml
1 lb	Ripe tomatoes	450 g
1	Garlic clove	1
2 tbsp	Tomato purée	2x15 ml
½ teasp	Sugar	2.5 ml
	Salt and pepper	
¼ pint	Dry white wine	150 ml
12 oz	Spaghetti	350 g
1 oz	Chopped almonds	25 g

Derind and dice the bacon. Wipe and trim the chicken, discarding skin. Cut the meat into strips. Heat half the butter and the oil in a flameproof casserole, add the bacon and chicken and fry for 5 minutes till browned all over.

Blanch, peel and chop the tomatoes. Add to the pan with the peeled and crushed garlic, tomato purée, sugar and salt and pepper. Add the wine and bring to the boil, stirring. Reduce the heat, cover the pan tightly and simmer for 20 minutes.

Meanwhile, cook the spaghetti in boiling salted water till just tender. Drain in a colander.

Melt remaining butter in the saucepan, add the almonds and fry over a high heat till golden. Return the spaghetti to the pan with half the tomato chicken sauce, toss lightly and adjust seasoning to taste. Place in a warmed serving dish.

Season remaining sauce, pour into a warmed sauceboat and serve separately.

Turkey noodle bake

Overall timing 1½ hours

Freezing Not suitable

To serve 4

4 oz	Button mushrooms	125 g
8 oz	Noodles	225 g
	Salt and pepper	
3 tbsp	Plain flour	3x15 ml
1	Chicken stock cube	1
¼ teasp	Paprika	1.25 ml
5 tbsp	Single cream	5x15 ml
8 oz	Cooked turkey meat	225 g
2 oz	Cheddar cheese	50 g
1 oz	Fresh breadcrumbs	25 g
½ oz	Butter	15 g

Wipe and slice the mushrooms. Cook the noodles in boiling salted water for about 5 minutes till tender. Drain the noodles thoroughly, reserving 1 pint (560 ml) of the cooking water.

Blend the flour in a small bowl with a little of the measured cooking water. Put rest of water into a saucepan, stir in blended flour, crumbled stock cube, salt, pepper and paprika. Bring to the boil, stirring. Reduce the heat and add the mushrooms. Simmer for 10 minutes.

Preheat the oven to 350°F (180°C) Gas 4. Grease an 8 inch (20 cm) soufflé dish.

Remove pan from heat and stir in cream.

Spread half the drained noodles over the bottom of the soufflé dish. Dice the turkey and arrange half over the noodles. Cover with half the sauce. Repeat the layers, finishing with sauce. Grate cheese and scatter over top. Sprinkle with breadcrumbs and dot with butter. Bake for 30 minutes.

Cheesy noodles with ham

Overall timing 1 hour

Freezing Not suitable

To serve 4

8 oz	Tagliatelle	225 g
	Salt and pepper	
4 oz	Cheese	125 g
3	Eggs	3
¾ pint	White sauce	400 ml
4 oz	Sliced cooked ham	125 g

Preheat the oven to 400°F (200°C) Gas 6.

Cook the noodles in boiling salted water for about 10 minutes till tender.

Grate cheese. Separate eggs. Stir yolks, 3 oz (75 g) of the cheese and seasoning into sauce.

Cut ham into strips and stir into the sauce. Drain noodles thoroughly and fold into sauce. Season to taste. Whisk the egg whites in a bowl till stiff but not dry and fold into the mixture with metal spoon.

Pour the mixture into a greased ovenproof dish. Sprinkle remaining grated cheese over and bake for about 30 minutes till set and golden. Serve immediately with whole green beans mixed with flaked almonds and butter.

Spaghetti omelette

Overall timing 30 minutes

Freezing Not suitable

To serve 4–6

12 oz	Spaghetti	350 g
	Salt and pepper	
1 oz	Cheddar cheese	25 g
1	Garlic clove	1
1 oz	Grated Parmesan cheese	25 g
4	Eggs	4
1 tbsp	Chopped parsley	15 ml
6	Basil leaves	6
2 oz	Butter	50 g

Cook the spaghetti in boiling salted water till tender.

Meanwhile, grate the Cheddar cheese. Peel and crush the garlic. Mix together the garlic, cheeses, eggs, parsley, chopped basil and seasoning.

Drain the spaghetti and put into a large bowl. Pour the egg and cheese mixture over and mix well. Melt 1 oz (25 g) butter in frying pan. Add spaghetti mixture and press down well with the back of a spoon to form a cake. Fry over a low heat for about 5 minutes, pressing down to keep the cake flat.

Run a knife round the edge of the omelette to loosen it, then turn it out on to a board. Add remaining butter to the pan and, when melted, slide the omelette back into the pan. Fry for 3–5 minutes till firmly set. Place on a warmed serving dish and serve immediately, cut into wedges.

Lasagne col pesto

Overall timing 1 hour

Freezing Suitable: reheat, covered with foil, in 350°F (180°C) Gas 4 oven for 1 hour

To serve 4

12 oz	Lasagne	350 g
	Salt	
4 tbsp	Grated Parmesan cheese	4x15 ml
2 oz	Butter	50 g
Pesto		
2	Garlic cloves	2
4 tbsp	Chopped fresh basil	4x15 ml
4 tbsp	Olive oil	4x15 ml
1 oz	Grated Parmesan cheese	25 g
	Pinch of salt	

Cook the lasagne in boiling salted water for 15–20 minutes till tender. Drain thoroughly and spread out on a damp cloth to cool.

Preheat oven to 350°F (180°C) Gas 4.

To make the pesto, peel and chop garlic and put in mortar with basil. Pound with pestle, gradually adding oil, Parmesan and salt.

Spread one-third of the lasagne over the bottom of a greased ovenproof dish. Spread with one-third of the pesto and sprinkle over 1 tbsp (15 ml) Parmesan. Repeat layers twice, adding extra Parmesan to the top. Dot with butter and bake for 20 minutes till heated through.

Spaghetti with aubergines

Overall timing 45 minutes plus draining

Freezing Not suitable

To serve 4

1	Large aubergine	1
	Salt and pepper	
1 lb	Ripe tomatoes	450 g
1	Garlic clove	1
	Oil	
2 teasp	Chopped fresh basil	2x5 ml
12 oz	Spaghetti	350 g
2 oz	Grated Parmesan cheese	50 g
	Sprig of basil	

Wash and thinly slice the aubergine. Put into a colander and sprinkle with salt. Leave to drain for 1 hour.

Blanch, peel and chop the tomatoes. Peel and crush garlic. Heat 3 tbsp (3x15 ml) oil in a saucepan, add garlic and fry for 1 minute. Add tomatoes, basil and seasoning, stir well and cook over a low heat for 15 minutes.

Cook spaghetti in boiling salted water till tender.

Meanwhile, rinse aubergine slices under running water and gently squeeze dry. Heat ½ inch (12.5 mm) oil in a frying pan and fry aubergine slices, a few at a time, till crisp on both sides. Drain on kitchen paper and keep hot.

Drain spaghetti thoroughly. Put into a warmed serving dish and pour tomato sauce over. Add aubergine slices, sprinkle with cheese, garnish with sprig of basil and serve.

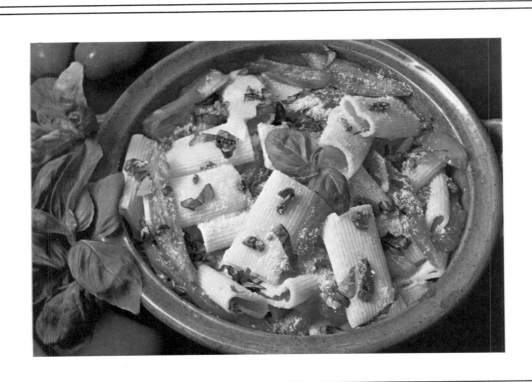

Macaroni niçoise

Overall timing 30 minutes

Freezing Not suitable

To serve 4

3	Anchovy fillets	3
12 oz	Tomatoes	350 g
1	Garlic clove	1
12 oz	Rigatoni	350 g
	Salt	
2 oz	Butter	50 g
2 oz	Grated Parmesan cheese	50 g
1 tbsp	Chopped fresh basil	15 ml

Chop the anchovies. Blanch, peel and cut tomatoes into thin slices. Place in a serving bowl with the anchovies and peeled and crushed garlic.

Cook the rigatoni in a large saucepan of boiling salted water till just tender. When cooked, drain in colander.

Melt butter in the saucepan and when frothy, add rigatoni and toss well. Add to the tomatoes and garlic, toss, then sprinkle with Parmesan and basil and serve immediately.

Spaghetti with bacon sauce

Overall timing 45 minutes

Freezing Not suitable

To serve 4

12 oz	Piece of smoked streaky bacon	350 g
1 tbsp	Oil	15 ml
1	Small red pepper	1
14 oz	Can of tomatoes	397 g
	Salt and pepper	
12 oz	Spaghetti	350 g
6 tbsp	Grated Parmesan cheese	6x15 ml

Remove the rind and any bones from the bacon. Cut into $\frac{1}{4}$ inch (6 mm) thick slices, then cut across into strips. Heat the oil in a saucepan, add the bacon and fry till golden all over.

Deseed and finely chop the pepper. Add to the pan and fry for 1 minute. Press the tomatoes and juice through a sieve into the pan and bring to the boil, stirring. Add seasoning, cover and simmer for 15 minutes.

Meanwhile, cook the spaghetti in boiling salted water till tender. Drain thoroughly and return to the pan. Add the sauce and all but 1 tbsp (15 ml) of the cheese. Toss lightly over a low heat for 2 minutes. Adjust the seasoning to taste.

Place spaghetti in a warmed serving dish and sprinkle with the remaining cheese. Serve immediately with fresh crusty bread.

Boer-style noodle supper

Overall timing 20 minutes

Freezing Not suitable

To serve 2

1 pint	Milk	560 ml
	Blade of mace	
6 oz	Noodles	175 g
1 oz	Butter	25 g
2	Eggs	2
¼ teasp	Ground cinnamon	1.25 ml
	Salt and pepper	

Put the milk in a saucepan with the mace and bring to the boil. Add the noodles and cook for about 5 minutes till tender. Drain, reserving the milk. Divide noodles between individual soup bowls and add half butter to each. Keep hot.

Separate the eggs. Beat the egg yolks in a bowl with the cinnamon and seasoning. Gradually strain the reserved milk on to the yolks, stirring constantly. Return to the pan.

Whisk the egg whites till stiff and fold into the yolk mixture. Cook over a low heat for 2–5 minutes without stirring till mixture begins to thicken. Do not allow to boil.

Pour egg mixture over the noodles and serve immediately with bread and a mixed salad.

Spaghetti with piquant sauce

Overall timing 50 minutes

Freezing Not suitable

To serve 4

1	Can of anchovy fillets	1
4 tbsp	Milk	4x15 ml
1 lb	Ripe tomatoes	450 g
1	Garlic clove	1
1	Dried red chilli	1
3 fl oz	Olive oil	90 ml
1 tbsp	Tomato purée	15 ml
2 tbsp	Capers	2x15 ml
12 oz	Spaghetti	350 g
	Salt and pepper	
4 oz	Stoned black olives	125 g

Drain the anchovies and put into a small bowl with the milk. Soak for 10 minutes. Blanch, peel and chop the tomatoes. Peel and crush the garlic; deseed and finely chop the chilli.

Heat the oil in a saucepan, add the garlic and cook for 2 minutes. Drain the anchovies, discarding the milk. Chop and add to the pan with the chilli. Fry for 3 minutes, pressing the anchovies with the back of a wooden spoon to break them up.

Add the tomatoes, tomato purée and capers. Bring to the boil, then cover and simmer for 15 minutes.

Meanwhile, cook the spaghetti in boiling salted water till tender. Drain thoroughly. Return to the pan and add the tomato and anchovy sauce and the black olives. Stir over a low heat for 3 minutes. Adjust seasoning to taste and serve hot.

Mushroom ravioli

Overall timing 45 minutes

Freezing Suitable: cook from frozen

To serve 4

12 oz	Strong flour	350 g
	Salt and pepper	
3	Eggs	3
1 lb	Mushrooms	450 g
1	Onion	1
2 oz	Butter	50 g

Sift flour and 1 teasp (5 ml) salt into a bowl. Add eggs and mix to a smooth, glossy dough.

Chop the mushrooms. Peel and finely chop onion. Melt half the butter in a frying pan and fry the onion for 5 minutes till transparent. Add mushrooms and seasoning and stir-fry over a high heat for about 5 minutes to evaporate any liquid. Reduce heat and cook gently for a further 5 minutes. Remove from heat and leave to cool.

Roll out the dough on a lightly floured surface and cut into 3 inch (7.5 cm) squares with a pastry wheel. Divide the mushroom mixture between the squares, then fold them over, pressing the edges together well to seal.

Put plenty of lightly salted water in a large saucepan and bring to the boil. Add the ravioli and cook for 10–15 minutes, then drain and place in a warmed serving dish. Melt the remaining butter, pour over the ravioli and toss well.

Neapolitan cannelloni

Overall timing 1½ hours

Freezing Suitable: reheat from frozen in 350°F (180°C) Gas 4 oven for 1 hour

To serve 4

12	Sheets of lasagne	12
8 oz	Mozzarella cheese	225 g
2 oz	Cooked ham	50 g
8 oz	Cream cheese	225 g
2	Eggs	2
	Salt and pepper	
1½ oz	Grated Parmesan cheese	40 g
Tomato sauce		
1	Onion	1
1	Garlic clove	1
1 tbsp	Oil	15 ml
14 oz	Can of tomatoes	397 g
1 tbsp	Chopped fresh basil	15 ml

Cook lasagne in boiling salted water for 10–15 minutes till tender. Drain and spread on a damp cloth to cool.

Thinly slice the Mozzarella. Dice ham. Place in a bowl with the cream cheese, eggs and seasoning. Mix well.

For the sauce, peel and finely chop onion. Peel and crush garlic. Heat oil in a saucepan, add onion and garlic and fry until golden. Add tomatoes in their juice, basil, salt and pepper. Cook for 10 minutes, stirring occasionally.

Preheat oven to 425°F (220°C) Gas 7.

Divide cheese mixture between lasagne sheets. Roll lasagne around filling and arrange, joins down, in greased ovenproof dish. Pour over the tomato sauce. Sprinkle half the Parmesan on top and bake for 15 minutes or until golden. Sprinkle with the rest of the Parmesan and serve immediately.

Spaghetti with sardine dressing

Overall timing 20 minutes

Freezing Not suitable

To serve 4

12 oz	Spaghetti	350 g
	Salt and pepper	
11½ oz	Can of sardines	326 g
2	Garlic cloves	2
3 oz	Butter	75 g

Cook the spaghetti in boiling salted water till tender.

Drain the sardines and put into a mortar. Peel and crush garlic and add to sardines. Pound to a paste with a pestle. Add the butter and mix well. Season to taste.

Drain the spaghetti and return to the pan. Add the sardine paste and toss lightly over a low heat till the spaghetti is coated. Place in a warmed serving dish and serve immediately with wedges of lemon.

Spaghetti with tomato sauce

Overall timing 30 minutes

Freezing Not suitable

To serve 4

1	Onion	1
2 lb	Cherry or plum tomatoes	900 g
	Bouquet garni	
	Pinch of sugar	
	Cayenne pepper or Tabasco sauce	
	Salt and pepper	
1 tbsp	Chopped fresh basil or parsley	15 ml
12 oz	Spaghetti	350 g

Peel and chop the onion. Halve the tomatoes. Put the onion and tomatoes in a saucepan with the bouquet garni and simmer gently until mushy.

Discard the bouquet garni, then rub the tomato sauce through a sieve, or purée in a blender. Return to the pan and add the sugar, a little cayenne or Tabasco sauce and seasoning. Stir in the herbs and reheat gently.

Meanwhile, cook the spaghetti in boiling salted water till just tender. Drain well and turn into a warmed serving dish. Pile the tomato sauce on top and serve.

Neapolitan rigatoni

Overall timing 50 minutes

Freezing Not suitable

To serve 2

2	Streaky bacon rashers	2
1	Onion	1
1	Garlic clove	1
1 oz	Lard	25 g
6 oz	Minced beef	175 g
5 tbsp	Beef stock	5x15 ml
5 tbsp	Red wine	5x15 ml
1 tbsp	Tomato purée	15 ml
1 teasp	Chopped fresh basil	5 ml
	Salt and pepper	
8 oz	Rigatoni	225 g

Derind and finely chop bacon. Peel and chop onion. Peel and crush garlic. Melt the lard in a saucepan, add bacon, onion and garlic and fry for 10 minutes till golden.

Add the minced beef and fry, stirring, till brown. Gradually stir in the stock, wine, tomato purée, basil and seasoning. Cover and simmer for 30 minutes.

Meanwhile, cook rigatoni in boiling salted water till tender. Drain thoroughly and pile on to a warmed serving dish. Keep hot.

Taste the sauce and adjust seasoning. Purée in a blender or press through a sieve, then reheat and spoon over rigatoni. Serve immediately with a mixed salad and grated Parmesan cheese.

Macaroni with mushrooms

Overall timing 30 minutes

Freezing Not suitable

To serve 4

4 oz	Button mushrooms	125 g
4 oz	Butter	125 g
8 fl oz	Carton of single cream	227 ml
12 oz	Short-cut macaroni	350 g
	Salt and pepper	
4 oz	Cooked ham	125 g
2 oz	Grated Parmesan cheese	50 g
½ pint	White sauce	300 ml

Finely chop the mushrooms. Place in a small saucepan with 2 oz (50 g) of the butter and cook gently for 5 minutes. Remove from heat and stir in cream.

Cook macaroni in boiling salted water till tender. Drain.

Cut the ham into pieces and add to the macaroni with 1 oz (25 g) of cheese, 1 oz (25 g) of butter and seasoning. Place macaroni in a flameproof dish with mushroom mixture and stir well. Cook gently for 10 minutes.

Preheat grill.

Pour white sauce over macaroni, sprinkle with remaining cheese and dot with remaining butter. Grill for 5 minutes.

Pasta with lamb and tomato sauce

Overall timing 1¼ hours

Freezing Not suitable

To serve 2

2	Bacon rashers	2
8 oz	Tomatoes	225 g
1	Onion	1
1	Garlic clove	1
2 tbsp	Oil	2x15 ml
6 oz	Minced lamb	175 g
¼ pint	Red wine	150 ml
	Salt and pepper	
8 oz	Pasta shapes	225 g

Derind and chop bacon. Blanch, peel and chop tomatoes. Peel and chop onion and garlic. Heat the oil in a saucepan, add the bacon and fry for 5 minutes. Add onion and garlic and fry gently till transparent. Add the minced lamb and fry for about 15 minutes till browned.

Stir in the red wine, tomatoes and seasoning. Cover and simmer for 40 minutes.

Meanwhile, cook pasta in boiling salted water till tender. Drain and place in warmed serving dish.

Spoon meat sauce over pasta and serve hot with a green salad.

Spaghetti with tuna

Overall timing 30 minutes

Freezing Not suitable

To serve 4

1	Onion	1
2	Garlic cloves	2
7 oz	Can of tuna	198 g
1 tbsp	Olive oil	15 ml
12 oz	Spaghetti	350 g
	Salt and pepper	
4	Anchovy fillets	4
2 tbsp	Tomato purée	2x15 ml
½ teasp	Sugar	2.5 ml
6 tbsp	Water	6x15 ml
1 tbsp	Chopped parsley	15 ml
2 teasp	Chopped fresh basil	2x5 ml

Peel and finely chop the onion; peel and crush the garlic. Drain the oil from the tuna into a saucepan. Add the olive oil and heat. Add the onion and garlic and fry till just golden.

Put the spaghetti into a saucepan of boiling salted water and cook gently till just tender.

Meanwhile, chop the anchovies and add to the onion with the tomato puree, sugar and water. Bring to the boil.

Flake the tuna fish and add to the pan with seasoning. Cover and simmer for 5 minutes.

Drain the spaghetti and add to the pan with the herbs. Toss lightly over a low heat for 2–3 minutes. Adjust seasoning to taste and serve immediately.

Striped vermicelli

Overall timing 45 minutes

Freezing Not suitable

To serve 4

1	Can of anchovies	1
6 tbsp	Milk	6x15 ml
1	Large onion	1
1	Garlic clove	1
2 tbsp	Oil	2x15 ml
14 oz	Can of tomatoes	397 g
	Salt and pepper	
	Chilli powder	
1 tbsp	Chopped parsley	15 ml
12 oz	Vermicelli	350 g
¼ pint	Carton of double cream	150 ml

Drain the anchovies and soak in the milk for 10 minutes.

Meanwhile, peel and finely chop the onion; peel and crush the garlic. Heat the oil in a small saucepan, add onion and garlic and fry till transparent. Add tomatoes and juice, salt, a pinch of chilli powder and parsley. Simmer for 20 minutes, stirring frequently.

Drain the anchovies and add to the tomato mixture. Purée in a blender or rub through a sieve. Season and reheat gently.

Cook the vermicelli in boiling salted water for 3 minutes till tender. Drain thoroughly and arrange on a warmed flat serving dish. Smooth the top and keep hot.

Warm the cream, then spread it in a wide band across the centre of the vermicelli. Spread the tomato sauce in a wide band on either side of the cream. Serve with hot garlic bread.

Tagliatelli with ham

Overall timing 25 minutes

Freezing Not suitable

To serve 4

12 oz	Tagliatelli	350 g
	Salt and pepper	
1	Large onion	1
2 oz	Butter	50 g
2 tbsp	Oil	2x15 ml
1	Garlic clove	1
4 oz	Lean cooked ham	125 g
2 teasp	Dried marjoram	2x5 ml
14 oz	Can of tomatoes	397 g
6 tbsp	Grated Parmesan cheese	6x15 ml

Cook the tagliatelli in boiling salted water till tender.

Meanwhile, peel and finely chop the onion. Heat the butter and oil in a large saucepan and fry the onion till transparent. Peel and crush the garlic and add to the pan. Chop the ham very finely and add to the pan with the marjoram and tomatoes with their juice. Season and cook for 10 minutes, stirring to break up the tomatoes.

Drain the tagliatelli and place in a warmed bowl. Add the sauce and Parmesan and toss well, adding seasoning to taste. Serve immediately with a watercress, cucumber and lettuce salad.

Spinach ravioli

Overall timing 1¼ hours

Freezing Suitable: cook ravioli from frozen, then add to tomato sauce

To serve 4–6

12 oz	Strong flour	350 g
	Salt and pepper	
3	Eggs	3
2	Bacon rashers	2
1	Large onion	1
1	Garlic clove	1
1 tbsp	Oil	15 ml
4 oz	Minced veal	125 g
4 oz	Sausagemeat	125 g
¼ teasp	Grated nutmeg	1.25 ml
6 tbsp	Dry white wine	6x15 ml
1 lb	Spinach	450 g
14 oz	Can of tomatoes	397 g
2 oz	Butter	50 g

Sift flour and 1 teasp (5 ml) salt into a bowl. Add eggs and mix to smooth, glossy dough.

Derind and dice bacon. Peel and finely chop onion; peel and crush garlic. Heat oil in a saucepan, add bacon, onion and garlic and fry for 5 minutes. Add the veal, sausagemeat and nutmeg and fry for 5 minutes. Stir in wine and seasoning and bring to the boil. Cover and simmer for 15 minutes.

Shred spinach and add to meat. Cover and simmer for a further 5 minutes.

Roll out dough to a large rectangle. Cut out rounds. Dot spoonfuls of spinach mixture on rounds. Fold in half and pinch edges to seal. Roll each half-moon round your forefinger and pinch ends together.

Cook ravioli in boiling salted water till tender. Drain. Press tomatoes through a sieve. Melt butter in pan, stir in tomatoes and seasoning and heat. Return ravioli to pan and toss lightly till coated.

Spaghetti with lamb sauce

Overall timing 1¾ hours

Freezing Not suitable

To serve 4

1½ lb	Boned shoulder of lamb	700 g
	Salt and pepper	
3 tbsp	Plain flour	3x15 ml
1	Large onion	1
3 tbsp	Olive oil	3x15 ml
2 teasp	Paprika	2x5 ml
¾ pint	Chicken stock	400 ml
2 tbsp	Tomato purée	2x15 ml
12 oz	Spaghetti	350 g

Cut the lamb into bite-size pieces. Season the flour and toss the meat in it till evenly coated. Peel and thinly slice the onion. Heat the oil in a saucepan, add the onion and fry till transparent. Add the meat and fry till browned all over. Sprinkle in any remaining flour and the paprika and cook for 1 minute, stirring.

Gradually add the stock and bring to the boil, stirring constantly. Add the tomato purée and seasoning, cover and simmer gently for about 1 hour till tender.

Break the spaghetti into 4 inch (10 cm) lengths. Add 1 pint (560 ml) water to the lamb and bring to the boil. Add the spaghetti and simmer till tender, stirring frequently.

Taste and adjust seasoning. Divide between warmed individual serving dishes, arranging the meat on top. Serve immediately.

Aubergine cheese bake

Overall timing 2¼ hours

Freezing Suitable: bake from frozen in 350°F (180°C) Gas 4 oven for 45 minutes

To serve 4

1¼ lb	Aubergines	600 g
	Salt and pepper	
2 tbsp	Plain flour	2x15 ml
	Oil	
1	Small onion	1
14 oz	Can of tomatoes	397 g
½ teasp	Dried basil	2.5 ml
8 oz	Mozzarella cheese	225 g
3 oz	Grated Parmesan cheese	75 g

Remove stalks from aubergines and cut lengthways into ½ inch (12.5 mm) thick slices. Sprinkle with salt. Leave for 1 hour, then rinse and pat dry. Coat with flour.

Preheat the oven to 350°F (180°C) Gas 4.

Heat oil in a large frying pan and fry aubergine slices on both sides till golden. Drain on kitchen paper and keep warm.

Peel and finely chop onion. Fry till transparent, adding more oil to pan if necessary. Mash tomatoes and juice and add to pan with seasoning. Cook for 10 minutes. Stir in basil and simmer for a further 5 minutes.

Place a layer of aubergines in oiled ovenproof dish. Cover with slices of Mozzarella and spoon on a little tomato sauce. Sprinkle with Parmesan and a pinch of salt. Repeat layering, ending with Parmesan. Sprinkle a little oil over surface and bake for 15 minutes or until top begins to brown.

Aubergine boxes

Overall timing 1½ hours

Freezing Not suitable

To serve 4

1 lb	Aubergines	450 g
	Salt and pepper	
3	Anchovy fillets	3
2 oz	Mozzarella cheese	50 g
1 teasp	Dried basil	2x5 ml
2 teasp	Capers	2x5 ml
1	Large onion	1
2	Garlic cloves	2
2 tbsp	Oil	2x15 ml
14 oz	Can of tomatoes	397 g
1 tbsp	Worcestershire sauce	15 ml
4–5	Fresh tomatoes (optional)	4–5

Cook aubergines in boiling salted water for 5 minutes. Drain and leave to cool, then cut off stalks and make a lengthways cut through the aubergines leaving the halves still attached at one side. Ease open and remove most of the flesh with a teaspoon. Finely chop or mash the flesh and put into a bowl.

Drain and chop anchovies. Dice Mozzarella. Mix together aubergine flesh, anchovies, basil, Mozzarella, capers and seasoning. Stuff the hollowed-out aubergine shells with mixture.

Preheat the oven to 350°F (180°C) Gas 4.

Peel and chop onion. Peel and crush garlic. Heat oil in flameproof casserole and fry onion till brown. Stir in garlic, tomatoes, Worcestershire sauce and seasoning. Simmer gently for about 10 minutes or until the sauce has become quite "mushy".

Arrange the stuffed aubergines on top of sauce and bake for 45 minutes. You can add 4–5 fresh tomatoes about 15 minutes before the end of the cooking time – they add attractive colour as well as taste.

Cabbage parcels

Overall timing 1¼ hours

Freezing Not suitable

To serve 4

1	White cabbage	1
3 oz	Long grain rice	75 g
1	Small onion	1
6 tbsp	Oil	6x15 ml
8 oz	Minced beef	225 g
	Salt and pepper	
¼ teasp	Grated nutmeg	1.25 ml
1 teasp	Dried oregano	5 ml
8 fl oz	Stock	220 ml
1 oz	Butter	25 g
1 tbsp	Plain flour	15 ml
1	Egg	1
2	Egg yolks	2
6 tbsp	Lemon juice	6x15 ml
¾ pint	White sauce	400 ml

Remove core from cabbage and cook in boiling water for 5 minutes. Drain and cool, then peel away 16–20 leaves. Add rice to same pan of boiling water and cook till tender. Drain.

Peel and chop onion. Heat 4 tbsp (4x15 ml) oil in a frying pan and cook onion till transparent. Add mince, salt, pepper, nutmeg and oregano. Cook for 5–8 minutes. Cool, then mix in rice.

Place a little stuffing on each cabbage leaf. Fold in sides and roll into tight parcels. Heat rest of oil in flameproof casserole. Pack cabbage rolls tightly in casserole and pour in stock. Cut leftover cabbage heart in two and place on top. Cover and simmer gently for 40 minutes.

Transfer cabbage rolls to warmed serving dish. Pour cooking liquor into a measuring jug and make up to 8 fl oz (220 ml) with water if necessary.

Melt butter in saucepan, then stir in flour and cooking liquor and simmer until thickened. Beat egg and egg yolks with lemon juice till foamy. Add to pan off heat. Return to a gentle heat. Don't allow sauce to boil. Stir in white sauce and heat. Pour sauce over rolls

Braised lettuce

Overall timing 40 minutes

Freezing Not suitable

To serve 4

4	Small round lettuces	4
	Salt and pepper	
2	Onions	2
2	Carrots	2
4 oz	Streaky bacon rashers	125 g
1 oz	Butter	25 g
½ pint	Chicken stock	300 ml

Trim lettuces. Blanch in boiling salted water for 2 minutes, then drain thoroughly.

Peel and slice onions and carrots. Derind and thinly slice bacon. Melt butter in saucepan, add onions, carrots and bacon and fry gently for 10 minutes, stirring occasionally.

Pour in stock and add blanched lettuces and seasoning. Cover and simmer for 20 minutes.

Transfer bacon and vegetables to warmed serving dish and keep hot. Boil cooking liquor rapidly to reduce by half. Taste and adjust seasoning. Pour over lettuce and serve immediately with roast meats.

Casseroled lettuce rolls

Overall timing 1 hour

Freezing Not suitable

To serve 4

8 oz	Streaky bacon	225 g
10	Large lettuce leaves	10
2	Onions	2
2	Carrots	2
	Salt and pepper	
¼ pint	Stock	150 ml
2 tbsp	Lemon juice	2x15 ml
Stuffing		
1	Onion	1
2 tbsp	Oil	2x15 ml
8 oz	Chicken livers	225 g
2 oz	Long grain rice	50 g
½ pint	Chicken stock	300 ml
	Bouquet garni	
	Salt and pepper	

To make the stuffing, peel and chop onion. Heat oil in pan and fry onion till golden. Chop chicken livers. Add to pan and brown on all sides.

Add rice, stock, bouquet garni and seasoning. Bring to the boil. Cover and simmer for 15 minutes, shaking pan frequently.

Meanwhile, derind and halve bacon rashers, then use them to line bottom and sides of an ovenproof dish. Wash and dry lettuce leaves. Peel and slice onions into rings. Peel and thinly slice carrots. Blanch lettuce, onions and carrots in boiling salted water for 3 minutes. Drain thoroughly.

Preheat the oven to 350°F (180°C) Gas 4.

Spread out lettuce leaves. Taste stuffing and adjust seasoning. Divide between lettuce leaves. Fold in sides of leaves, then roll up tightly round stuffing. Arrange, join side down, in ovenproof dish. Add blanched onions and carrots. Mix stock, lemon juice and seasoning. Pour over lettuce. Cover tightly and bake for 25–30 minutes.

Tomatoes stuffed with vegetables

Overall timing 30 minutes

Freezing Not suitable

To serve 4

3	Large waxy potatoes	3
3	Large carrots	3
4 oz	Green beans	125 g
2	Stalks of celery	2
	Salt and pepper	
4 oz	Frozen peas	125 g
6 tbsp	Mayonnaise	6 x 15 ml
	Lemon juice	
4	Large tomatoes	4
	Basil leaves	

Peel the potatoes. Scrape the carrots. Top and tail the beans. Wash and trim the celery. Dice all the vegetables. Cook in boiling salted water for 5 minutes. Add the peas and cook for a further 5 minutes or until tender. Drain well and cool.

Add the mayonnaise to the vegetables with a few drops of lemon juice and seasoning and mix well.

Halve the tomatoes and scoop out the seeds and centres. Fill with the vegetable mixture and arrange on a serving plate. Serve garnished with basil leaves.

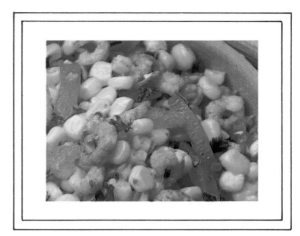

Chicory bake

Overall timing 45 minutes

Freezing Not suitable

To serve 2

2	Heads of chicory	2
	Salt and pepper	
½ teasp	Sugar	2.5 ml
1 oz	Butter	25 g
½ teasp	Lemon juice	2.5 ml
2	Slices of Gruyère cheese	2
2	Tomatoes	2
	Lettuce leaves	

Place chicory in saucepan of boiling water. Add pinch of salt, sugar, a knob of butter and lemon juice. Cook for 30 minutes.

Preheat the oven to 425°F (220°C) Gas 7.

Drain chicory. Wrap each head in slice of cheese. Place seam-side down in greased ovenproof dish and surround with halved tomatoes. Season well, dot with the rest of the butter and bake for 15 minutes. Garnish with lettuce leaves and serve hot.

Corn prawn salad

Overall timing 15 minutes plus 1 hour chilling

Freezing Not suitable

To serve 2

11½ oz	Can of sweetcorn kernels	326 g
3	Tomatoes	3
8 oz	Shelled prawns	225 g
Dressing		
1	Onion	1
2 tbsp	Herb vinegar	2x15 ml
3 tbsp	Oil	3x15 ml
	Salt and pepper	
1 tbsp	Chopped fresh sage	15 ml
1 tbsp	Chopped parsley	15 ml
1 tbsp	Chopped chives	15 ml

Drain sweetcorn. Blanch and peel tomatoes and cut into strips. Put sweetcorn, tomatoes and prawns in a serving dish.

To make the dressing, peel and finely chop onion. Mix together vinegar, oil and seasoning, then add the onion, sage, parsley and chives.

Pour dressing over salad, mix in well, cover and chill for 1 hour before serving.

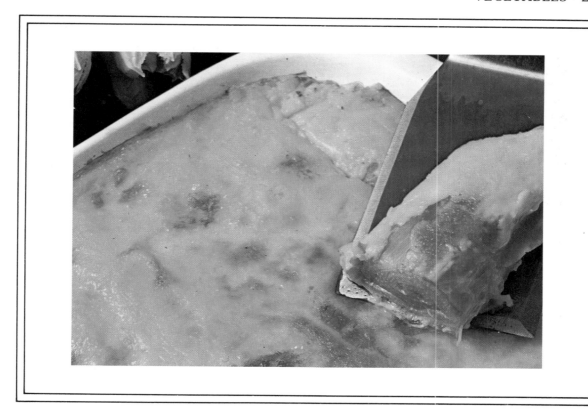

Chicory rolls in cheese sauce

Overall timing 1¼ hours

Freezing Suitable: bake from frozen in cold oven set to 350°F (180°C) Gas 4 for 1 hour; increase to 450°F (230°C) Gas 8 for extra 10 minutes

To serve 4-6

4 oz	Butter	125 g
8	Large heads of chicory	8
2 tbsp	Lemon juice	2x15 ml
1 teasp	Sugar	5 ml
	Salt and pepper	
1 oz	Plain flour	25 g
½ pint	Milk	300 ml
	Grated nutmeg	
2	Egg yolks	2
2 oz	Grated Parmesan cheese	50 g
8	Thin slices of cooked ham	8

Melt half butter in a saucepan and add chicory, lemon juice, sugar and seasoning. Cover and cook gently for about 30 minutes, turning the chicory occasionally.

Meanwhile, make the sauce. Melt 1 oz (25 g) of remaining butter in another saucepan and stir in the flour. Remove from heat and gradually add milk. Return to heat and bring to the boil, stirring until thickened. Remove from heat and stir in a pinch of nutmeg, egg yolks, cheese and seasoning.

Preheat the grill.

Lift out chicory with draining spoon. Reserve cooking liquor. Wrap each chicory head in a slice of ham and arrange in a greased ovenproof dish. Add reserved liquor to sauce, beat well, then pour over chicory. Dot with the rest of the butter and grill for 5–10 minutes till golden on top. Serve immediately.

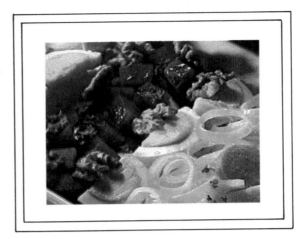

Asparagus milanese

Overall timing 30 minutes

Freezing Not suitable

To serve 4

1 lb	Asparagus	450 g
	Salt	
2 oz	Grated Parmesan cheese	50 g
2 oz	Butter	50 g

Cook asparagus in boiling salted water for 15–20 minutes till tender. Drain carefully on a tea-towel or kitchen paper, then place on a warmed serving dish and cool slightly. Sprinkle Parmesan over the asparagus tips.

Melt the butter in a small saucepan over a low heat. When golden brown, pour over the Parmesan. Serve immediately.

Alsace salad

Overall timing 15 minutes

Freezing Not suitable

To serve 6

2	Dessert apples	2
3	Boiled potatoes	3
1	Small cooked beetroot	1
2	Frankfurters	2
1	Onion	1
1	Hard-boiled egg	1
2 teasp	Chopped parsley	2x5 ml
	Sprigs of parsley	
8	Walnuts	8
3 tbsp	Olive oil	3x15 ml
1 tbsp	Wine vinegar	15 ml
1 teasp	Powdered mustard	5 ml
	Salt and pepper	

Peel, core and chop apples. Peel and dice potatoes and beetroot. Slice frankfurters. Peel onion and cut into rings. Shell egg and cut into 6 wedges.

Arrange prepared ingredients in rows in a serving dish and sprinkle with parsley. Garnish with parsley sprigs and walnuts.

To make dressing, mix oil with vinegar, mustard and seasoning. Pour dressing over salad and serve immediately.

Country-style peas

Overall timing 45 minutes

Freezing Not suitable

To serve 6

4 oz	Button onions	125 g
2 lb	Fresh peas	900 g
3	Carrots	3
8 oz	New potatoes	225 g
1	Round lettuce	1
1	Thick streaky bacon rasher	1
2 oz	Butter	50 g
	Sprig of thyme	
	Sprig of tarragon	
	Bay leaf	
	Salt and pepper	

Blanch and peel onions. Shell peas; scrape and dice carrots. Scrub potatoes. Tear lettuce into pieces. Derind bacon and cut into strips.

Melt butter in a flameproof casserole and fry bacon and onions till bacon fat begins to run. Add remaining vegetables, herbs tied together, seasoning and ¼ pint (150 ml) water. Cover and simmer for 25 minutes till vegetables are tender. Remove herbs before serving.

Cheese and potato bake

Overall timing 1¼ hours

Freezing Not suitable

To serve 6

2 lb	New potatoes	900 g
3	Onions	3
2 tbsp	Oil	2 x 15 ml
1	Red pepper	1
8 oz	Sliced cooked ham	225 g
14 oz	Can of tomatoes	397 g
5	Small gherkins	5
12 oz	Red Leicester cheese	350 g
¼ pint	Soured cream	150 ml
2	Egg yolks	2
	Salt and pepper	
¼ teasp	Grated nutmeg	1.25 ml
2 oz	Butter	50 g

Preheat the oven to 400°F (200°C) Gas 6.

Scrub potatoes. Cook in boiling water for 30 minutes.

Peel and thinly slice onions. Fry in oil for 5 minutes. Deseed and slice red pepper, add to onion and fry for 5 minutes. Shred ham; add to pan with tomatoes, sliced gherkins and seasoning.

Drain potatoes and cool. Slice thickly. Slice cheese. Layer potatoes, cheese and tomato mixture in greased ovenproof dish. Mix soured cream, egg yolks, seasoning and nutmeg and pour over top. Dot with butter. Bake for 20 minutes.

Swiss style potatoes

Overall timing 1 hour

Freezing Not suitable

To serve 4

2 lb	Potatoes	900 g
3 tbsp	Caraway seeds	3x15 ml
1 tbsp	Sea-salt	15 ml
2 oz	Butter	50 g
8 oz	Curd cheese	225 g
4 fl oz	Milk	120 ml
1	Onion	1
2 tbsp	Chopped parsley	2x15 ml
2 tbsp	Chopped mustard and cress	2x15 ml
	Salt and pepper	
Garnish		
	Parsley sprigs	
	Mustard and cress	

Preheat the oven to 350°F (180°C) Gas 4.

Halve potatoes. Mix caraway seeds and sea-salt together in a bowl. Dip the cut sides of potatoes into mixture. Place potatoes in greased ovenproof dish with the caraway seeds facing up.

Melt the butter and pour a little over each potato half. Bake for 45 minutes.

Mix cheese with milk in a bowl. Peel and finely chop onion and add to bowl with parsley, mustard and cress and seasoning.

Divide cheese mixture between warmed serving plates and place the potatoes on top. Garnish with parsley and cress.

Courgettes with mozzarella

Overall timing 30 minutes plus chilling

Freezing Suitable: reheat from frozen in 350°F (180°C) Gas 4 oven for 45 minutes

To serve 2

1	Onion	1
1	Garlic clove	1
1 oz	Butter	25 g
3 tbsp	Oil	3x15 ml
8 oz	Can of tomatoes	226 g
¼ teasp	Dried basil	1.25 ml
4	Courgettes	4
2 tbsp	Plain flour	2x15 ml
	Salt and pepper	
4 oz	Mozzarella cheese	125 g

Peel and finely chop onion. Peel and crush garlic. Heat butter and 1 tbsp (15 ml) oil in a frying pan and fry onion and garlic till transparent.

Drain tomatoes. Add to pan with basil and cook over a low heat for 20 minutes. Purée mixture in a blender or push through a sieve.

Trim and slice courgettes. Coat slices with flour. Heat remaining oil in another frying pan and fry courgettes till lightly golden and tender. Drain on kitchen paper and season with salt and pepper.

Thinly slice Mozzarella. Layer courgettes, Mozzarella and tomato sauce in serving dish. Chill for 2–3 hours. Serve with hot garlic bread or toast and butter curls.

Deep-fried courgettes

Overall timing 2¼ hours

Freezing Not suitable

To serve 4

1¼ lb	Courgettes	600 g
	Salt	
3 tbsp	Plain flour	3x15 ml
	Oil for frying	

Trim courgettes and cut into thin strips. Sprinkle with salt and leave for 1½ hours.

Dry courgettes well on kitchen paper and coat in flour. Shake in a sieve to remove excess flour.

Heat oil in a deep-fryer.

Fry courgettes till lightly golden, then drain well on kitchen paper. Serve hot with tartare sauce.

Variations

Season the flour with a little paprika or ground coriander before coating courgettes.

Braised fennel

Overall timing 1 hour

Freezing Suitable

To serve 6

5	**Bulbs of fennel**	5
	Salt and pepper	
4 oz	**Streaky bacon**	125 g
1	**Onion**	1
2 oz	**Butter**	50 g
½ pint	**Chicken stock**	300 ml
	Bouquet garni	
	Sprigs of parsley	

Trim fennel. Cut each bulb in half and blanch in boiling salted water for 10 minutes. Drain.

Derind and finely chop bacon. Peel and chop onion. Melt butter in flameproof casserole and fry bacon for 5 minutes.

Arrange onion and fennel pieces on top of bacon. Cover with stock and add bouquet garni and seasoning. Cover and simmer for about 45 minutes till tender.

Remove bouquet garni. If liked, sprinkle fennel with grated Parmesan cheese. Garnish with parsley and serve with chicken or a bacon joint.

Tunisian stuffed courgettes

Overall timing 1¼ hours

Freezing Suitable: bake from frozen, covered, in 350°F (180°C) Gas 4 oven for about 45 minutes

To serve 4

1 lb	Courgettes	450 g
1	Onion	1
8 oz	Minced lamb	225 g
1 tbsp	Chopped parsley	15 ml
2	Eggs	2
	Cayenne	
	Salt and pepper	
4 tbsp	Plain flour	4 x 15 ml
4 tbsp	Oil	4 x 15 ml
8 oz	Can of tomatoes	227 g
	Parsley	

Trim courgettes. Using a long thin knife or melon-baller, scoop out centre of each whole courgette, working from both ends if necessary and trying to keep the sides an even thickness. Reserve cut-out flesh.

Peel and finely chop onion and mix with chopped courgette flesh, minced lamb, parsley, 1 egg, a pinch of cayenne and seasoning.

Fill courgettes with prepared mixture. Roll any leftover mixture into little meat balls. Beat remaining egg in a bowl and dip stuffed courgettes and meat balls in it. Coat lightly with flour.

Heat oil in a large frying pan. Add courgettes and meat balls and cook for about 20 minutes, turning to brown all sides. Remove from pan and drain on kitchen paper.

Sieve tomatoes and their juice. Add to pan juices with seasoning and cook over a moderate heat for about 15 minutes.

Return courgettes and meat balls to pan and cook for a further 15 minutes. Serve hot, sprinkled with chopped parsley.

Avocado soufflé

Overall timing 45 minutes

Freezing Not suitable

To serve 2

1 oz	Butter	25 g
1 oz	Plain flour	25 g
¼ pint	Milk	150 ml
2	Ripe avocados	2
1 teasp	Lemon juice	5 ml
	Pinch of grated nutmeg	
	Salt and pepper	
	Pinch of ground cinnamon *or*	
1 teasp	Grated lemon rind (optional)	5 ml
3	Eggs	3

Preheat the oven to 400°F (200°C) Gas 6.

Melt the butter in a saucepan, stir in the flour and cook for 1 minute. Gradually stir in the milk. Bring to the boil, stirring till thickened. Remove from the heat.

Cut the avocados in half lengthways and lift out the stones. Cut out four very thin slices, sprinkle with lemon juice and reserve for the garnish. Remove remaining flesh with a teaspoon, place it in a bowl and mash well. Add to the sauce and beat vigorously until well blended. Add nutmeg, seasoning and cinnamon or lemon rind, if used.

Separate the eggs. Add the yolks one by one to the saucepan, beating well after each addition. Whisk egg whites with a pinch of salt till very stiff, then gently fold into the sauce.

Pour mixture into a greased 2 pint (1.1 litre) soufflé dish. Place on a baking tray and bake for about 30 minutes till well risen. Garnish with reserved avocado slices and serve immediately.

French stuffed lettuce

Overall timing 40 minutes

Freezing Not suitable

To serve 4

4	Round lettuces	4
1 pint	Chicken stock	560 ml
2 oz	Butter	50 g
1 oz	Plain flour	25 g
½ pint	Milk	300 ml
	Salt	
	Grated nutmeg	
4 oz	Cooked ham	125 g
3 oz	Mozzarella cheese	75 g
2	Egg yolks	2

Preheat the oven to 350°F (180°C) Gas 4.

Trim lettuces, discarding outer leaves if necessary. Bring stock to the boil in a large saucepan. Add lettuces, cover and cook for 5 minutes. Drain thoroughly, reserving cooking liquor. Allow lettuces to cool.

Melt 1 oz (25 g) of the butter in another saucepan. Add flour and cook, stirring, for 2 minutes. Gradually stir in milk. Bring to the boil, stirring, and cook for 3 minutes. Season with salt and a pinch of grated nutmeg.

Dice ham and Mozzarella and stir into sauce with egg yolks. Cook over a low heat for 2 minutes. Remove from heat and taste and adjust seasoning.

Cut cooled lettuces in half lengthways. Arrange four lettuce halves in a greased ovenproof dish, cut sides uppermost. Spoon sauce into each half and top with remaining lettuce halves. Add ¼ pint (150 ml) of the reserved cooking liquor and dot with remaining butter.

Cover with foil and bake for 15 minutes. Serve hot with French bread.

Baked sweet potatoes

Overall timing 1 hour

Freezing Not suitable

To serve 4

4x8 oz	Sweet potatoes	4x225 g
	Salt and pepper	
2 oz	Butter	50 g

Preheat the oven to 400°F (200°C) Gas 6,

Wash the sweet potatoes gently to avoid breaking the skins. Arrange on a greased baking tray and bake in the centre of the oven for about 45 minutes till tender when pierced with a skewer.

Arrange the sweet potatoes on a warmed serving dish and cut open along the top. Sprinkle a little salt and pepper into each and top with a knob of butter. Serve immediately.

Cauliflower ring

Overall timing 1¼ hours

Freezing Not suitable

To serve 4–6

1	Large cauliflower	1
	Salt and pepper	
4 oz	Butter	125 g
2 oz	Plain flour	50 g
¾ pint	Milk	400 ml
¼ teasp	Grated nutmeg	1.25 ml
4 oz	Gruyère or Cheddar cheese	125 g
3	Eggs	3
1 tbsp	Dried breadcrumbs	15 ml
	Sprigs of parsley	

Preheat oven to 375°F (190°C) Gas 5.

Trim cauliflower and divide into florets. Cook for 7–10 minutes in boiling salted water. Drain, chop and put in bowl.

To make sauce, melt 2 oz (50 g) of the butter in a pan, stir in flour and cook for 1 minute. Gradually stir in milk. Bring to the boil, stirring, and cook for 1 minute. Add seasoning and nutmeg. Grate cheese and stir 3 oz (75 g) into sauce.

Remove pan from heat. Pour about two-thirds of the sauce into a bowl and set aside. Stir eggs into sauce left in pan. Mix sauce thoroughly into cauliflower.

Grease a 9½ inch (24 cm) ring mould with half remaining butter. Sprinkle breadcrumbs on bottom. Fill with cauliflower mixture, pressing down well, and bake for 30–35 minutes.

Remove from oven and immerse mould up to rim in cold water. Turn up oven to 450°F (230°C) Gas 8. Run a knife blade around the sides of the mould, then carefully turn out on to ovenproof dish (if any of the mixture sticks to mould, quickly smooth it back into position with a knife and a little of remaining sauce).

Spread reserved sauce over cauliflower ring and sprinkle with remaining cheese. Melt remaining 1 oz (25 g) butter and pour over. Return to oven and bake for about 15 minutes until golden brown. Serve hot.

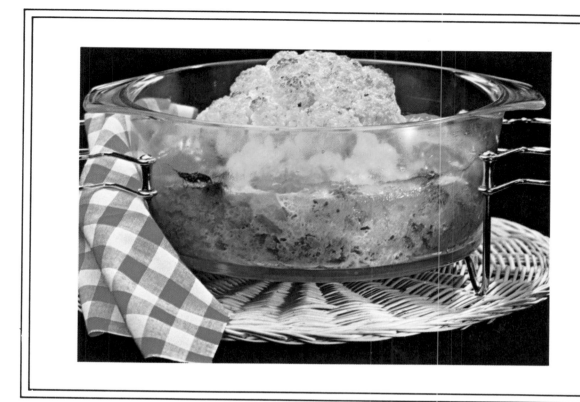

Cauliflower bake

Overall timing 1½ hours

Freezing Not suitable

To serve 4

1	Cauliflower	1
	Salt and pepper	
	Grated nutmeg	
1	Soft bread roll	1
1 pint	Milk	560 ml
1	Onion	1
4	Tomatoes	4
8 oz	Minced beef	225 g
5	Eggs	5
½ teasp	Paprika	2.5 ml
2 oz	Butter	50 g

Remove any leaves and trim cauliflower stalk. Put whole cauliflower into a pan containing 1½ inches (4 cm) of boiling, salted water. Add a pinch of grated nutmeg, cover and cook for 10 minutes.

Crumble the bread roll into a little of the milk in a large bowl. Peel and chop the onion. Chop three of the tomatoes. Add the mince, onion, chopped tomatoes and 1 egg to the bowl. Season with salt and pepper and mix well.

Preheat oven to 400°F (200°C) Gas 6.

Drain cauliflower; place in greased oven-proof dish. Spoon meat mixtur round. Mix remaining eggs with the rest of the milk. Season with salt, pepper, a pinch of nutmeg and paprika. Pour over cauliflower and meat.

Cut the butter into pieces and put on top. Cut remaining tomato into quarters and place round cauliflower. Bake in oven for 1 hour.

Broccoli vinaigrette

Overall timing 20 minutes plus 20 minutes marination

Freezing Not suitable

To serve 6

1 lb	Broccoli	450 g
	Salt and pepper	
10 tbsp	Oil	10x15 ml
1 teasp	Powdered mustard	5 ml
4 tbsp	White wine vinegar	4x15 ml
1 teasp	Brown sugar	5 ml
1	Onion	1
2 tbsp	Chopped chives	2x15 ml
2 tbsp	Chopped parsley	2x15 ml
1 tbsp	Chopped fresh tarragon	15 ml
5	Small gherkins	5
2	Hard-boiled eggs	2
2	Tomatoes	2
5	Radishes	5

Trim broccoli leaves and coarse stems, then cook in boiling salted water for about 10 minutes. Drain well, then chop and divide pieces between six serving dishes or place in salad bowl.

Beat together oil, mustard, vinegar, sugar and seasoning. Peel and finely chop the onion and add to dressing with herbs. Finely chop gherkins and eggs and stir into dressing.

Blanch, peel and finely chop tomatoes. Chop radishes and stir both into dressing. Pour over broccoli and mix well. Leave for 20 minutes until completely cold. Serve with buttered toast.

Stuffed tomatoes au gratin

Overall timing 50 minutes

Freezing Not suitable

To serve 4

4	Large tomatoes	4
1½ lb	Fresh peas	700 g
1	Onion	1
2 tbsp	Oil	2x15 ml
	Salt and pepper	
2 oz	Butter	50 g
3 tbsp	Plain flour	3x15 ml
½ pint	Milk	300ml
4 oz	Cheese	125 g
1 tbsp	Fresh breadcrumbs	15 ml

Preheat the oven to 400°F (200°C) Gas 6.

Halve the tomatoes and scoop out the flesh. Discard the seeds and chop the flesh. Shell the peas. Peel and finely chop the onion.

Heat the oil in a frying pan and fry the onion till transparent. Add the peas, cover and cook for 5 minutes. Stir in the chopped tomato flesh, season and continue cooking, covered, for 10 minutes.

Meanwhile, melt the butter in a saucepan. Stir in the flour and cook for 1 minute. Gradually stir in the milk and bring to the boil, stirring until thickened.

Grate the cheese. Mix three-quarters into the sauce with the pea mixture. Use to fill the tomato halves and arrange in an ovenproof dish. Mix the remaining cheese with the breadcrumbs and sprinkle over the tomatoes. Bake for 20 minutes and serve hot.

Vegetable croquettes

Overall timing 1¼ hours plus chilling

Freezing Suitable: deep fry after thawing

To serve 4

1½ lb	Floury potatoes	700 g
1	Large parsnip	1
	Salt and pepper	
2	Large leeks	2
1	Stalk of celery	1
2	Large carrots	2
2 oz	Butter	50 g
2 tbsp	Chopped parsley	2x15 ml
¼ teasp	Grated nutmeg	1.25 ml
2	Eggs	2
	Oil for deep frying	
4 tbsp	Plain flour	4x15 ml
	Sprigs of parsley	

Peel and chop the potatoes and parsnip. Cook in boiling salted water for 15–20 minutes till tender.

Meanwhile, trim and finely shred leeks and celery. Peel and grate carrots. Melt butter in a frying pan, add leeks and celery and fry till golden.

Drain potatoes and parsnip, return to pan and shake over a low heat to dry throughly. Remove from heat and mash to a smooth purée. Stir in fried vegetables and any pan juices. Add carrots, parsley, nutmeg and seasoning. Beat in eggs. Spread the mixture on a plate, cool, then chill for 2–3 hours till firm.

Heat oil in a deep-fryer to 340°F (170°C). Shape vegetable mixture into 20 balls with floured hands. Fry, a few at a time, for 5–6 minutes, till crisp and golden. Drain on kitchen paper. Serve hot, garnished with parsley.

Cauliflower polonaise

Overall timing 35 minutes

Freezing Not suitable

To serve 4

1	Small cauliflower	1
	Salt	
4	Hard-boiled eggs	4
4 oz	Butter	125 g
2 tbsp	Dried breadcrumbs	2x15 ml
1 teasp	Paprika	5 ml

Trim cauliflower and cook whole in boiling salted water for about 20 minutes till just tender.

Meanwhile, shell and finely chop eggs.

Drain cauliflower. Place in a warmed serving dish and sprinkle with the eggs. Keep warm.

Melt butter in frying pan. Add breadcrumbs and paprika and stir-fry until crisp. Sprinkle over cauliflower and serve.

Cauliflower fritters

Overall timing 25 minutes

Freezing Not suitable

To serve 4

1	Large cauliflower	1
	Salt	
1	Egg	1
1	Egg white	1
2 oz	Plain flour	50 g
4 oz	Dried breadcrumbs	125 g
	Oil for frying	
	Grated Parmesan cheese	
	Chopped parsley	

Trim cauliflower and divide into 25–30 florets. Cook in boiling salted water for 7–10 minutes or till just tender. Drain and allow to cool.

In a bowl, beat together egg, egg white and a pinch of salt till frothy. Dip each floret into flour, then into egg mixture, then roll in breadcrumbs till well coated.

Heat oil to 320°F (160°C). Deep fry cauliflower till golden brown and crisp. Remove cauliflower from pan with a draining spoon and drain on kitchen paper. Serve hot, sprinkled with salt and a little grated Parmesan and chopped parsley mixed together.

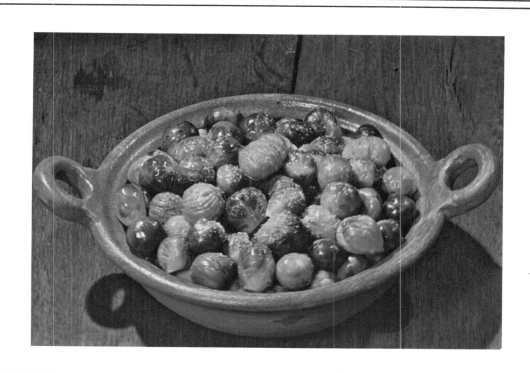

Brussels sprouts with chestnuts

Overall timing 1 hour

Freezing Not suitable

To serve 4–6

12 oz	Chestnuts	350 g
¾ pint	Hot beef stock	400 ml
1½ lb	Brussels sprouts	700 g
	Salt	
	Grated nutmeg	
2 oz	Butter	50 g

Make a cut in each chestnut with a sharp knife, then place them in a saucepan. Cover with cold water, bring to the boil and cook for 10 minutes.

Drain chestnuts and peel off both outer and inner skins. Add to the stock and simmer gently for about 20 minutes till tender.

Meanwhile, trim the sprouts and cut a cross in the base of each one. Cook in boiling salted water for 10–12 minutes till tender. Drain and season with nutmeg.

Melt the butter in a pan, then add the drained chestnuts and sprouts. Gently shake the pan to coat the vegetables with butter. Turn into a warmed serving dish and serve.

Potato and onion bake

Overall timing 1 hour

Freezing Not suitable

To serve 4

1½ lb	Potatoes	700 g
12 oz	Onions	350 g
3 oz	Butter	75 g
	Salt and pepper	

Preheat the oven to 400°F (200°C) Gas 6.

Peel the potatoes and slice very thinly (use a mandolin for best results). Put into a bowl of cold water to prevent discoloration. Peel and thinly slice the onions.

Drain the potatoes and dry with kitchen paper. Butter an ovenproof dish and cover the bottom with a layer of potato. Dot with butter, season and cover with a layer of onion. Dot with butter, season and repeat the layers till all the ingredients have been used, finishing with potato. Dot the top with the remaining butter.

Bake for about 40 minutes till the potatoes are tender and golden. Serve immediately.

Potato gnocchi

Overall timing 1½ hours plus chilling

Freezing Not suitable

To serve 6

2 lb	Floury potatoes	900 g
	Salt and pepper	
8 oz	Plain flour	225 g
1 teasp	Baking powder	5 ml
2	Eggs	2
6 oz	Slices of cheese	175 g
2 oz	Butter	50 g
3 tbsp	Grated Parmesan cheese	3x15 ml

Scrub the potatoes and cook in boiling salted water for about 30 minutes till tender. Drain, peel and press through a sieve into a large bowl.

Sift the flour and baking powder together, add to the potatoes and mix in with a wooden spoon. Beat in the eggs and seasoning. Spread out on a plate and chill for 2–3 hours till firm.

Preheat oven to 425°F (220°C) Gas 7.

Bring a large pan of salted water to the boil, then reduce heat till simmering. Put teaspoonfuls of the potato mixture into the water and cook for about 4 minutes or till they rise to the surface. Remove with a draining spoon and keep hot while you cook the rest.

Layer cooked dumplings in an ovenproof dish with slices of cheese and butter and sprinkle Parmesan on top. Brown in the oven for 5–10 minutes.

Fried ham and spinach

Overall timing 30 minutes

Freezing Not suitable

To serve 4

2 lb	Spinach	900 g
	Salt and pepper	
6 oz	Slice of cooked ham	175 g
1	Garlic clove	1
3 tbsp	Oil	3 x 15 ml
2	Hard-boiled eggs	2
2 tbsp	Pine nuts (optional)	2 x 15 ml

Wash and pick over the spinach, discarding any withered leaves or coarse stalks. Drain thoroughly and blanch in lightly salted boiling water for 1 minute. Remove from heat, rinse under cold water and drain thoroughly. Chop coarsely.

Dice the ham and peel the garlic. Heat the oil in a large frying pan, add ham and garlic and fry for 2–3 minutes. Stir in the spinach, add plenty of pepper and fry gently for 5 minutes, stirring occasionally.

Meanwhile, shell and finely chop the eggs. Add to the pan with the pine nuts, if used, and cook for 2 minutes.

Discard garlic clove. Adjust seasoning to taste and arrange on a warmed serving dish. Serve immediately with thick slices of crusty bread.

Carrot soufflé

Overall timing 1 hour

Freezing Not suitable

To serve 4

1 lb	Carrots	450 g
2 oz	Butter	50 g
	Salt and pepper	
Sauce base		
2 oz	Butter	50 g
2 oz	Plain flour	50 g
1 pint	Milk	560 ml
	Salt and pepper	
3	Eggs	3

Peel and thinly slice the carrots, then cook in boiling water for 15 minutes. Drain and plunge into cold water to cool carrots quickly.

Melt butter in another pan, add drained carrots and cook for 5 minutes. Season with salt and pepper.

Preheat oven to 375°F (190°C) Gas 5.

For the sauce base, melt butter in a saucepan and stir in flour. Gradually add milk and bring to the boil, stirring until thickened. Season with salt and pepper and cool.

Separate the eggs. Mix the egg yolks and carrots into the sauce. Whisk the whites in a bowl until very stiff, then carefully fold into the carrot mixture. Pour into a greased 3 pint (1.7 litre) soufflé dish. Bake for about 30 minutes until the soufflé is golden and well risen. Serve immediately.

Potato pancakes

Overall timing 45 minutes

Freezing Not suitable

To serve 4

1¼ lb	Waxy potatoes	600 g
2	Eggs	2
1 tbsp	Plain flour	15 ml
	Salt and pepper	
4 tbsp	Oil	4x15 ml

Peel the potatoes and grate coarsely into a bowl of cold water. Drain and squeeze dry in a cloth, then put into a dry bowl. Add the eggs, flour and seasoning and mix well.

Heat a little of the oil in a frying pan and add one-quarter of the potato mixture. Flatten into a pancake with the back of a fish slice and fry over a moderate heat for about 5 minutes till the edges are golden. Turn carefully and brown the other side. Remove from the pan and keep hot while rest of mixture is cooked.

Serve hot with roast or grilled meats and a green vegetable.

Rumanian vegetable casserole

Overall timing 1¼ hours

Freezing Not suitable

To serve 6–8

2	Waxy potatoes	2
2	Turnips	2
2	Medium-size onions	2
2	Garlic cloves	2
2	Carrots	2
1	Medium-size aubergine	1
2	Courgettes	2
2	Small leeks	2
4 oz	French beans	125 g
3	Large tomatoes	3
1 oz	Butter	25 g
2 tbsp	Oil	2x15 ml
4 oz	Shelled fresh peas	125 g
2 tbsp	Tomato purée	2x15 ml
	Bouquet garni	
	Salt and pepper	

Peel the potatoes, turnips, onions, garlic and carrots. Cut the potatoes, turnips, carrots, aubergine and courgettes into ¾ inch (2 cm) chunks. Cut the leeks and beans into 1 inch (2.5 cm) lengths. Quarter the tomatoes; slice the onions.

Heat the butter and oil in a flameproof casserole and fry the onions, leeks and garlic till golden. Add the remaining vegetables, tomato purée, bouquet garni and 1 pint (560 ml) water and mix well. Season and bring to the boil. Simmer gently for about 45 minutes till the vegetables are tender.

German broad beans

Overall timing 45 minutes

Freezing Suitable

To serve 4

2 lb	Unshelled broad beans	900 g
	Salt and pepper	
1	Chicken stock cube	1
2 oz	Streaky bacon	50 g
2	Onions	2
3 tbsp	Plain flour	3x15 ml
	Pinch of grated nutmeg	
½ pint	Carton of single cream	284 ml
1 tbsp	Chopped parsley	15 ml

Shell beans. Place in boiling, salted water and cook for 20 minutes or until tender. Drain cooking liquid into measuring jug and top up to ½ pint (300 ml) with water. Crumble in stock cube. Set beans and liquid in jug aside for the moment.

Derind and dice bacon; peel and chop onions. Put bacon and onions into a saucepan and fry gently for about 10 minutes. Remove pan from heat and stir in the flour. Gradually stir in the stock from the jug. Return pan to heat and cook gently for about 5 minutes, stirring constantly until sauce thickens. Remove from heat and season to taste with salt, pepper and nutmeg.

Stir in beans and cream and heat gently for a further 5 minutes, stirring. Transfer to warmed serving dish, garnish with parsley and serve.

Italian cauliflower omelette

Overall timing 20 minutes

Freezing Not suitable

To serve 2

12 oz	Cauliflower	350 g
	Salt and pepper	
1	Onion	1
2 oz	Butter	50 g
6	Eggs	6
2 tbsp	Grated Parmesan cheese	2x15 ml
½ teasp	Grated nutmeg	2.5 ml

Preheat the grill.

Cut cauliflower into tiny florets and cook in boiling salted water for 3–5 minutes till just tender.

Meanwhile, peel and finely chop onion. Melt butter in a frying pan and fry onion till golden. Add the drained cauliflower and seasoning and cook for 2 minutes, spreading evenly in the pan.

Beat the eggs in a bowl with the Parmesan and nutmeg. Pour evenly over the cauliflower and cook over a moderate heat till the omelette is nearly set.

Put the frying pan under the grill and cook till the top of the omelette is golden. Slide omelette on to a warmed serving plate and cut in two to serve.

Stuffed baked potatoes

Overall timing 1½ hours

Freezing Not suitable

To serve 8

8x8 oz	Waxy potatoes	8x225 g
1	Large onion	1
3 oz	Butter	75 g
8 oz	Cooked ham	225 g
6 tbsp	Dry white wine or cider	6x15 ml
2 oz	Fresh breadcrumbs	50 g
2 tbsp	Chopped parsley	2x15 ml
	Salt and pepper	
¼ pint	Chicken stock	150 ml

Preheat the oven to 400°F (200°C) Gas 6.

Peel the potatoes. Cut a slice from one end of each so they stand upright. Cut a slice from the other end of each and hollow out the centres with a sharp knife, leaving a thick shell. Finely chop the scooped out pieces and slices cut from the tops of the potatoes.

Peel and finely chop the onion. Melt 1 oz (25 g) of the butter in a saucepan and fry the onion till transparent. Dice the ham and add to the pan with the wine or cider, chopped potatoes and breadcrumbs. Cover and cook for 5 minutes, then stir in the parsley and seasoning.

Spoon the mixture into the potatoes, pressing it down firmly. Stand potatoes upright in a greased ovenproof dish. Melt remaining butter with the stock and pour into the dish.

Bake for 50 minutes to 1 hour, basting frequently, till the potatoes are tender. Serve hot with a green salad.

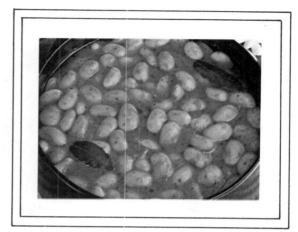

Stuffed cabbage

Overall timing 2 hours 10 minutes

Freezing Not suitable

To serve 6

8 oz	Streaky bacon	225 g
2	Onions	2
2 tbsp	Oil	2x15 ml
1	Green cabbage	1
2	Tomatoes	2
1	Garlic clove	1
1¾ lb	Sausagemeat	750 g
4 oz	Rice	125 g
4 oz	Frozen peas	125 g
	Salt and pepper	
1¾ pints	Hot beef stock	1 litre

Derind and chop bacon. Peel and finely chop onions. Heat oil in frying pan. Add bacon and cook till crisp. Add onions and cook gently for 10 minutes.

Remove all large outer leaves of cabbage. On a large piece of muslin make two layers of leaves in a circular shape. Finely chop remaining cabbage.

Finely chop tomatoes. Peel and crush garlic. Add tomatoes and garlic to chopped cabbage with sausagemeat, rice, peas, bacon and onion and seasoning. Mix well and form into a ball. Place in centre of cabbage leaves, then remake cabbage shape so leaves cover stuffing. Lift corners of muslin and tie at top. Place cabbage in stock, cover and simmer for 1½ hours.

Breton beans

Overall timing 1½ hours

Freezing Suitable

To serve 4–6

8 oz	Dried butter beans	225 g
2	Onions	2
2	Cloves	2
1	Carrot	1
1	Garlic clove	1
¼ teasp	Dried mixed herbs	1.25 ml
2	Bay leaves	2
	Salt and pepper	
1 lb	Tomatoes	450 g
2 oz	Butter	50 g

Place beans in a saucepan, cover with water and simmer for 15 minutes.

Peel one onion and spike with cloves; peel and slice carrot. Peel and crush garlic. Drain beans and return to pan. Add onion, carrot, garlic and herbs. Cover with water and bring to the boil. Cover and cook for 50 minutes; add salt and cook for another 20.

Meanwhile, peel and chop remaining onions. Blanch, peel and quarter tomatoes. Melt butter in a saucepan and add onions, tomatoes and seasoning. Simmer for 20 minutes.

Drain beans and mix into tomato sauce.

Italian fried vegetables

Overall timing 1 hour

Freezing Not suitable

To serve 6

1	Large aubergine	1
	Salt and pepper	
8 oz	Courgettes	225 g
½	Cauliflower	½
8 oz	Large flat mushrooms	225 g
2	Large dessert apples	2
4	Eggs	4
6 oz	Fine breadcrumbs	175 g
3 oz	Plain flour	75 g
	Oil for deep frying	
	Sprigs of parsley	

Cut aubergine into ¼ inch (6 mm) thick slices. Sprinkle with salt and leave for 15 minutes.

Meanwhile, halve courgettes lengthways, then cut into 2 inch (5 cm) lengths. Divide cauliflower into florets. Blanch in boiling salted water for 3 minutes, then drain and rinse under cold water.

Quarter mushrooms. Peel and core apples and cut into thick rings. Rinse aubergines and pat dry with kitchen paper.

Beat eggs in shallow dish and spread breadcrumbs on a board. Coat vegetables in seasoned flour, then dip into egg and breadcrumbs.

Heat oil in a deep-fryer to 340°F (170°C). Fry aubergine slices for about 4 minutes, turning occasionally, till crisp and golden. Drain on kitchen paper and keep hot.

Fry courgettes and cauliflower florets for 5–6 minutes, and mushrooms and apples for 3–4 minutes. Drain on kitchen paper and keep hot.

Arrange all the fried vegetables on a warmed serving dish and garnish with parsley. Serve immediately with Tartare sauce and a green salad.

Stuffed cucumbers

Overall timing 1 hour

Freezing Suitable

To serve 6

3	Large cucumbers	3
2 oz	Cooked ham	50 g
4 oz	Minced beef	125 g
2 tbsp	Fresh breadcrumbs	2x15 ml
1 tbsp	Chopped parsley	15 ml
3 tbsp	Milk	3x15 ml
1	Egg	1
	Salt and pepper	
Sauce		
1	Onion	1
1	Leek	1
2 oz	Butter	50 g
1 oz	Plain flour	25 g
½ pint	Stock	300 ml
1 tbsp	Chopped parsley	15 ml
	Paprika	
	Salt	
1 tbsp	Vinegar	15 ml
4 fl oz	Top of milk	120 ml

Peel cucumbers. Halve them lengthways and scoop out seeds. Finely chop ham and mix with beef, breadcrumbs, parsley, milk, egg and seasoning. Stuff cucumbers with mixture.

To make sauce, peel and finely chop onion. Trim and finely chop leek. Melt butter in a saucepan and fry onion and leek till golden. Sprinkle flour into pan and cook for 1 minute, stirring. Gradually stir in stock, then add parsley, a pinch each of paprika and salt and the vinegar. Bring to the boil, stirring.

Arrange cucumbers on top of sauce and surround with any leftover stuffing. Cover and cook gently for 30 minutes. Turn cucumbers over halfway through cooking time.

Stir milk into sauce and heat through uncovered for 2 minutes.

Romanian peppers

Overall timing 1¼ hours

Freezing Not suitable

To serve 6

1 lb	Lean pork	450 g
2	Onions	2
2 oz	Butter	50 g
4 oz	Button mushrooms	125 g
8 oz	Tomatoes	225 g
½ pint	Water	300 ml
	Salt and pepper	
½ teasp	Paprika	2.5 ml
6	Green peppers	6
2 teasp	Cornflour	2x5 ml
4 tbsp	Top of milk	4x15 ml
	Tabasco sauce	

Dice the pork. Peel and finely chop onions. Melt butter in saucepan. Fry onions and pork for 10 minutes.

Slice mushrooms. Blanch, peel and chop tomatoes. Add mushrooms and tomatoes to the saucepan. Pour in water and cook for 40 minutes over a low heat. Season with salt, pepper and paprika.

Cut tops off peppers. Remove seeds. Place peppers and their tops in a saucepan of boiling water and cook for 5 minutes or until just soft. Lift out and drain. Keep warm.

Blend cornflour with top of milk. Stir into pork mixture, then bring just to the boil to thicken. Season with a few drops of Tabasco sauce. Mix well, then use mixture to fill peppers. Place tops on peppers to serve.

Leeks with mustard sauce

Overall timing 30 minutes

Freezing Not suitable

To serve 4–6

2 lb	Leeks	900 g
	Salt and pepper	
4 oz	Cheese	125 g
1	Small onion	1
1	Garlic clove	1
2 oz	Butter	50 g
2 tbsp	Plain flour	2x15 ml
¾ pint	Milk	400 ml
1 tbsp	Made mustard	15 ml

Trim leeks. Cook in boiling salted water for 15–20 minutes till tender. Drain, saving ¼ pint (150 ml) cooking liquor. Arrange leeks in warmed serving dish. Keep hot.

Grate cheese. Peel and chop onion and garlic. Melt the butter in a saucepan and fry the onion and garlic till golden. Stir in the flour and cook for 1 minute. Gradually add reserved cooking liquor and milk. Bring to the boil, stirring, and cook for 3 minutes. Stir in mustard, cheese and seasoning and heat through gently without boiling. Pour over leeks and serve immediately.

Leek and cheese soufflé

Overall timing 1 hour

Freezing Not suitable

To serve 4

2 oz	Butter	50 g
2 oz	Plain flour	50 g
¼ pint	Warm milk	300 ml
2 oz	Red Leicester cheese	50 g
8 oz	Leeks	225 g
	Salt and pepper	
3	Large eggs	3

Melt the butter in a pan, stir in the flour and cook for 1 minute. Gradually add warm milk and bring to the boil, stirring. Simmer for 2 minutes. Remove from heat and leave to cool.

Grate the cheese. Trim and finely chop leeks. Blanch in boiling water for 5 minutes and drain thoroughly. Stir the grated cheese and leeks into sauce and season. Separate eggs. Beat the yolks into the sauce.

Whisk egg whites in a bowl till stiff but not dry. Stir 1 tbsp (15 ml) whisked whites into sauce to lighten it, then carefully fold in the rest. Turn mixture into greased 2 pint (1.1 litre) soufflé dish, place on baking tray and bake for 30–35 minutes till well risen and golden. Serve immediately.

Irish cabbage

Overall timing 40 minutes

Freezing Not suitable

To serve 4–6

14 oz	Potatoes	400 g
2	Small leeks	2
	Milk	
1 lb	Green cabbage	450 g
	Salt and pepper	
	Pinch of mace	
4 oz	Butter	125 g
	Sprigs of parsley	

Cook unpeeled potatoes in lightly salted water till just tender. Meanwhile, trim the leeks, then roughly chop both white and green parts. Just cover with milk and cook gently till soft.

Roughly chop cabbage and cook in boiling, lightly salted water for 7 minutes. Drain and cut into smaller pieces. Keep cabbage warm.

Drain potatoes; peel and put through a food mill or mash well. Mash in the leeks/milk mixture and season well with salt, pepper and mace. Place bowl over a pan of boiling water and gradually beat in the cabbage till light and fluffy.

Melt butter. Place vegetable mixture in warmed serving dish, make a well in the centre and pour in the hot butter. Garnish with parsley sprigs and serve immediately.

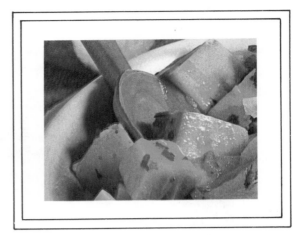

Cheesy vegetables

Overall timing 10 minutes

Freezing Not suitable

To serve 6

8 oz	Cream cheese	225 g
¼ pint	Carton of single cream	150 ml
2 lb	Hot cooked mixed vegetables (including beans, cauliflower, peas, carrots and mushrooms)	900 g
2 tbsp	Grated Parmesan cheese	2x15 ml
	Salt and pepper	

Beat the cream cheese and cream together in a bowl. Place the bowl over a pan of simmering water and heat through gently, stirring occasionally. Do not boil.

Arrange the vegetables in a warmed serving dish. Keep hot.

Beat the Parmesan into the cream cheese mixture and season to taste. Pour the hot sauce over the vegetables and serve immediately with roast or grilled meat, or as vegetarian lunch.

Greek pumpkin

Overall timing 1 hour

Freezing Not suitable

To serve 4–6

2 lb	Pumpkin	900 g
2	Medium onions	2
3 tbsp	Olive oil	3x15 ml
14 oz	Can of tomatoes	397 g
¼ teasp	Ground cumin	1.25 ml
2	Sprigs of flat-leafed parsley	2
	Salt and pepper	
½ pint	Water	300 ml

Scrape the seeds and fibrous centre out of the pumpkin. Cut into chunks, leaving the skin on. Peel the onions and cut through the root into eight wedges.

Heat the oil in a saucepan, add onions and fry till transparent. Add the tomatoes and juice, cumin and pumpkin. Chop the parsley and add with seasoning and the water. Bring to the boil, then cover and simmer for 25–35 minutes till the pumpkin is tender.

Adjust the seasoning and pour into a warmed serving dish. Serve hot with roast or grilled meat.

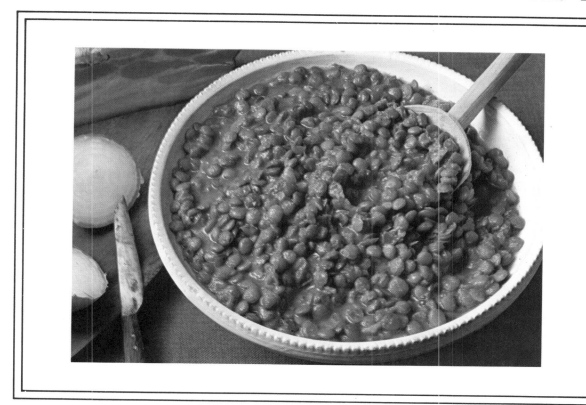

Lentils with bacon

Overall timing 1½ hours

Freezing Suitable

To serve 4

8 oz	Continental lentils	225 g
1	Large onion	1
8 oz	Smoked streaky bacon	225 g
3 tbsp	Oil	3x15 ml
1 teasp	Salt	5 ml
3 tbsp	Tomato purée	3x15 ml
1½ pints	Stock	850 ml

Wash and pick over the lentils. Peel and finely chop the onion. Derind and dice the bacon. Heat oil in a saucepan and fry onion and bacon till golden. Add the lentils and salt and cook for 10 minutes, stirring frequently.

Stir in the tomato purée and the stock and simmer for about 1 hour until the lentils are tender. Taste and adjust seasoning. Serve on slices of fried bread with a mixed salad.

Russian potatoes with cream

Overall timing 1¼ hours

Freezing Not suitable

To serve 4

1½ lb	Waxy potatoes	700 g
	Salt and pepper	
2 oz	Button mushrooms	50 g
1	Small onion	1
2 oz	Butter	50 g
¼ pint	Soured cream	150 ml
2 tbsp	Chopped parsley	2x15 ml

Cook the potatoes in boiling salted water for about 30 minutes till tender. Drain and peel the potatoes, then cut into ¼ inch (6 mm) thick slices. Slice the mushrooms. Peel and thinly slice the onion.

Melt the butter in a frying pan and fry the onion till transparent. Add the mushrooms and fry for 2–3 minutes, stirring. Add the sliced potatoes and fry for 5 minutes, turning once.

Pour the cream over and season well. Turn potatoes gently till coated and continue cooking over a low heat for about 10 minutes till the potatoes have absorbed most of the cream.

Stir in the parsley, adjust the seasoning and serve hot.

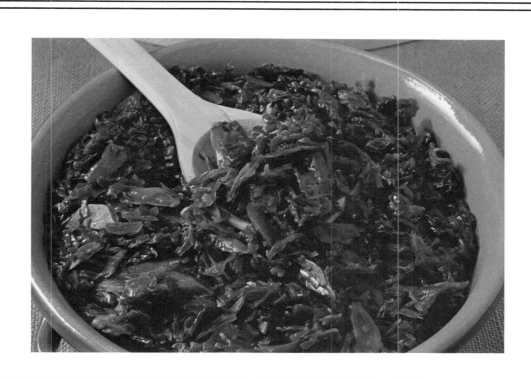

Sweet-sour red cabbage

Overall timing 1 hour 20 minutes

Freezing Suitable

To serve 4

2 lb	Red cabbage	about 1 kg
2 oz	Streaky bacon	50 g
1	Onion	1
1	Cooking apple	1
6	Whole allspice	6
½ teasp	Salt	2.5 ml
2 teasp	Honey	2x5 ml
3 fl oz	Red wine or wine vinegar	90 ml

Discard any damaged outer leaves from the cabbage. Quarter, cut away core and thick ribs and shred leaves.

Derind and chop bacon. Peel and chop onion. Cook bacon in flameproof casserole over a low heat until fat starts to run. Add onion and cook for 5 minutes, stirring.

Peel, core and chop apple and add to casserole with cabbage. Crush allspice and add to casserole with salt, honey and wine or vinegar. Mix well, then cover and simmer for 1 hour.

If there's too much liquid at the end of cooking time, remove the lid and continue simmering. Serve hot.

Stir-fried celery

Overall timing 15 minutes

Freezing Not suitable

To serve 4

1	Large bunch of celery	1
2 teasp	Salt	2x5 ml
3 tbsp	Oil	3x15 ml
2 tbsp	Soy sauce	2x15 ml
½ teasp	Sugar	2.5 ml

Cut off leaves from celery, then chop into 2 inch (5 cm) pieces. Sprinkle with salt.

Heat oil in frying pan. When oil is very hot, add the celery and stir-fry for 5 minutes. Add soy sauce and sugar, mix well and serve immediately.

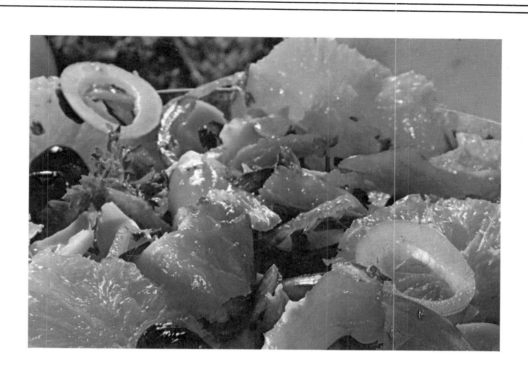

Sunshine salad

Overall timing 15 minutes plus chilling

Freezing Not suitable

To serve 2

8 oz	Poached smoked haddock	225 g
1	Orange	1
1	Grapefruit	1
1	Green pepper	1
1	Onion	1
1 tbsp	Chopped parsley	15 ml
3 tbsp	Olive oil	3x15 ml
1 tbsp	Lemon juice	15 ml
	Salt and pepper	
2 oz	Black olives	50 g

Cut the haddock into small strips. Peel orange and grapefruit and slice or chop the flesh. Deseed and slice pepper. Peel onion and cut into thin rings.

Put prepared ingredients into salad bowl with the parsley. Add oil, lemon juice and seasoning. Toss salad well and chill. Garnish with stoned olives just before serving.

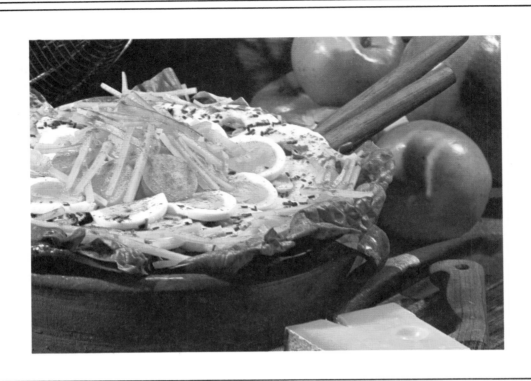

Swiss salad

Overall timing 35 minutes

Freezing Not suitable

To serve 4

12 oz	Boiled new potatoes	350 g
1	Dessert apple	1
2 tbsp	White wine vinegar	2x15 ml
1 teasp	Made mustard	5 ml
4 tbsp	Oil	4x15 ml
	Salt and pepper	
$\frac{1}{2}$	Round lettuce	$\frac{1}{2}$
6 oz	Gruyère cheese	175 g
4	Hard-boiled eggs	4
2 teasp	Chopped chives	2x5 ml
1 teasp	Paprika	5 ml

Peel and slice the potatoes into a bowl. Peel, core and slice the apple and toss in the vinegar. Add to the potatoes.

Mix the mustard, oil and seasoning together in a bowl and pour over the potatoes and apple. Toss lightly.

Wash and dry the lettuce leaves and use to line salad bowl. Arrange the potato mixture on the lettuce.

Cut the cheese into matchsticks. Scatter the cheese round the edge and in the centre of the salad. Shell and slice the eggs and arrange on the salad. Sprinkle with the chives and paprika and serve immediately with crusty or wholemeal bread or rolls and butter.

Bacon and potato salad

Overall timing 55 minutes

Freezing Not suitable

To serve 6–8

2 lb	Medium-size waxy potatoes	900 g
	Salt and pepper	
8 oz	Streaky bacon rashers	225 g
1	Large onion	1
4 tbsp	White wine vinegar	4×15 ml
4 tbsp	Water	4×15 ml
1 teasp	Powdered mustard	5 ml
1 tbsp	Chopped chives	15 ml

Scrub the potatoes, cover with cold salted water and bring to the boil. Cook for about 30 minutes till tender.

Meanwhile, derind and dice the bacon and fry over a moderate heat till crisp and brown. Lift out of the pan with a draining spoon and put into a warmed serving dish. Cover with foil to keep hot.

Drain the potatoes and cut into $\frac{1}{2}$ inch (12.5 mm) thick slices. Add to the bacon and cover again.

Peel and roughly chop the onion, add to the bacon fat in the pan and fry over a moderate heat till golden. Add the vinegar, water, salt, pepper and mustard and bring to the boil.

Pour over the potatoes and bacon, turning them carefully till coated. Sprinkle with chives and serve immediately with fresh crusty bread.

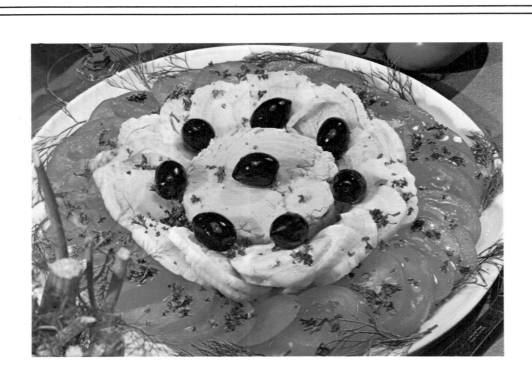

Tuna salad

Overall timing 15 minutes

Freezing Not suitable

To serve 4

1	Bulb of fennel	1
	Salt and pepper	
4	Tomatoes	4
6½ oz	Can of tuna	184 g
3 tbsp	Oil	3x15 ml
1 tbsp	Wine vinegar	15 ml
	Chopped parsley	
1 oz	Black olives	25 g

Trim and slice the fennel. Blanch in boiling salted water for 5 minutes. Drain. Slice tomatoes. Drain tuna.

Place tuna in centre of serving dish and arrange fennel and tomato slices around it.

In a bowl, mix together oil, vinegar and seasoning. Pour dressing over salad and sprinkle with chopped parsley. Garnish with black olives and fennel leaves, if available.

Avocado and pine nut salad

Overall timing 15 minutes plus chilling

Freezing Not suitable

To serve 2

1	Large ripe avocado	1
1½ teasp	Lemon juice	7.5 ml
2	Gherkins	2
1 tbsp	Pine nuts	15 ml
1½ tbsp	Olive oil	22.5 ml
	Salt and pepper	
1	Garlic clove	1
4	Fresh mint leaves	4
2 tbsp	Plain yogurt	2x15 ml

Cut the avocado in half and remove the stone. Peel away the skin, dice the flesh and put into a bowl. Sprinkle with lemon juice and toss lightly till the avocado is coated.

Slice the gherkins thinly and add to the avocado with the pine nuts. Sprinkle with oil, season and toss.

Peel and crush the garlic into a small bowl. Wash the mint leaves and shred finely. Add to the garlic with the yogurt and mix well. Pour over the avocado and toss lightly. Chill for 1 hour.

Divide salad between two individual dishes and serve immediately with crusty rolls.

Asparagus and potato salad

Overall timing 25 minutes plus chilling

Freezing Not suitable

To serve 4

1 lb	New potatoes	450 g
	Salt and pepper	
1	Small onion	1
1 tbsp	Lemon juice	15 ml
¼ pint	Thick mayonnaise	150 ml
12 oz	Can of asparagus spears or tips	340 g
1	Hard-boiled egg	1
4	Anchovy fillets	4
2 teasp	Drained capers	2x5 ml

Scrape the potatoes and cut into even-sized chunks. Cook in boiling salted water for about 5 minutes till tender. Drain and place in a large bowl.

Peel the onion and chop finely. Stir gently into the potatoes with the lemon juice and plenty of seasoning. Add the mayonnaise and mix well.

Drain the asparagus (if using spears, cut into 2 inch/5 cm lengths), and fold gently into the salad. Arrange in a serving dish.

Shell the hard-boiled egg and cut into quarters lengthways. Arrange round the dish. Arrange anchovy fillets in a cross on the salad. Garnish with capers and chill for 30 minutes before serving with wholemeal or black bread.

Fennel and tomato salad

Overall timing 30 minutes

Freezing Not suitable

To serve 4

1	Large bulb of fennel	1
	Salt and pepper	
1	Onion	1
4	Tomatoes	4
3 tbsp	Oil	3x15 ml
1 tbsp	Wine vinegar or lemon juice	15 ml

Trim fennel. Cut into thin slices and blanch in boiling salted water for 5 minutes. Drain.

Peel onion and cut into rings. Slice tomatoes. Arrange fennel, onion and tomatoes in layers in salad bowl.

In another bowl, mix together oil, vinegar or lemon juice and seasoning. Pour over salad. Chill for 15 minutes before serving.

Vegetable and herb salad

Overall timing 30 minutes

Freezing Not suitable

To serve 6

1 lb	Potatoes	450 g
	Salt and pepper	
8 oz	Cauliflower	225 g
4 oz	Green beans	125 g
4 oz	Frozen peas	125 g
4 tbsp	Oil	4x15 ml
2 tbsp	Vinegar	2x15 ml
2 tbsp	Chopped fresh mixed herbs	2x15 ml

Scrub the potatoes and cut into small chunks. Place in a saucepan, cover with water, add salt and bring to the boil. Boil gently for 2 minutes.

Divide cauliflower into florets. Add to the pan. Bring back to the boil. Cut beans into 1 inch (2.5 cm) lengths and add to pan with the peas. Simmer gently for 5 minutes or until the potatoes are tender.

Meanwhile, whisk together the oil, vinegar, herbs and seasoning.

Drain the vegetables well and place in salad bowl. While still hot, pour dressing over the vegetables and toss well. Allow to cool before serving.

Egg and parsley mayonnaise

Overall timing 15 minutes plus chilling

Freezing Not suitable

To serve 4

8	Hard-boiled eggs	8
2	Spring onions	2
3 tbsp	Chopped parsley	3x15 ml
¼ pint	Thick mayonnaise	150 ml
¼ pint	Carton of soured cream	150 ml
	Salt and pepper	

Shell and slice the hard-boiled eggs. Trim the spring onions and slice thinly. Arrange half the eggs in a shallow dish and sprinkle the spring onions and 2 tbsp (2x15 ml) of the parsley over.

Mix together the mayonnaise and soured cream and add seasoning to taste. Spoon three-quarters of the mayonnaise mixture over the eggs. Arrange the remaining egg slices decoratively on top and spoon the rest of the mayonnaise between them.

Chill for 1 hour before serving. Sprinkle with the reserved parsley and serve with slices of crusty brown bread.

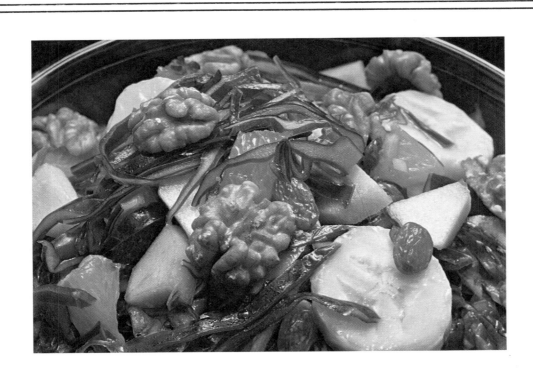

Walnut cabbage salad

Overall timing 30 minutes plus maceration

Freezing Not suitable

To serve 4

½	Red cabbage	½
4 tbsp	Walnut or olive oil	4x15 ml
2 tbsp	Lemon juice	2x15 ml
2	Large oranges	2
1	Large dessert apple	1
1	Banana	1
2 oz	Walnut halves	50 g
1 oz	Seedless raisins	25 g

Shred the cabbage and toss with the oil and lemon juice. Leave to macerate in the refrigerator for 1 hour.

Peel the oranges and separate into segments. Peel, core and chop the apple. Peel and thickly slice the banana. Add the fruit to the cabbage with the walnuts and raisins. Toss together well, then serve.

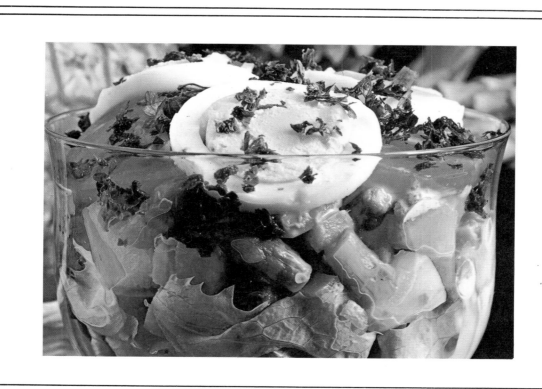

Asparagus and ham salad

Overall timing 20 minutes plus chilling

Freezing Not suitable

To serve 4

12 oz	Can of asparagus spears	340 g
4 oz	Cooked ham	125 g
4	Pineapple rings	4
	Lettuce leaves	
8 tbsp	Mayonnaise	8x15 ml
$\frac{1}{2}$ teasp	Brandy (optional)	2.5 ml
2 tbsp	Lemon juice	2x15 ml
	Pinch of cayenne	
Garnish		
2	Tomatoes	2
2	Hard-boiled eggs	2
	Chopped parsley	

Drain and chop asparagus and place in a mixing bowl. Dice ham. Chop the pineapple rings. Add both to asparagus and mix together well.

Place lettuce in the bottom of individual glasses. Divide asparagus mixture evenly between them.

Mix mayonnaise with brandy, if using, lemon juice and cayenne. Divide dressing equally between glasses. Garnish with chopped tomato, sliced hard-boiled egg and chopped parsley. Chill for 10 minutes before serving.

Caesar salad

Overall timing 15 minutes plus chilling

Freezing Not suitable

To serve 4

6 tbsp	Oil	6x15 ml
2 tbsp	Vinegar	2x15 ml
2	Garlic cloves	2
	Salt and pepper	
½	Cos lettuce	½
4	Eggs	4
2	Slices of bread	2
2 oz	Roquefort or Parmesan cheese	50 g
4	Anchovy fillets	4

Beat together 4 tbsp (4x15 ml) of the oil, the vinegar, 1 peeled and crushed garlic clove and seasoning in a bowl. Cover and chill for 30 minutes.

Wash and dry lettuce. Tear leaves into pieces, put in a bowl and leave in the refrigerator to crisp.

Put eggs in a pan of cold water, bring to the boil and cook for 4–5 minutes. Drain and place in a bowl of cold water. Shell.

Rub bread slices all over with remaining halved garlic clove, then cut into 1 inch (2.5 cm) cubes. Fry in rest of oil till golden. Drain croûtons on kitchen paper.

Divide lettuce and croûtons between serving plates. Arrange eggs on top of lettuce, sprinkle over crumbled or grated cheese, then spoon dressing over. Garnish with rolled anchovy fillets and serve with crusty bread.

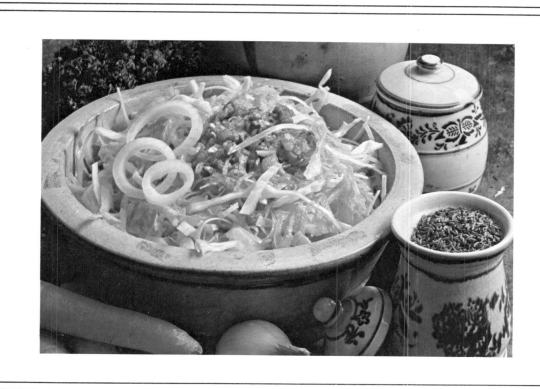

Carrot and cabbage slaw

Overall timing 15 minutes plus chilling

Freezing Not suitable

To serve 4

8 oz	Carrots	225 g
8 oz	White cabbage	225 g
4 tbsp	Wine vinegar	4x15 ml
5 tbsp	Oil	5x15 ml
½ teasp	Caraway seeds	2.5 ml
¼ teasp	Sugar	1.25 ml
	Salt and pepper	
2 oz	Streaky bacon	50 g
1	Large onion	1

Peel and grate carrots. Shred cabbage. In a salad bowl, mix together vinegar, 4 tbsp (4x15 ml) of the oil, caraway seeds, sugar and seasoning. Add carrots and cabbage and mix well. Cover the bowl and chill for 30 minutes.

Derind and chop the bacon. Heat remaining 1 tbsp (15ml) oil in frying pan and fry bacon for 3 minutes till crisp. Peel and finely chop onion, saving a few rings for garnish. Add chopped onion to pan and fry for a few minutes.

Remove salad from refrigerator. Put the hot bacon and onion mixture on top and garnish with onion rings. Serve with roasts or cold meat.

Chef's salad

Overall timing 20 minutes

Freezing Not suitable

To serve 4–6

1	Round lettuce	1
2	Heads of radicchio *or*	2
$\frac{1}{4}$	Red cabbage	$\frac{1}{4}$
4 oz	Cooked ham	125 g
3 oz	Gruyère or Emmenthal cheese	75 g
1	Small onion	1
2	Tomatoes	2
Dressing		
2 tbsp	Oil	2x15 ml
1 tbsp	Wine vinegar	15 ml
1 teasp	Dijon mustard or made English mustard	5 ml
	Salt and pepper	

Wash and dry lettuce. Line salad bowl with crisp whole leaves. Tear the rest into bite-size pieces and arrange on top.

Wash and dry radicchio and tear into pieces, or shred cabbage. Cut ham into $\frac{1}{2}$ inch (12.5 mm) dice. Slice cheese, then cut into small strips. Peel and slice onion and separate into individual rings. Cut tomatoes into wedges. Arrange all the prepared ingredients on top of the lettuce.

Mix together the dressing ingredients and pour over the salad. Toss thoroughly but gently. Garnish with garlic croûtons if liked.

Waldorf salad

Overall timing 15 minutes plus 1 hour refrigeration

Freezing Not suitable

To serve 4

4	Stalks of celery	4
8 oz	Dessert apples	225 g
1 tbsp	Lemon juice	15 ml
	Salt and pepper	
6 tbsp	Thick mayonnaise	6x15 ml
2 oz	Nuts	50 g

Chop celery. Peel, core and dice apples. Place in salad bowl with celery, lemon juice and a little salt. Chill for about 1 hour.

Remove from refrigerator and stir in mayonnaise, chopped nuts and seasoning to taste.

If serving this salad on a special occasion, divide mixture between hollowed-out apples that have been sprinkled with lemon juice. For a simpler, yet still effective presentation, serve on lettuce (shredded or leaves) in individual glass dishes and garnish with fine lemon slices.

Salade niçoise

Overall timing 25 minutes

Freezing Not suitable

To serve 4

1 lb	Waxy potatoes	450 g
	Salt and pepper	
8 oz	Green beans	225 g
4 oz	Large black olives	125 g
2 tbsp	Drained capers	2x15 ml
1	Garlic clove	1
4 tbsp	Olive oil	4x15 ml
1 tbsp	Tarragon vinegar	15 ml
1 teasp	Lemon juice	5 ml
1 tbsp	Chopped parsley	15 ml
1	Large firm tomato	1
6	Anchovy fillets	6

Peel and dice the potatoes. Cook in boiling salted water for about 5 minutes till just tender. Top, tail and string the beans and cut into 1 inch (2.5 cm) lengths. Cook in another pan of boiling salted water for 5 minutes till tender.

Drain the vegetables and rinse under cold water. Drain thoroughly and put into a salad bowl. Add half the olives and the capers.

Peel and crush the garlic clove into a bowl. Add the oil, vinegar, lemon juice, parsley and pepper to taste and mix well, then pour over vegetables. Toss lightly till evenly coated.

Cut the tomato into thin wedges. Arrange on the salad with the remaining olives. Cut the anchovies into strips and arrange in a lattice on top of the salad. Serve immediately with French bread.

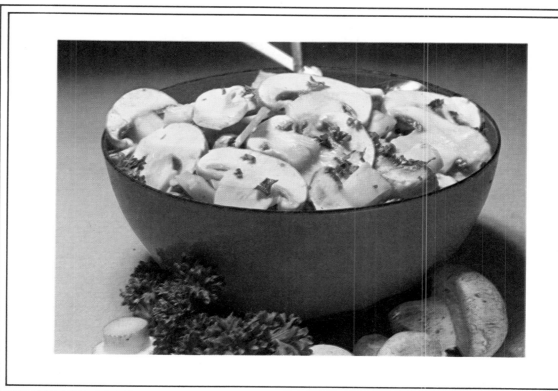

Raw mushroom salad

Overall timing 20 minutes plus chilling

Freezing Not suitable

To serve 4

12 oz	Button mushrooms	350 g
1 teasp	Lemon juice	5 ml
1 teasp	Made mustard	5 ml
2 tbsp	Single cream	2x15 ml
2 tbsp	Oil	2x15 ml
1½ teasp	White wine vinegar	7.5 ml
	Salt and pepper	
	Chopped parsley	

Thinly slice the mushrooms. Put into a salad bowl and sprinkle with the lemon juice.

Mix together the mustard, cream, oil, vinegar and seasoning. Pour this dressing over the mushrooms and toss carefully. Sprinkle chopped parsley on top. Chill for 30 minutes before serving.

Spanish salad

Overall timing 45 minutes plus 1 hour refrigeration

Freezing Not suitable

To serve 4

½	Cucumber	½
	Salt and pepper	
12 oz	Potatoes	350 g
12 oz	Can of asparagus spears	340 g
8 fl oz	Mayonnaise	220 ml
1 tbsp	French mustard	15 ml
½ teasp	Dried tarragon	2.5 ml
½	Red pepper	½

Peel and slice cucumber. Sprinkle with salt and chill for 1 hour.

Peel and dice potatoes, then cook in boiling salted water for 10 minutes. Drain and leave to cool.

Drain asparagus and dry spears on kitchen paper.

Mix together potatoes, mayonnaise, mustard, tarragon and seasoning and put into a shallow dish. Arrange asparagus on top like the spokes of a wheel. Drain cucumber slices and place one between each asparagus spear and one in the centre. Deseed and dice pepper and place on top of cucumber to add colour.

Israeli sweet-sour salad

Overall timing 20 minutes plus chilling

Freezing Not suitable

To serve 4

2 tbsp	Sultanas	2x15 ml
1 lb	Carrots	450 g
4	Oranges	4
2	Avocados	4
2 tbsp	Lemon juice	2x15 ml
3 tbsp	Oil	3x15 ml
1 tbsp	Wine or cider vinegar	15 ml
	Salt and pepper	
	Ground ginger	

Put the sultanas into a bowl, cover with warm water and leave to soak.

Peel carrots and grate into serving dish. Add the juice of two of the oranges and mix well. Peel remaining oranges and separate into segments.

Peel avocados and remove stones. Cut flesh into chunks and sprinkle with lemon juice.

Drain sultanas and add to serving dish with oranges and avocados.

In a small bowl, beat the oil and vinegar with a pinch each of salt, pepper and ground ginger. Pour over salad and toss. Chill for 15 minutes before serving.

Rice salad with anchovy dressing

Overall timing 40 minutes plus chilling

Freezing Not suitable

To serve 4

8 oz	Long grain rice	225 g
	Salt and pepper	
1	Can of anchovy fillets	1
2	Large hard-boiled eggs	2
1 teasp	Powdered mustard	5 ml
5 tbsp	Olive oil	5 x 15 ml
1	Carrot	1
1	Small onion	1
1	Green chilli	1
1	Red pepper	1
1	Small bulb of fennel	1
2 oz	Stoned black olives	50 g
1 teasp	Chopped chives	5 ml

Cook rice in boiling salted water for 15 minutes till tender. Drain and rinse under cold water to cool.

Drain anchovies and reserve half for garnish. Put the rest into a mortar and pound to a paste with the pestle. Shell and finely chop eggs. Add to mortar with mustard and pound together, gradually adding oil a few drops at a time. Season.

Peel carrot and cut shallow grooves at intervals along its length. Slice thinly and place in large bowl with rice.

Peel and finely chop onion; thinly slice chilli: deseed and slice pepper. Add these to the rice. Thinly slice fennel; chop fennel tops and add to salad. Toss lightly. Chill salad and dressing for 30 minutes.

Put salad into a serving dish and arrange reserved anchovies on top with olives and chives. Serve with dressing.

Greek salad

Overall timing 40 minutes including chilling

Freezing Not suitable

To serve 2

2	Large tomatoes	2
$\frac{1}{4}$	Cucumber	$\frac{1}{4}$
1	Small onion	1
2 oz	Black olives	50 g
8	Anchovy fillets	8
4 oz	Fetta or Wensleydale cheese	125 g
Dressing		
3 tbsp	Olive oil	3x15 ml
1 tbsp	Lemon juice	15 ml
	Salt and pepper	
	Pinch of dried marjoram	

Quarter tomatoes. Slice cucumber. Peel onion and cut into rings. Stone olives (optional). Roll up anchovy fillets. Cut cheese into chunks. Place all these ingredients in a serving bowl or divide them between two serving dishes.

To make the dressing, mix the oil and lemon juice with pinch of salt, pepper to taste and marjoram. Pour over salad, mix well and chill for 30 minutes before serving.

Another good alternative to Fetta is white Stilton – the important thing is to use a crumbly white cheese with a slightly sour taste. As in the authentic Greek version, it will absorb all the flavour of the oil dressing.

Tunisian mixed salad

Overall timing 25 minutes plus chilling

Freezing Not suitable

To serve 4

1½ lb	Cooked waxy potatoes	700 g
8 oz	Cooked carrots	225 g
3	Canned artichoke hearts	3
6 oz	Cooked peas	175 g
2 tbsp	Drained capers	2x15 ml
12	Stoned black olives	12
12	Stoned green olives	12
4 tbsp	Olive oil	4x15 ml
2 tbsp	Lemon juice	2x15 ml
1 tbsp	Chopped parsley	15 ml
¼ teasp	Ground coriander	1.25 ml
	Salt and pepper	

Dice the potatoes and carrots. Drain the artichokes and cut into quarters. Put all the vegetables into a serving dish with the capers and olives.

Whisk the oil and lemon juice together with the parsley, coriander and plenty of seasoning. Pour the dressing over the salad and toss lightly. Chill for 30 minutes before serving with crusty bread.

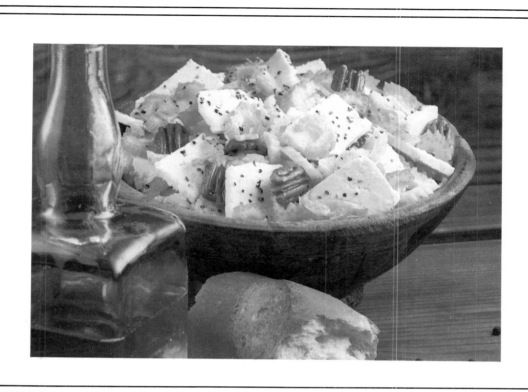

Goat's cheese salad

Overall timing 15 minutes plus 1 hour chilling

Freezing Not suitable

To serve 4

12 oz	Goat's cheese	350 g
	Salt and pepper	
4 tbsp	Olive oil	4x15 ml
2 tbsp	Wine vinegar	2x15 ml
4	Stalks of celery	4
2 oz	Walnuts	50 g
	Fennel seed (optional)	

Slice cheese and put into serving bowl. Grind black pepper over it. Beat 2 tbsp (2x15 ml) oil and 1 tbsp (15 ml) vinegar together and pour over cheese.

Chop celery. Add celery and nuts to bowl. Toss lightly.

Beat together the rest of the oil and vinegar and pour over. Sprinkle with salt and crushed fennel seed, if used, and chill for 1 hour. Serve with crusty French bread.

Gouda salad

Overall timing 15 minutes

Freezing Not suitable

To serve 4–6

Salad		
1	Webb's lettuce	1
2 oz	Corn salad or watercress	50 g
1	Head of white chicory	1
4	Tomatoes	4
1	Hard-boiled egg	1
1	Onion	1
2 oz	Black olives	50 g
4 oz	Gouda cheese	125 g
Dressing		
2 tbsp	Oil	2x15 ml
1 tbsp	Wine vinegar	15 ml
1 tbsp	Chopped fresh fines herbes or	15 ml
1 teasp	Dried fines herbes	5 ml
	Salt and pepper	

Trim and wash lettuce and corn salad or watercress. Dry thoroughly. Trim, wash and shred chicory. Arrange lettuce leaves in salad bowl, scatter the chicory over and arrange corn salad or watercress in the centre.

Wipe and slice tomatoes. Shell and quarter hard-boiled egg. Peel and finely slice onion. Arrange on top of lettuce with the olives.

Cut cheese into thin matchstick strips. Sprinkle over top of salad.

To make dressing, put the oil, vinegar, herbs, salt and pepper into a bowl and mix well together. Pour over salad just before serving and toss.

Mimosa salad

Overall timing 15 minutes

Freezing Not suitable

To serve 4

3 tbsp	Single cream	3x15 ml
1 tbsp	Lemon juice	15 ml
	Salt and pepper	
1	Lettuce	1
1	Orange	1
4 oz	Black and white grapes	125 g
1	Banana	1
1	Hard-boiled egg yolk	1

In a salad bowl, mix together the cream, lemon juice and seasoning.

Wash and dry lettuce leaves. Peel the orange and cut into thin slices. Wash grapes. Peel and slice banana. Place the lettuce, orange, grapes and banana in salad bowl on top of dressing. Toss just before serving and garnish with sieved egg yolk.

Prawn and chicory salad

Overall timing 30 minutes plus chilling

Freezing Not suitable

To serve 4

2	Small heads of chicory	2
3 tbsp	Lemon juice	3x15 ml
4	Tomatoes	4
1	Fresh green chilli	1
8 oz	Shelled prawns	225 g
1 tbsp	White wine vinegar	15 ml
	Salt and pepper	
4 oz	Cream cheese	125 g
3 tbsp	Plain yogurt	3x15 ml
1	Garlic clove	1
¼ teasp	Powdered mustard	1.25 ml
2 tbsp	Oil	2x15 ml

Remove any wilted outside leaves from the chicory, cut off the bases and scoop out the cores. Cut across into ½ inch (12.5 mm) thick slices. Put into a bowl, add 2 tbsp (2x15 ml) of the lemon juice and toss.

Blanch, peel and quarter the tomatoes. Deseed and thinly slice the chilli. Put into a salad bowl with the tomatoes, prawns, vinegar and seasoning. Add the chicory and toss together lightly.

Put the cheese and yogurt into a bowl and beat till smooth. Add the peeled and crushed garlic, mustard, oil and remaining lemon juice. Season to taste and trickle over the salad. Chill for 15 minutes.

Just before serving, toss salad lightly till ingredients are evenly coated.

Prawn and egg salad

Overall timing 35 minutes

Freezing Not suitable

To serve 4–6

1	Lemon	1
12 oz	Shelled prawns	350 g
¼ teasp	Tabasco sauce	1.25 ml
	Salt and pepper	
4–6	Hard-boiled eggs	4–6
¼ pint	Thick mayonnaise	150 ml
1 teasp	Tomato purée	5 ml
½ teasp	Anchovy essence	2.5 ml
	Lettuce leaves	
2 oz	Black olives	50 g
4 oz	Unshelled prawns	125 g

Cut lemon in half across the segments; reserve one half. Finely grate rind of the other and reserve. Squeeze juice into a bowl.

Add shelled prawns to lemon juice with Tabasco sauce and seasoning. Leave to marinate for 15 minutes.

Meanwhile, shell eggs and cut in half lengthways. Divide the mayonnaise between two bowls. Add tomato purée and anchovy essence to one and grated lemon rind to the other.

Put the yellow mayonnaise mixture into a piping bag fitted with a star nozzle and pipe on to half the eggs. Pipe the pink mixture on to the remaining eggs.

Line a serving dish with lettuce leaves. Arrange the marinated prawns in a circle in the centre. Place eggs around the edge, alternating the colours, and garnish with the black olives.

Cut remaining lemon half into a basket shape and place in centre of the dish. Hang the whole unshelled prawns on the lemon and serve immediately.

Chicory and anchovy salad

Overall timing 15 minutes

Freezing Not suitable

To serve 4

4	Heads of chicory	4
4	Anchovy fillets	4
2 tbsp	Lemon juice	2x15 ml
½ teasp	Salt	2.5 ml
2 tbsp	Chopped parsley	2x15 ml
2	Hard-boiled egg yolks	2
Dressing		
1 tbsp	Wine or cider vinegar	15 ml
1 teasp	French mustard	5 ml
	Salt and pepper	
3 tbsp	Oil	3x15 ml

Trim and chop chicory. Drain and chop anchovy fillets. Place both in salad bowl. Add lemon juice and salt.

To make the dressing, mix together vinegar, mustard and seasoning in a small bowl. Gradually beat in oil until the dressing thickens.

Pour dressing over salad and toss. Sprinkle with chopped parsley and sieved or crumbled egg yolks.

Cockle salad

Overall timing 1 hour 20 minutes

Freezing Not suitable

To serve 4

2 lb	Fresh cockles	900 g
	Coarse salt	
1	Small onion	1
¼ pint	Dry white wine	150 ml
1	Lettuce	1
1 tbsp	Strong made mustard	15 ml
3 tbsp	Oil	3x15 ml
1 tbsp	Vinegar	15 ml
1 tbsp	Chopped parsley or chives	15 ml
	Salt and pepper	

Scrub cockles well under running cold water. Add as much coarse salt to a bowl of water as will dissolve and place the cockles in the water so that they open and release any sand or grit.

Remove cockles from bowl, then rinse under cold running water and drain.

Peel and chop onion. Put into saucepan with wine and boil till wine begins to evaporate. Add cockles and cook, stirring, for about 3 minutes till the shells open. Discard any that do not open. Strain the juice and reserve.

Line salad bowl with lettuce leaves. Remove cockles from shells and pile them on the lettuce. Mix together the reserved strained juice, mustard, oil, vinegar, parsley or chives and seasoning. Pour over cockles just before serving.

Crispy lettuce and cheese salad

Overall timing 15 minutes plus chilling

Freezing Not suitable

To serve 4–6

1	Large bulb of fennel	1
	Salt and pepper	
1	Cos lettuce	1
1	Onion	1
4 tbsp	Oil	4x15 ml
1 tbsp	Lemon juice	15 ml
3 oz	Grated Parmesan cheese	75 g
1 tbsp	Chopped parsley	15 ml

Trim fennel. Cut into small pieces and blanch in boiling salted water for 2 minutes. Drain.

Wash and dry lettuce. Shred finely. Peel and thinly slice onion. Put into a salad bowl with blanched fennel and lettuce and mix well together. Chill for 15 minutes to crisp.

Meanwhile, beat the oil and lemon juice together in a small bowl. Add salt and lots of freshly-ground black pepper.

Add Parmesan and chopped parsley to salad bowl and pour dressing over. Toss and serve immediately.

This salad makes a good accompaniment to many Italian-style dishes incorporating pasta and tomato sauce.

Cucumber and cider salad

Overall timing 10 minutes plus 1 hour chilling

Freezing Not suitable

To serve 4

2	Cucumbers	2
¼ pint	Dry cider	150 ml
3 tbsp	Chopped parsley	3x15 ml
1 teasp	Sugar	5 ml
	Salt and pepper	

Peel cucumbers. Cut them in half lengthways and scoop out the seeds with a spoon. Thinly slice cucumbers and put into a bowl.

Mix together the cider, parsley, sugar and seasoning. Pour over the cucumber and chill for at least 1 hour. Toss gently before serving.

Cucumber and fruit salad

Overall timing 15 minutes

Freezing Not suitable

To serve 2

½	Cucumber	½
1	Orange	1
¼	Honeydew melon	¼
2 oz	Black grapes	50 g
	Sprigs of dill	
Dressing		
3 tbsp	Soured cream	3 x 15 ml
1½ teasp	Lemon juice	7.5 ml
1 tbsp	Caster sugar	15 ml
1 tbsp	Chopped fresh dill	15 ml
	Salt and pepper	

Thinly slice cucumber. Put into a bowl. Peel orange, remove pips and cut flesh into pieces. Peel melon, remove seeds and cut flesh into thin slices. Add orange and melon to cucumber with grapes. Chill for 20 minutes.

To make the dressing, beat soured cream, lemon juice, sugar, dill and seasoning in a bowl.

Divide salad between two serving glasses and spoon a little of the dressing over each. Garnish with dill sprigs and keep in refrigerator till ready to serve.

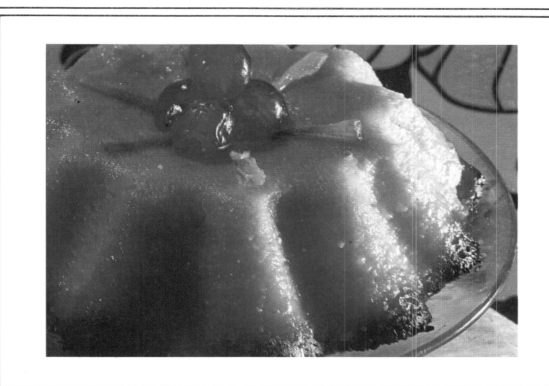

Spicy pumpkin dessert

Overall timing 45 minutes plus chilling

Freezing Not suitable

To serve 6

14 oz	Can of pumpkin purée	398 ml
2 oz	Butter	50 g
½ pint	Milk	300 ml
5 tbsp	Sugar	5x15 ml
3	Eggs	3
½ teasp	Ground cinnamon	2.5 ml
¼ teasp	Ground ginger	1.25 ml
¼ teasp	Grated nutmeg	1.25 ml
	Salt	
¼ pint	Carton of whipping cream	150 ml
	Glacé cherries	
	Candied angelica	

Preheat the oven to 350°F (180°C) Gas 4.

Put the pumpkin purée into a bowl and beat in the melted butter, milk, sugar, eggs, spices and a pinch of salt. In a separate bowl, whip the cream till it forms soft peaks, and fold into the mixture.

Pour the mixture into a greased 2 pint (1.1. litre) brioche mould and bake for about 30 minutes. Remove from the oven and leave to cool completely, then chill for 3–4 hours till firm.

Turn out the dessert on to a serving dish and decorate with glacé cherries and angelica. Serve with pouring cream.

Singapore coconut pudding

Overall timing 45 minutes plus 30 minutes soaking

Freezing Not suitable

To serve 4

3 oz	Desiccated coconut	75 g
4 fl oz	Boiling water	120 ml
8 oz	Caster sugar	225 g
3	Eggs	3
	Pinch of salt	
4 tbsp	Grated fresh coconut	4x15 ml

Put desiccated coconut in a bowl and pour over boiling water. Soak for 30 minutes, then pour through muslin or a fine sieve into a jug. Squeeze out liquid from coconut. Discard coconut.

Preheat the oven to 350°F (180°C) Gas 4.

Beat the sugar, eggs and salt till thick and foamy. Gradually add reserved coconut liquid.

Turn the mixture into a lightly greased 1 pint (560 ml) mould or four ovenproof dishes and place in roasting tin half-filled with hot water. Bake for 30 minutes.

Allow to cool, then invert over a serving plate to turn out. Chill until ready to serve, sprinkled with grated fresh coconut.

Upside-down cheesecake

Overall timing 1¼ hours plus chilling

Freezing Suitable

To serve 8

8 oz	Nice biscuits	225 g
4 oz	Butter	125 g
3 tbsp	Light soft brown sugar	3 x 15 ml
1 teasp	Ground cinnamon	5 ml
Filling		
12	Petits suisses	12
4 tbsp	Single cream	4 x 15 ml
4 teasp	Plain flour	4 x 5 ml
3 oz	Caster sugar	75 g
1 teasp	Vanilla essence	5 ml
1	Lemon	1
4	Eggs	4

Preheat the oven to 350°F (180°C) Gas 4.

Crush biscuits. Put butter, sugar and cinnamon into a saucepan and heat gently till sugar dissolves. Remove from heat and stir in biscuit crumbs. Press all but 4 tbsp (4x15 ml) over bottom and sides of greased 9 inch (23 cm) loose-bottomed flan tin.

Beat cheese with cream, flour, sugar, vanilla essence, grated rind of the lemon and 1 tbsp (15 ml) of the juice. Separate eggs. Beat yolks into the cheese mixture. Whisk whites till stiff and fold into cheese mixture. Pour into crumb case and smooth the top. Sprinkle remaining crumbs on top and press down lightly.

Bake for 45 minutes till set. Switch off the oven, open the door slightly and leave cheesecake in oven till cold. Chill for 2–3 hours, then invert on to a serving dish.

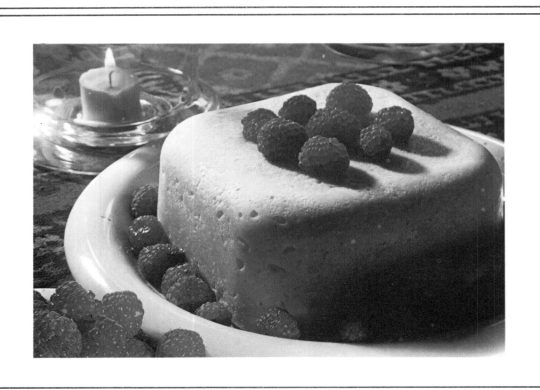

Raspberries jubilee

Overall timing 10 minutes plus 2 hours
maceration

Freezing Not suitable

To serve 6

12 oz	Fresh or frozen raspberries	350 g
2–4 oz	Caster sugar	50–125 g
3 tbsp	Lemon juice	3x15 ml
1½ pints	Vanilla ice cream	850 ml
3 tbsp	Kirsch or brandy	3x15 ml

Put raspberries, sugar (add according to taste) and lemon juice in a bowl and macerate for 2 hours in the refrigerator. Chill serving plate.

Transfer raspberries and soaking juices to a saucepan and heat through gently.

Remove ice cream from freezer and place on serving plate. Spoon raspberries and syrup over. Warm Kirsch or brandy in ladle. Set alight and pour over ice cream. Serve immediately.

Marbled ice cream with chocolate sauce

Overall timing 20 minutes

Freezing Not suitable

To serve 4-6

2 teasp	Cornflour	2x5 ml
½ pint	Cold milk	300 ml
2 oz	Plain dessert chocolate or chocolate dots	50 g
2 tbsp	Granulated sugar	2x15 ml
½ teasp	Vanilla essence	2.5 ml
	Chocolate and vanilla ice cream	
4-6	Sponge fingers	4-6

Blend the cornflour in a bowl with a little milk. Put rest of milk in saucepan with the broken up chocolate or chocolate dots. Heat slowly until the chocolate melts, then stir in cornflour. Cook, stirring constantly, until the sauce comes to the boil and thickens. Stir in sugar and vanilla essence and cook, stirring, for 3 minutes more.

Turn ice cream out on to chilled serving plate and press sponge fingers into the top. Pour some of the sauce over. Serve immediately with the remaining sauce.

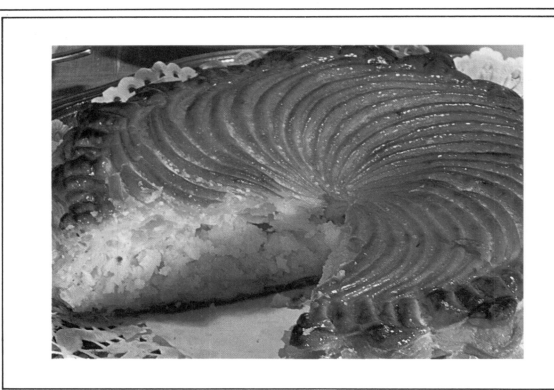

Rum and almond pastry cake

Overall timing 2¼ hours

Freezing Suitable: refresh from frozen in 350°F (180°C) Gas 4 oven for 30 minutes

Serves 6–8

13 oz	Frozen puff pastry	375 g
3 oz	Butter	75 g
3 oz	Caster sugar	75 g
2	Eggs	2
4 oz	Ground almonds	125 g
2 tbsp	Rum	2x15 ml
1 tbsp	Icing sugar	15 ml

Thaw pastry. To make filling, cream butter with sugar till light and fluffy. Beat in one whole egg and one egg yolk, reserving white. Fold in the ground almonds and rum. Cover and chill for 40 minutes.

Roll out dough to ¼ inch (6 mm) thickness. Cut out two rounds, one 8 inch (20 cm) and the other 9 inch (23 cm). Place smaller one on a dampened baking tray. Place almond filling in a ball in centre of dough round, leaving at least a 2 inch (5 cm) border all round. Brush edges with water.

Place second dough round on top and press edges together to seal. Using a knife, trim, then knock up edges and crimp. Chill for 15 minutes.

Preheat the oven to 450°F (230°C) Gas 8.

Brush pie with reserved beaten egg white. Leave for 1 minute, then brush again. Using the tip of a sharp knife, score top of pie to make a swirl pattern. Bake for 20 minutes, then reduce temperature to 400°F (200°C) Gas 6 and bake for a further 25 minutes, or until well risen and golden brown.

Remove from oven and increase heat to 475°F (240°C) Gas 9. Sift icing sugar over pie and return to oven to bake for 4–5 minutes to glaze. Remove from baking tray with palette knife and place on serving plate.

Strawberries and cream

Overall timing 15 minutes plus chilling

Freezing Not suitable

To serve 4

1 lb	Strawberries	450 g
Crème Chantilly		
8 fl oz	Carton of double cream	227 ml
¼ teasp	Vanilla essence	1.25 ml
	Icing sugar	

Hull and wipe the strawberries. Divide between individual serving dishes and chill for 1 hour.

Whip the cream till stiff peaks form, then fold in the vanilla essence and sugar to taste. Pipe the cream on top of the strawberries and serve immediately.

Variation

Sprinkle the strawberries with fresh orange juice, or an orange liqueur such as Cointreau, before chilling.

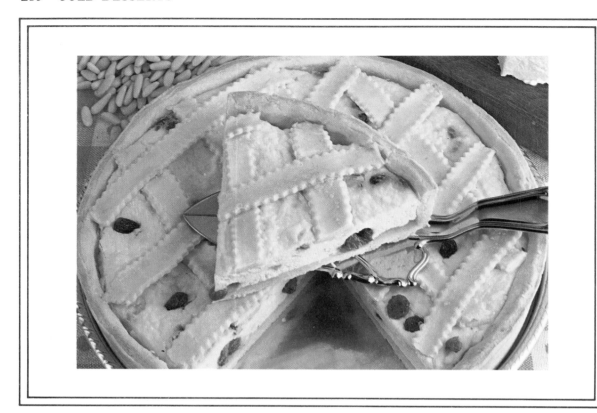

Honey and lemon cheesecake

Overall timing 1¼ hours plus cooling

Freezing Suitable

To serve 12

6 oz	Rich shortcrust pastry	175 g
2	Eggs	2
1 lb	Curd cheese	450 g
6 tbsp	Thick honey	6x15 ml
2	Lemons	2
4 oz	Sultanas	125 g

Preheat the oven to 400°F (200°C) Gas 6.

Roll out dough and use to line 8½ inch (22 cm) loose-bottomed flan tin, reserving any trimmings. Prick bottom. Bake blind for 10 minutes, then remove from oven and reduce temperature to 350°F (180°C) Gas 4.

Separate the eggs. Put the yolks into a bowl with the cheese, honey and the grated rind of one of the lemons. Squeeze juice from both lemons and add to the bowl with the sultanas. Mix well.

In another bowl, whisk the egg whites to soft peaks and fold into the cheese mixture with a metal spoon. Pour into flan case and smooth the surface.

Roll out dough trimmings and cut into thin strips with a pastry wheel. Arrange in a lattice pattern over the filling. Bake for 50–55 minutes till set. Cool in tin, then turn out and serve cold.

Strawberries melba

Overall timing 15 minutes plus maceration

Freezing Not suitable

To serve 4-6

1 lb	Strawberries	450 g
4 oz	Raspberries	125 g
4 tbsp	Caster sugar	4x15 ml
2 teasp	Lemon juice	2x5 ml
1 oz	Slivered almonds	25 g

Hull the strawberries and pile in a serving dish.

Sieve the raspberries, then stir in the sugar and lemon juice until the sugar has dissolved. Pour over the strawberries and toss gently to coat. Leave to macerate for 1 hour.

Scatter the almonds over the top and serve.

Clementines niçoise

Overall timing 15 minutes plus 2 hours maceration

Freezing Not suitable

To serve 8

8	Large clementines	8
1	Peach	1
4 oz	Cherries	125 g
8 oz	Can of pineapple rings	227 g
2 oz	Caster sugar	50 g
2 tbsp	Cointreau	2x15 ml
	Vanilla ice cream	

Slice the top off each clementine with a sharp knife and reserve. Scoop out the flesh with a teaspoon, taking care not to break the shell. Cover the empty shells and the tops and chill.

Cut the flesh into neat pieces, discarding the pips and pith. Peel the peach, cut in half and discard the stone. Cut into cubes. Stone the cherries, then chop flesh. Drain the pineapple and cut into pieces.

Put all the fruit into a bowl with the sugar and liqueur and leave to macerate for 2 hours.

Remove clementine shells and tops from the refrigerator. Divide the fruit and juices between the shells, add a scoop of ice cream and place the lids on top. Serve immediately in individual glass dishes.

Clementine rice mould

Overall timing 1¼ hours plus cooling

Freezing Not suitable

To serve 4–6

4 oz	Pudding rice	125 g
5	Clementines	5
¾ pint	Milk	400 ml
1 teasp	Vanilla essence	5 ml
	Salt	
4 oz	Caster sugar	125 g
1	Egg	1
1 oz	Butter	25 g
	Candied angelica	
Syrup		
¼ pint	Water	150 ml
3 oz	Sugar	75 g

Put the rice in a large saucepan of water, bring to the boil and boil for 5 minutes. Drain well.

Finely chop the peel and flesh of one clementine. Put into a saucepan with milk and bring almost to the boil. Remove from the heat, cover and leave to infuse for 10 minutes. Strain milk and return to pan. Add vanilla essence, a pinch of salt and rice. Cook gently, stirring occasionally, for 25–30 minutes till all milk has been absorbed. Add sugar and cook for a further 5 minutes.

Lightly beat egg. Remove cooked rice from heat and mix in egg and butter. Pour into a greased 2 pint (1.1 litre) soufflé dish. Cool, then chill for 2–3 hours.

To make syrup, put water and sugar into a saucepan and heat gently, stirring, till sugar has dissolved. Cut remaining clementines into wedges and add to syrup. Boil gently for 25 minutes till tender and syrup has caramelized.

Turn out rice mould onto serving plate. Arrange clementine wedges and angelica on top and around sides. Spoon over any remaining caramel, if liked, and serve with cream.

Coffee water ice

Overall timing 2 hours

Freezing See method

To serve 6–8

9 oz	Granulated sugar	250 g
1 tbsp	Vanilla sugar	15 ml
1 pint	Water	560 ml
8 teasp	Instant coffee granules	8x5 ml
½ pint	Carton of whipping cream	300 ml
	Peppermint essence (optional)	

Put granulated and vanilla sugar and water in a saucepan. Stir until sugar has completely dissolved, then bring to the boil and boil for 5 minutes. Skim if necessary. Stir in the coffee granules and remove pan from heat. Allow mixture to cool completely.

Pour coffee mixture through a fine sieve or muslin-lined sieve into a freezer tray. Place in freezer or freezing compartment of refrigerator and leave for about 1 hour or until the mixture forms a granular mass. Do not stir.

In a bowl whip cream till just holding soft peaks, then add a few drops of peppermint essence, if using, to taste. Scrape out contents of freezer tray with a fork and divide ice between chilled serving glasses. Top each glass with peppermint-flavoured cream and serve with biscuits.

Rum and apricot pudding cake

Overall timing 55 minutes

Freezing Not suitable

To serve 6

1 pint	Milk	560 ml
½ teasp	Vanilla essence	2.5 ml
4	Eggs	4
4 tbsp	Caster sugar	4x15 ml
4 oz	Sponge cake	125 g
2 tbsp	Rum	2x15 ml
4 oz	Chopped glacé fruits	125 g
1 oz	Butter	25 g
8 oz	Apricot jam	225 g

Preheat the oven to 375°F (190°C) Gas 5.

Put the milk and vanilla essence into a saucepan and bring to the boil. Meanwhile, separate the eggs. Add the sugar to the yolks and beat together with a fork. Pour the hot milk over the yolks, stirring constantly.

Crumble the sponge cake into a bowl. Strain the custard over the cake and mix in half the rum, the glacé fruits and butter. Leave to cool.

Whisk the egg whites till stiff. Fold into the crumb mixture with a metal spoon. Pour the mixture into a greased and lined 2 pint (1.1 litre) soufflé dish and smooth the top. Bake for about 35–40 minutes till well risen and golden.

Put the apricot jam into a saucepan with remaining rum and heat gently till melted.

Serve the cake hot from the dish, with the apricot sauce separately in a sauceboat. Or, leave the cake to cool completely and turn out on to a serving dish. Pour the hot apricot sauce on top and serve immediately.

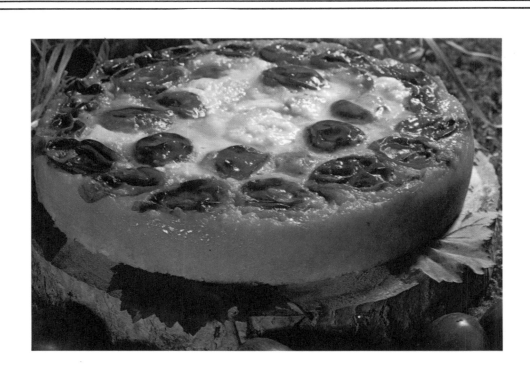

Plum crumb pudding

Overall timing 1½ hours plus chilling

Freezing Not suitable

To serve 8

4 oz	Sponge cake	125 g
3	Eggs	3
2 oz	Caster sugar	50 g
1 pint	Milk	560 ml
1 oz	Butter	25 g
	Grated rind of 1 lemon	
½ teasp	Ground cinnamon	2.5 ml
1 lb	Red plums	450 g

Preheat oven to 350°F (180°C) Gas 4. Grease and base-line a 9 inch (23 cm) springform tin.

Crumble the cake into a bowl. Separate two of the eggs, putting the yolks and remaining whole egg into a bowl with the sugar. Put the milk and butter into a saucepan and bring almost to the boil.

Beat the yolks and sugar together and pour the milk on to them, stirring constantly. Strain over the cake crumbs. Add the lemon rind and cinnamon, mix well and leave to stand for 15 minutes.

Meanwhile, wash and halve the plums, discarding the stones. Dry thoroughly on kitchen paper.

Whisk the 2 egg whites in a large bowl till stiff but not dry and fold into the crumb mixture with a metal spoon. Pour the mixture into the tin.

Arrange the plums cut sides down on the mixture and bake in the centre of the oven for about 50 minutes till set.

Remove from the oven and leave to cool in the tin, then chill for 3–4 hours. Remove pudding from tin and place on a serving dish. Serve cut into slices, with pouring cream.

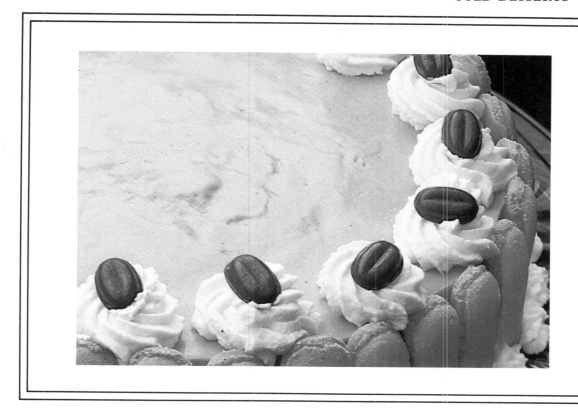

Coffee charlotte

Overall timing 50 minutes plus chilling

Freezing Suitable

To serve 8

2 tbsp	Brandy	2x15 ml
30	Sponge fingers	30
5 oz	Caster sugar	150 g
¼ pint	Strong black coffee	150 ml
2 teasp	Powdered gelatine	2x5 ml
4	Egg yolks	4
2 tbsp	Vanilla sugar	2x15 ml
½ pint	Carton of double cream	300 ml
15	Sugar coffee beans	15

Mix brandy with ¼ pint (150 ml) water in a shallow dish. Dip sponge fingers quickly in mixture to moisten them, then use to line sides of greased 10 inch (25 cm) springform tin. Place biscuits upright, sugared sides against tin, and trim ends to height of tin. Press lightly into place.

Put caster sugar and 3 tbsp (3x15 ml) water in heavy-based saucepan. Stir to dissolve sugar, then heat until golden brown. Stir in coffee and simmer for 2 minutes till caramel dissolves. Cool.

Dissolve gelatine in 2 tbsp (2x15 ml) cold water.

Put egg yolks and vanilla sugar in a bowl over a pan of hot water and whisk together till light and foamy. Stir coffee caramel into egg mixture and whisk till it starts to thicken. Stir in gelatine, then leave to cool until just on the point of setting.

Whip two-thirds of the cream until it holds soft peaks. Using a metal spoon, fold lightly into coffee mixture. Pour into centre of sponge finger-lined tin and chill till set.

Unclip tin and carefully transfer charlotte to a serving plate. Whip remaining cream until it holds stiff peaks. Pipe 15 rosettes round edge of charlotte. Place a coffee bean on top of each one. Pipe smaller rosettes round base.

Strawberry vacherin

Overall timing 2¼ hours plus cooling

Freezing Not suitable

To serve 8

6	Egg whites	6
12 oz	Caster sugar	350 g
1 lb	Strawberries	450 g
Crème Chantilly		
½ pint	Carton of double cream	284 ml
1 tbsp	Cold milk	15 ml
1	Ice cube	1
1 tbsp	Caster sugar	15 ml
¼ teasp	Vanilla essence	1.25 ml

Preheat the oven to 300°F (150°C) Gas 2.

Line two baking trays with non-stick paper. Draw a 10 inch (25 cm) square on one, and a 6 inch (15 cm) square on the other.

Whisk egg whites till stiff and dry. Sprinkle over 2 tbsp (2x15 ml) of the sugar and whisk in, then gradually whisk in remaining sugar to make a stiff, glossy meringue.

Using the marked squares as a guide, put large spoonfuls of meringue on to paper to make two squares with scalloped edges. Swirl into peaks. Place large square in centre of oven with small square below. Bake for about 1¼ hours till slightly browned and crisp. Cool.

Meanwhile, hull strawberries. To make the Crème Chantilly, whip cream with milk, ice cube, sugar and vanilla essence till it forms soft peaks. Chill till required.

Just before serving, carefully peel the paper from the meringue squares and place the large one on a flat board or serving dish. Spread or pipe two-thirds of the Crème Chantilly over and arrange two-thirds of the strawberries on top. Place the small meringue square on top and spread with the remaining crème. Decorate with remaining strawberries and serve immediately.

Champagne sorbet

Overall timing 20 minutes plus freezing

Freezing See method

To serve 6

8 oz	Caster sugar	225 g
1 pint	Water	560 ml
¼ pint	Champagne or dry cider	150 ml
1 tbsp	Lemon juice	15 ml
2	Egg whites	2

Put the sugar and water in a pan and heat gently, stirring until sugar dissolves. Bring to the boil and simmer for 10 minutes without stirring. Do not let the mixture colour. Remove from the heat and cool.

Add the Champagne or cider and lemon juice to the syrup, then pour into a 2 pint (1.1 litre) freezer tray. Freeze till mushy.

Remove mixture from freezer, turn into a bowl and beat well to break down any ice crystals. Whisk the egg whites until stiff and fold into the mixture. Return to the freezer tray and freeze till firm.

Strawberry milk ring

Overall timing 30 minutes plus setting

Freezing Not suitable

To serve 6

1	Lemon	1
5 teasp	Powdered gelatine	5x5 ml
5 tbsp	Caster sugar	5x15 ml
1	Large can of evaporated milk	1
½ pint	Buttermilk	300 ml
	Pink food colouring	
1	Egg white	1
¼ pint	Carton of double cream	150 ml
1 lb	Fresh strawberries	450 g

Grate the rind from the lemon and reserve. Squeeze out the juice and place in a small bowl. Sprinkle the gelatine over and dissolve. Stir in the sugar. Allow to cool slightly.

Pour the well-chilled evaporated milk into a large bowl and whisk till very thick and foamy. Whisk in the buttermilk, gelatine mixture, reserved lemon rind and a few drops of food colouring. Pour into a dampened 2 pint (1.1 litre) ring mould and chill for 3–4 hours till set.

Dip the mould up to the rim in hot water for a few seconds and turn out on to a serving plate.

Whisk the egg white till stiff. Whip the cream till stiff and fold into the whisked egg white. Hull the strawberries and pile half in the centre of the ring. Pipe the cream mixture on top and around the base of the ring. Decorate with the remaining strawberries and serve immediately.

Crème caramel

Overall timing 45 minutes

Freezing Not suitable

To serve 6

1 pint	Milk	560 ml
½	Vanilla pod	½
1	Piece lemon rind	1
4	Eggs	4
4 oz	Caster sugar	125 g

Preheat the oven to 350°F (180°C) Gas 4.

Put the milk, vanilla pod and lemon rind in a saucepan and bring to the boil. Remove from heat and lift out the vanilla pod and lemon rind.

In a bowl, beat eggs with half sugar and gradually pour in the hot milk, stirring constantly.

Melt the remaining sugar in a saucepan over a moderate heat till golden brown. Divide between six small moulds and turn them so the caramel coats the bottoms and sides.

Strain the custard mixture into the moulds and place them in a roasting tin half-filled with hot water. Bake for 45 minutes till set. Allow to cool in moulds and chill before turning out.

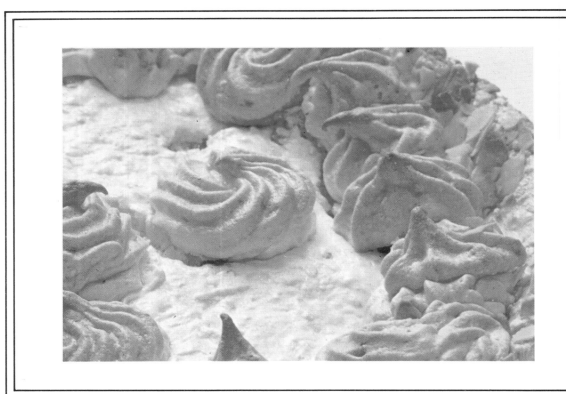

Blackberry special

Overall timing 4 hours including chilling but not cooling

Freezing Not suitable

To serve 6–8

6 oz	Plain flour	150 g
2	Egg yolks	2
3 oz	Caster sugar	75 g
3 oz	Butter	75 g
¼ teasp	Salt	1.25 ml
Filling		
1 lb	Blackberries	450 g
2 oz	Chopped mixed peel	50 g
3	Egg whites	3
6 oz	Caster sugar	175 g
6 oz	Ground almonds	175 g
1 teasp	Grated lemon rind	5 ml
¼ teasp	Ground cinnamon	1.25 ml
2 oz	Flaked almonds	25 g

Sift flour into a mixing bowl. Add egg yolks, sugar, small flakes of butter and salt. Mix to a pliable dough. Chill for 2 hours.

Preheat the oven to 375°F (190°C) Gas 5.

Roll out dough and use to line 9 inch (23 cm) flan ring on a baking tray. Bake blind for 15 minutes.

Remove flan case from oven and reduce heat to 300°F (150°C) Gas 2. Remove foil and beans. Add blackberries to flan and sprinkle with peel.

Whisk egg whites until very stiff. Fold in sugar followed by ground almonds, lemon rind and cinnamon. Put 3 tbsp (3x15 ml) of the mixture in a piping bag fitted with a large rose nozzle. Spread the remainder over blackberries. Sprinkle edges of flan with flaked almonds and decorate the top with swirls of piped egg white mixture.

Bake for 1 hour 10 minutes. Remove from oven and cut flan into wedges before it cools. When cold, remove flan ring and serve.

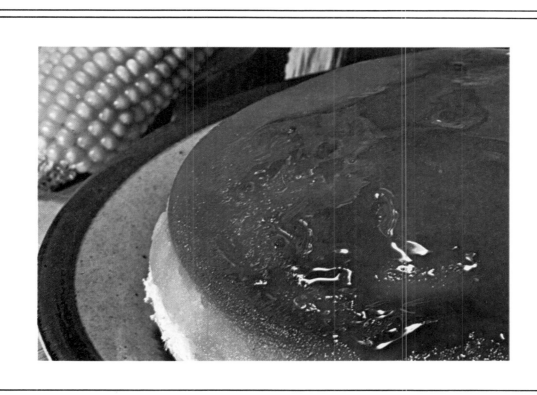

Caramel cornmeal mould

Overall timing 1 hour

Freezing Not suitable

To serve 6–8

¾ pint	Milk	400 ml
	Pinch of salt	
4 oz	Sugar	125 g
1	Bay leaf	1
18	Sugar lumps	18
9 tbsp	Warm water	9x15 ml
1 tbsp	Lemon juice	15 ml
5	Eggs	5
3 oz	Fine maizemeal	75 g

Preheat the oven to 400°F (200°C) Gas 6.

Put the milk in a saucepan with the salt, sugar and bay leaf. Bring to the boil. Remove from the heat, cover and leave to infuse for 10 minutes.

Put the sugar lumps, water and lemon juice into a small saucepan and heat gently, stirring till sugar dissolves. Bring to the boil and boil without stirring till a deep golden caramel colour. Watch pan carefully to see that caramel does not burn. Pour into an 8 inch (20 cm) round deep cake tin, turning it so that the bottom and sides are coated with the caramel.

Separate the eggs. Put the egg yolks and maizemeal into a bowl and mix together with a wooden spoon. Remove bay leaf from the milk. Gradually pour the hot milk on to the egg yolks, stirring continuously. Whisk the egg whites till stiff and fold into the mixture.

Pour the mixture into the prepared tin and place in a roasting tin containing 1 inch (2.5 cm) hot water. Bake for 35–40 minutes. While still warm; run knife round edge of mould and invert on to serving plate. Serve warm or cold, with pouring cream.

Cider and grape ring

Overall timing 15 minutes plus setting

Freezing Not suitable

To serve 4–6

1 pint	Medium-sweet cider	600 ml
1 tbsp	Powdered gelatine	15 ml
1 tbsp	Lemon juice	15 ml
8 oz	White grapes	225 g
8 oz	Black grapes	225 g
2 tbsp	Caster sugar	2x15 ml

Put 6 tbsp (6x15 ml) of the cider in a heatproof bowl, sprinkle over the gelatine and leave until spongy – about 5 minutes.

Dissolve gelatine over a pan of hot water, then stir in the remaining cider and lemon juice. Remove bowl from the heat. Spoon enough of the cider jelly into a dampened 1½ pint (850 ml) ring mould just to cover it. Leave it to set in the refrigerator.

Reserve half of each kind of grape. Wash and cut remainder in half and remove pips. Arrange halves over the set jelly, then cover with more liquid jelly and leave to set. Continue layers, ending with jelly, then chill in refrigerator till set. Wash remaining grapes and remove most of moisture. Toss in caster sugar.

Dip the mould quickly in and out of hot water and invert over a serving plate so jelly slides out. Fill centre with sugared grapes. Serve with whipped cream and ginger biscuits.

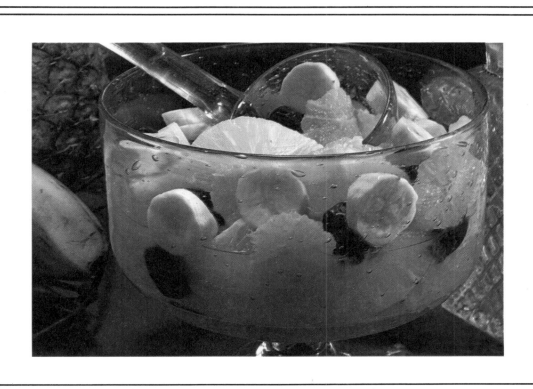

Fruit salad with prunes

Overall timing 30 minutes

Freezing Not suitable

To serve 4

	Selection of any firm fresh fruit: apple, banana, cherries, orange, clementine, pear, peach, strawberries and grapes	
1	Lemon	1
1 oz	Butter	25 g
3 tbsp	Caster sugar	3×15 ml
2 oz	Flaked almonds	50 g
3 tbsp	Rum	3×15 ml

Prepare the fruit and chop it into pieces. Mix these together in a bowl. Grate lemon and squeeze out juice. Add juice to fruit.

Put the butter and caster sugar into a saucepan. Heat without stirring, until the sugar caramelizes and becomes light brown. This will take about 5 minutes. Add the grated lemon rind and almonds. Cook for about 5 minutes, stirring occasionally, until the caramel and nuts are golden brown.

Remove pan from the heat. Add juices from mixed fruits and stir until caramel becomes a smooth syrup. Add the fruit and heat through for about 5 minutes, turning the mixture over frequently to distribute the syrup. Remove from heat.

Warm rum in a metal ladle, then set it alight and pour over fruit. Serve immediately with whipped cream or ice cream.

Rum trifle

Overall timing 35 minutes plus chilling

Freezing Not suitable

To serve 4–6

2 tbsp	Cocoa powder	2x15 ml
4 oz	Caster sugar	125 g
1¼ pints	Milk	700 ml
4	Egg yolks	4
2 oz	Plain flour	50 g
4 tbsp	Rum	4x15 ml
4 tbsp	Water	4x15 ml
8	Trifle sponges	8

Mix the cocoa with 1 oz (25 g) of the sugar. Heat the milk in a saucepan and add ¼ pint (150 ml) of it to the cocoa mixture. Stir till well blended.

In another bowl, beat the egg yolks with remaining sugar and flour. Gradually add the remaining hot milk. Return to the saucepan and bring to the boil, stirring. Cook for 2 minutes till custard thickens. Pour half of the custard back into bowl and stir in cocoa mixture.

Line a glass bowl with greaseproof paper. Put rum and water on a plate. Split the sponges in half, then halve each half. Dip sponges in rum mixture just to moisten. Line bottom and sides of bowl with half the sponges.

Pour in the plain custard and cover with a layer of sponges. Pour the chocolate custard into the mould and cover with remaining sponges. Cover with foil or cling film and chill for at least 3 hours but preferably overnight.

Turn trifle out on to a plate, carefully remove greaseproof paper and decorate with whipped cream, if liked.

Cherry bread pudding

Overall timing 1 hour

Freezing Not suitable

To serve 4–6

7	Slices of bread	7
15 oz	Can of cherries	425 g
4	Eggs	4
4 oz	Caster sugar	125 g
¾ pint	Milk	400 ml
	Grated rind of ½ lemon	
1 tbsp	Icing sugar	15 ml

Preheat the oven to 350°F (180°C) Gas 4.

Cut the slices of bread into quarters diagonally. Arrange eight of the bread triangles over the bottom of an ovenproof dish.

Drain the cherries; halve and remove stones. Spread half the cherries over bread and cover with eight more triangles. Sprinkle over the remaining cherries and cover with the remaining bread, arranged in overlapping rows.

Beat the eggs with the sugar and add the milk. Sprinkle lemon rind over the bread and strain the egg mixture over. Sprinkle the surface with icing sugar and bake for 35 minutes. Serve hot.

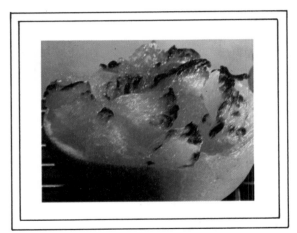

Baked apples

Overall timing 35 minutes

Freezing Not suitable

To serve 4

4	Large apples	4
8 tbsp	Jam	8x15 ml
1 oz	Butter	25 g
4 tbsp	Water	4x15 ml
4 tbsp	Caster sugar	4x15 ml

Preheat oven to 375°F (190°C) Gas 5.

Wash, dry and core apples. Place in a greased ovenproof dish and fill each apple with jam. Add small knob of butter to each.

Put water in bottom of dish, then bake for 25 minutes. Serve sprinkled with sugar.

Caramelized grapefruit

Overall timing 20 minutes

Freezing Not suitable

To serve 4

2	Grapefruit	2
1 teasp	Ground cinnamon	5 ml
4 tbsp	Caster sugar	4x15 ml

Preheat the grill.

Cut grapefruit in half. Remove flesh with grapefruit knife, separate segments and discard membranes. Put segments into a bowl. Mix cinnamon with half the sugar and sprinkle over fruit.

Fill grapefruit shells with segments and sprinkle with remaining sugar. Grill for a few minutes till golden brown. Serve hot.

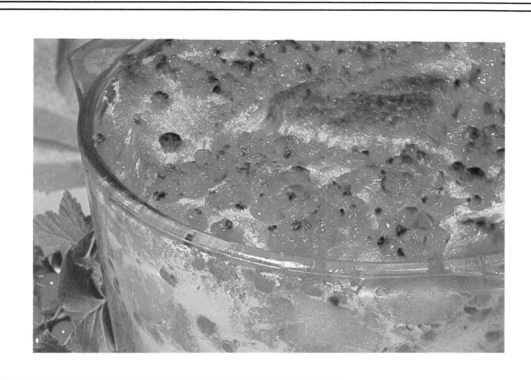

Redcurrant pudding

Overall timing 1½ hours

Freezing Suitable: reheat from frozen in 350°F (180°C) Gas 4 oven for 1 hour

To serve 6–8

12 oz	Redcurrants	350 g
12	Slices of stale bread	12
2 oz	Butter	50 g
1 pint	Milk	560 ml
1	Vanilla pod	1
2	Eggs	2
6 tbsp	Caster sugar	6x15 ml

Wash and drain the redcurrants. Remove the stalks. Remove the crusts from the bread. Spread with butter and cut into triangles.

Sprinkle a few redcurrants over the bottom of a well-greased 3 pint (1.7 litre) ovenproof dish and arrange some of the bread on top. Cover with redcurrants, then a layer of bread. Repeat the layers.

Put the milk and vanilla pod into a saucepan and bring to the boil. Remove from the heat and lift out the vanilla pod. Whisk the eggs with 5 tbsp (5x15 ml) of the sugar till frothy, then pour in the hot milk, whisking continuously. Strain the custard over the redcurrants and bread. Leave to soak for 20 minutes.

Preheat the oven to 375°F (190°C) Gas 5.

Sprinkle the remaining sugar over the pudding and bake for about 40 minutes till golden. Serve immediately.

Russian pudding

Overall timing 30 minutes

Freezing Not suitable

To serve 4–6

1½ pints	Milk	850 ml
	Pinch of salt	
	Grated rind of ½ lemon	
4 oz	Granulated sugar	125 g
3 oz	Semolina or ground rice	75 g
1	Egg	1
1 lb	Can of cherries	453 g
2 tbsp	Redcurrant jelly	2x15 ml

In a saucepan, heat the milk, salt, lemon rind and 2 oz (50 g) of the sugar. Stir in the semolina or ground rice. Remove from the heat.

Separate the egg and add the beaten yolk to the saucepan.

In a bowl, beat the egg white till stiff and carefully fold into the semolina or ground rice mixture.

Drain cherries. Place cherries and 2 tbsp (2x15 ml) of the juice in a pan. Stir in the redcurrant jelly and cook for 5 minutes.

Preheat the grill. Grease a flameproof serving dish. Pour in half the semolina or rice mixture, then all the cherry mixture and finally the rest of the semolina or rice. Sprinkle with the remaining sugar and place under the grill. Cook till the sugar caramelizes and turns golden but not brown – it should take about 3 minutes. Serve immediately.

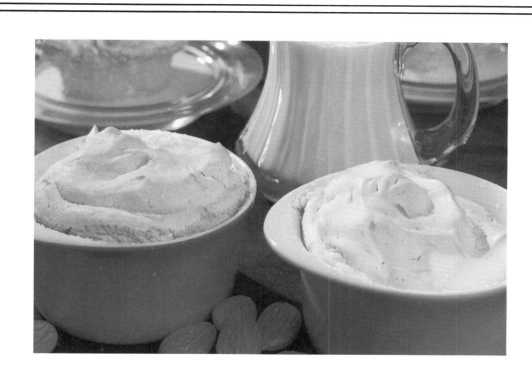

Almond apricot desserts

Overall timing 1¼ hours

Freezing Not suitable

To serve 6

1 oz	Butter	25 g
1 oz	Caster sugar	25 g
8 oz	Apricot jam	225 g
3 tbsp	Lemon juice	3 x 15 ml
3	Eggs	3
2 oz	Ground almonds	50 g

Preheat the oven to 300°F (150°C) Gas 2.

Melt the butter in a saucepan and use to grease six small ovenproof dishes. Coat the inside of each dish with sugar.

Put the apricot jam and lemon juice into a saucepan and heat gently, stirring. Put pan into water to cool mixture quickly.

Separate the eggs. Stir the yolks and almonds into the jam mixture. Beat the egg whites in a mixing bowl until very stiff. Gently fold into the jam mixture.

Fill each dish to the top with the mixture. Place on a baking tray and bake for about 45 minutes.

Serve in the dishes or turn desserts out on to serving plates. Serve hot with custard, whipped·cream or ice cream.

Coconut and cherry surprise

Overall timing 1 hour

Freezing Suitable: reheat in 375°F (190°C) Gas 5 oven for 10 minutes

To serve 8–10

8 oz	Shortcrust pastry	225 g
2½ oz	Ground almonds	65 g
14 oz	Can of cherry pie filling	379 g
1 oz	Desiccated coconut	25 g
Filling		
3 oz	Butter	75 g
3 oz	Caster sugar	75 g
2	Eggs	2
¼ teasp	Almond essence	1.25 ml
2 tbsp	Milk	2x15 ml
2 oz	Self-raising flour	50 g
2 oz	Desiccated coconut	50 g
1½ oz	Ground almonds	40 g

Topping		
3 tbsp	Desiccated coconut	3x15 ml
1	Egg yolk	1
1 teasp	Milk	5 ml

Roll out dough and use to line greased 10 inch (25 cm) springform tin. Sprinkle ground almonds over. Spread pie filling to within 1 inch (2.5 cm) of edge, then cover with coconut.

Preheat the oven to 400°F (200°C) Gas 6.

Make filling by creaming butter with sugar till pale and fluffy. Add eggs, essence and 1 tbsp (15 ml) milk and beat well. Fold in flour, followed by remaining milk, coconut and almonds.

Place mixture in blobs over pie filling and smooth evenly so no fruit is visible. Sprinkle with coconut and bake for 30 minutes.

Mix egg yolk and milk together. Brush over tart and bake for a further 10 minutes. Serve hot.

Flamed fruit salad

Overall timing 30 minutes

Freezing Not suitable

To serve 4

	Selection of any firm fresh fruit: apple, banana, cherries, orange, clementine, pear, peach, strawberries and grapes	
1	Lemon	1
1 oz	Butter	25 g
3 tbsp	Caster sugar	3 x 15 ml
2 oz	Flaked almonds	50 g
3 tbsp	Rum	3 x 15 ml

Prepare the fruit and chop it into pieces. Mix these together in a bowl. Grate lemon and squeeze out juice. Add juice to fruit.

Put the butter and caster sugar into a saucepan. Heat without stirring, until the sugar caramelizes and becomes light brown. This will take about 5 minutes. Add the grated lemon rind and almonds. Cook for about 5 minutes, stirring occasionally, until the caramel and nuts are golden brown.

Remove pan from the heat. Add juices from mixed fruits and stir until caramel becomes a smooth syrup. Add the fruit and heat through for about 5 minutes, turning the mixture over frequently to distribute the syrup. Remove from heat.

Warm rum in a metal ladle, then set it alight and pour over fruit. Serve immediately with whipped cream or ice cream.

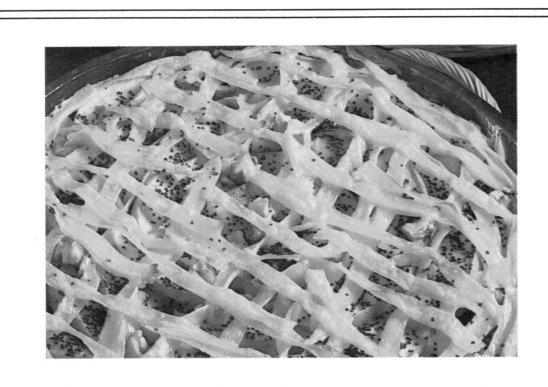

Baked noodle pudding

Overall timing 1 hour

Freezing Not suitable

To serve 4

½ pint	Milk	300 ml
1 pint	Water	560 ml
8 oz	Noodles	225 g
2 oz	Butter	50 g
2	Eggs	2
2	Large dessert apples	2
2 oz	Walnut pieces	50 g
3 oz	Caster sugar	75 g
2 teasp	Poppy seeds	2x5 ml

Preheat the oven to 325°F (170°C) Gas 3.

Put the milk and water into a saucepan and bring to the boil. Add the noodles, bring back to the boil and simmer till tender. Drain noodles and put into a large bowl. Stir in the melted butter and beaten eggs till lightly coated.

Spread one-third of the noodles over the bottom of a greased ovenproof dish. Core and thinly slice the apples. Arrange half the slices over the noodles with half the walnuts. Sprinkle with one-third of the sugar and poppy seeds.

Repeat the layers, finishing with a layer of noodles arranged in a lattice pattern. Sprinkle with the remaining sugar and poppy seeds.

Bake for about 35 minutes till the apples are tender. Remove from the oven and cool completely before serving.

Bananas flambé

Overall timing 15 minutes

Freezing Not suitable

To serve 4

¼ pint	Water	150 ml
3 oz	Caster sugar	75 g
8	Bananas	8
5 tbsp	Rum	5x15 ml
1	Small block of vanilla ice cream	1
2 oz	Flaked almonds	50 g

Put the water and sugar into a saucepan and cook until it starts to turn golden.

Peel the bananas. Leave whole or cut in half crossways. Add to the pan. Cook, uncovered, for 7 minutes, spooning syrup over occasionally. Remove from heat, stir in 4 tbsp (4x15 ml) of the rum and keep warm.

Place scoops of ice cream on a chilled serving dish. Cover with the bananas and spoon the syrup over.

Warm the remaining rum in a metal spoon or ladle. Set alight and pour over the bananas. Decorate with flaked almonds and serve immediately, while flaming.

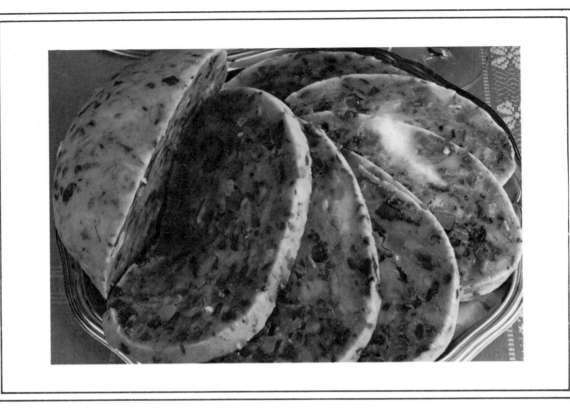

Plum pudding

Overall timing 5½ hours plus maceration

Freezing Suitable: boil from frozen for about 2 hours

To serve 8–10

1 lb	Mixed sultanas, raisins and currants	450 g
12 oz	Prunes	350 g
5 oz	Chopped mixed peel	150 g
4 tbsp	Rum	4x15 ml
¼ pint	Light ale or lager	150 ml
3	Eggs	3
8 oz	Flaked almonds	225 g
1	Apple	1
2 teasp	Mixed spice	2x5 ml
2 teasp	Salt	2x5 ml
12 oz	Brown sugar	350 g
2	Oranges	2
2	Lemons	2
8 oz	Shredded suet	225 g
6 oz	Plain flour	175 g
5 oz	Fresh breadcrumbs	150 g

Put dried fruits and candied peel in a large bowl, add 3 tbsp (3x15 ml) rum and ale or lager and leave to macerate overnight.

Drain fruit, reserving liquid. Stone prunes, then add eggs, almonds, grated apple, mixed spice, salt, sugar and the juice and grated rind of oranges and lemons. Mix well.

Put suet in a bowl and work in flour and breadcrumbs. Mix in any liquid from macerated fruit and add a little more beer if mixture is too dry. Knead to a dough and mix in all remaining ingredients. Tip mixture on to a clean, floured tea-towel and tie the corners together. Suspend from a long wooden spoon in a large saucepan half filled with boiling water. Boil for 5 hours.

Drain pudding for 5 minutes before removing tea-towel. Warm remaining rum, set alight and pour over pudding. Serve hot with custard.

Plum soufflé

Overall timing 1 hour

Freezing Not suitable

To serve 6

1½ lb	Ripe plums	700 g
2–4 oz	Sugar	50–125 g
6 tbsp	Water	6x15 ml
2½ oz	Butter	65 g
1 tbsp	Dried breadcrumbs	15 ml
2 oz	Plain flour	50 g
½ pint	Warm milk	300 ml
3	Large eggs	3
	Grated rind of 1 orange	

Preheat oven to 375°F (190°C) Gas 5.

Stone the plums and cut into quarters. Put into a saucepan with the sugar and water. Bring to the boil, cover and simmer for 10 minutes.

Grease a 3 pint (1.7 litre) soufflé dish with ½ oz (15 g) butter and coat with the breadcrumbs. Put two thirds of the plums in the dish with any juice.

Melt the remaining butter in a large saucepan, stir in the flour and cook for 1 minute. Gradually add the warm milk and bring to the boil, stirring constantly. Simmer for 2 minutes, then remove from the heat. Cool slightly.

Separate the eggs. Beat the yolks into the sauce with the orange rind and remaining plums. Whisk the egg whites till stiff but not dry. Stir one spoonful into sauce and fold in remainder. Pour mixture over the plums in the dish.

Stand dish in a roasting tin containing 1 inch (2.5 cm) hot water. Bake for 30–35 minutes till well risen and golden. Serve immediately.

Baked apricots

Overall timing 1 hour

Freezing Suitable: reheat from frozen in 400°F (200°C) Gas 6 oven for 15 minutes, then add syrup

To serve 6–8

12	Large apricots	12
½ pint	Milk	300 ml
2 tbsp	Custard powder	2x15 ml
1 tbsp	Caster sugar	15 ml
4 oz	Blanched almonds	125 g
5 oz	Macaroons	150 g
1½ oz	Candied orange peel	40 g
	Pinch of ground cinnamon	
6 tbsp	Redcurrant jelly	6x15 ml
4 tbsp	Water	4x15 ml

Preheat the oven to 400°F (200°C) Gas 6.

Halve apricots and remove stones. Arrange, cut sides up, in a greased ovenproof dish.

Prepare the custard according to packet instructions, using the milk, custard powder and sugar. Cool quickly by standing the pan in cold water. Stir the custard frequently to prevent a skin forming.

Chop almonds, macaroons and candied peel finely and stir into the custard with the cinnamon. Fill apricot halves with custard mixture. Bake for 30 minutes.

Meanwhile, mix together the redcurrant jelly and water in a small pan over a low heat. Spoon syrup carefully over the apricots and bake for a further 10 minutes.

Serve hot with whipped cream, or leave to cool, then chill and serve with ice cream or whipped cream.

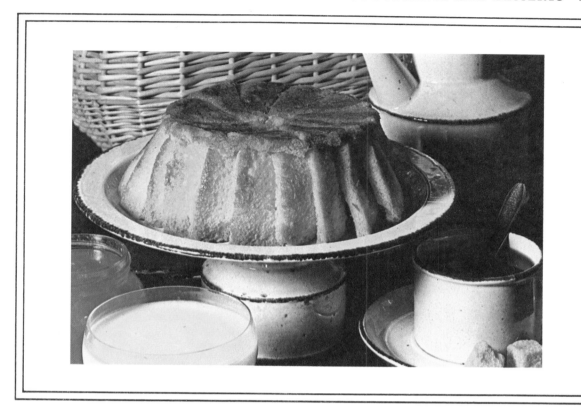

Apple and marmalade charlotte

Overall timing 1 hour

Freezing Suitable: reheat in 400°F (200°C) Gas 6 oven for 10 minutes

To serve 8

2½ lb	Cooking apples	1.1 kg
4 tbsp	Water	4x15 ml
1 oz	Sugar	25 g
4 oz	Marmalade	125 g
1½ lb	Stale sliced bread	700 g
3 oz	Butter	75 g

Preheat oven to 400°F (200°C) Gas 6.

To make the filling, peel apples, core and slice into a large saucepan. Add water, cover and bring to the boil. Cook over medium heat for 12 minutes without removing the lid at all during cooking. Remove from heat and beat in sugar and marmalade with a wooden spoon.

Remove crusts and butter bread. Cut a third of slices into triangles, and the rest into wide fingers.

Grease a 3 pint (1.7 litre) charlotte mould and line the bottom with some of the bread triangles, buttered-side out. Overlap the slices as the bread tends to shrink during cooking. Line sides of mould with over-lapping bread fingers, butter-side out.

Pour in apple mixture and top with remaining bread triangles, butter-side up. Cook on centre shelf of the oven for 30–40 minutes till golden brown.

Remove from oven. Leave to cool slightly in the mould. Run a knife around the edge and turn out on to a warmed serving plate. Serve hot with custard or cream.

Fruity rice pudding

Overall timing 1¼ hours

Freezing Suitable: reheat in 300°F (150°C) Gas 2 oven for 30 minutes

To serve 6–8

1¼ pints	Milk	700 ml
	Salt	
4	Strips of lemon rind	4
5 oz	Round grain rice	150 g
1½ lb	Apples	700 g
2	Bananas	2
1 oz	Butter	25 g
4 oz	Caster sugar	125 g
1 teasp	Ground cinnamon	5 ml
4 oz	Bottle of sweet cherries	125 g
2 oz	Shelled walnuts	50 g
3	Eggs	3

Preheat oven to 350°F (180°C) Gas 4.

Put the milk, pinch of salt and strips of lemon rind into a saucepan and bring to the boil. Add the rice. Cover and cook for 40 minutes on a low heat, stirring occasionally.

Meanwhile, peel and slice the apples and bananas. Melt the butter and 2 oz (50 g) of the sugar in a saucepan until golden brown. Add the apples and cook for 5 minutes, then add the bananas and cook for 2–3 minutes more. Sprinkle on the cinnamon, then stir in drained cherries and chopped walnuts.

Remove from heat, put mixture into a greased ovenproof dish and smooth over. Work quickly to prevent caramel setting.

Separate the eggs. Cream together the yolks and 1 oz (25 g) sugar in one bowl. In another, beat the whites and remaining sugar together until mixture is very stiff. Fold both mixtures into the cooked rice (take out the lemon peel first) then pour over the fruit. Bake for 30 minutes. Serve hot with cream.

Jam omelettes

Overall timing 10 minutes

Freezing Not suitable

To serve 2

3	Eggs	3
	Pinch of salt	
1 oz	Butter	25 g
3 tbsp	Jam	3x15 ml
1 tbsp	Caster sugar	15 ml

Beat eggs with salt in a bowl. Melt half butter in omelette pan. Add half the egg mixture and cook until set. Slip omelette out of pan on to plate, cooked side down.

Repeat with remaining egg mixture to make another omelette. Spoon jam into the middle of each omelette. Roll them up like pancakes and sprinkle with caster sugar.

To make the caramelized stripes, heat a skewer or toasting fork over a naked flame, then press lightly on top of the omelettes at intervals. Serve at once.

Nutty apple pudding

Overall timing 50 minutes

Freezing Not suitable

To serve 4–6

1½ lb	Cooking apples	700 g
¼ pint	Water	150 ml
2 oz	Flaked almonds	50 g
2 oz	Sultanas	50 g
7 oz	Wholemeal bread	200 g
4 oz	Demerara sugar	125 g
2 oz	Butter	50 g

Preheat the oven to 425°F (220°C) Gas 7.

Peel and core apples and slice into a saucepan. Add water, almonds and sultanas. Cover and cook over a gentle heat for 10 minutes. Remove from heat.

Crumble the bread into a bowl and mix in half the sugar. Grease an ovenproof dish with some of the butter and spread half the bread mixture over the bottom. Cover with apple mixture, then top with remaining bread. Sprinkle on rest of sugar and dot with remaining butter. Bake for about 20 minutes.

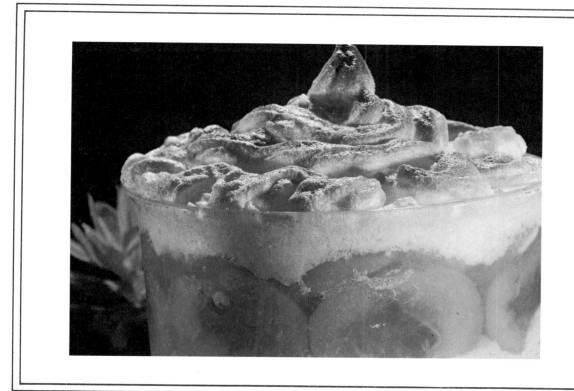

Peach meringue pudding

Overall timing 50 minutes

Freezing Not suitable

To serve 6

1 pint	Milk	560 ml
4 tbsp	Semolina	4x15 ml
2	Eggs	2
3 oz	Caster sugar	75 g
4	Ripe peaches	4
3 tbsp	Peach or raspberry jam	3x15 ml
1 oz	Toasted flaked almonds	25 g

Preheat the oven to 350°F (180°C) Gas 4.

Heat the milk in a saucepan and sprinkle in the semolina, stirring constantly. Bring to the boil and cook, stirring, for 3 minutes till thickened. Remove from the heat.

Separate the eggs. Beat the yolks into the semolina with 1 oz (25 g) of the sugar. Pour mixture into a 7 inch (18 cm) soufflé dish and smooth surface.

Peel and halve the peaches. Remove stones. Place a little jam in each peach half. Arrange in soufflé dish, some with the cut sides pressing against the sides of the dish and the rest jam-side down on the semolina.

Whisk the egg whites till stiff, then whisk in half the remaining sugar. Fold in the finely chopped almonds and the rest of the sugar. Pipe or spoon the meringue over the peaches.

Bake for 20 minutes till the meringue is lightly browned. Serve hot or leave to cool completely and chill before serving.

Pear brown betty

Overall timing 1 hour

Freezing Not suitable

To serve 6–8

2 lb	Ripe pears	900 g
8 oz	Stale breadcrumbs	225 g
4 oz	Caster sugar	125 g
2 oz	Butter	50 g

Preheat the oven to 375°F (190°C) Gas 5.

Peel and halve the pears. Remove the cores and cut flesh into ¼ inch (6 mm) slices.

Cover the bottom of a greased 8 inch (20 cm) springform tin with a quarter of the breadcrumbs. Arrange one-third of the pears on top and sprinkle with a little sugar. Repeat the layers till all the ingredients have been used.

Dot with the butter and bake for about 45 minutes till the pears are tender and the top is crisp and golden. Remove from the tin and serve hot or cold with pouring cream or custard.

Pear dumplings

Overall timing 1¼ hours plus chilling

Freezing Not suitable

To serve 4

12 oz	Plain flour	350 g
¼ teasp	Salt	1.25 ml
6 oz	Butter	175 g
	Grated rind of 1 orange	
2 tbsp	Caster sugar	2x15 ml
1	Egg yolk	1
Filling		
4	Ripe pears	4
2 oz	Butter	50 g
2 tbsp	Soft brown sugar	2x15 ml
½ teasp	Ground cinnamon	2.5 ml

Sift flour and salt into a bowl and rub in butter. Stir in the grated orange rind and caster sugar and add enough water to bind to a dough. Knead till smooth. Chill for 30 minutes.

Preheat the oven to 400°F (200°C) Gas 6.

Roll out dough and cut into four 8 inch (20 cm) squares.

Peel and halve pears and remove cores. Cream butter with soft brown sugar and cinnamon till pale and fluffy. Use to fill centres of pears. Press halves together and place one on each dough square.

Brush edges of dough squares with water. Bring the four corners of each square together at top of pears, sealing edges well. Roll out dough trimmings and cut into leaves. Lightly beat egg yolk with 1 tbsp (15 ml) water and brush over dough. Dip leaves in egg and press in place on top.

Place on a greased baking tray and bake for about 30 minutes ti¹¹ crisp and golden. Serve hot with whipped cream or vanilla ice cream.

Pineapple fritters

Overall timing 25 minutes

Freezing Not suitable

To serve 6

15½ oz	Can of pineapple rings	439 g
4 oz	Plain flour	125 g
1½ teasp	Caster sugar	7.5 ml
1	Whole egg	1
1 tbsp	Oil	15 ml
4 fl oz	Milk or water	120 ml
2	Egg whites	2
	Oil for frying	
3 tbsp	Icing sugar	3x15 ml

Drain the pineapple rings and dry on kitchen paper.

Sift flour and sugar into bowl. Beat in egg, oil and liquid till smooth. Whisk egg whites till stiff and fold into batter.

Heat oil in a deep-fryer to 340°F (170°C). Spear the pineapple rings on a fork, dip into the batter and carefully lower into the oil. Fry three at a time for 2–3 minutes till crisp and golden. Remove from the pan, drain on kitchen paper and keep hot while remaining fritters are cooked.

Arrange on a warmed serving plate, sift the icing sugar over and serve immediately with whipped cream.

French toast

Overall timing 25 minutes

Freezing Not suitable

To serve 4–6

10	Thin slices of bread	10
½–¾ pint	Milk	300–400 ml
2–3	Eggs	2–3
2 oz	Butter	50 g
2 oz	Caster sugar	50 g
1 teasp	Ground cinnamon (optional)	5 ml

Place bread on a baking tray or Swiss roll tin and pour over the milk. The more stale the bread, the more milk you will need to make the bread spongy. Soak for 10 minutes.

Whisk the eggs in a shallow dish till creamy. Lightly press bread with a fork to remove excess milk.

Melt butter in frying pan (reserve some if you cannot cook all slices at once). Dip bread in egg to coat, add to pan and fry for 3–4 minutes on each side. Sprinkle with caster sugar and cinnamon, if used, and serve immediately, with jam or golden or maple syrup.

Apple strudel

Overall timing 1¾ hours

Freezing Not suitable

To serve 8

10 oz	Strong plain flour	275 g
1	Large egg	1
4 oz	Butter	125 g
	Pinch of salt	
2½ lb	Bramley apples	1.1 kg
3 oz	Caster sugar	75 g
2 teasp	Ground cinnamon	2x5 ml
4 oz	Seedless raisins	125 g
1 tbsp	Grated lemon rind	15 ml
4 oz	Ground almonds	125 g
2 oz	Fresh breadcrumbs	50 g

Sift flour on to a work surface. Add egg. Melt half butter in a pan, then add 3 tbsp (3x15 ml) water and salt. Add mixture to flour and mix to a soft, sticky dough. Knead till smooth.

Leave in a warm place for 20 minutes.

Meanwhile, peel and core apples, then slice half very thinly. Coarsely grate rest into a bowl and mix in sugar, cinnamon, raisins, lemon rind, almonds and half breadcrumbs.

Place a large patterned tea-towel on a flat surface and sprinkle it with flour. Roll out dough on top till it is same shape as towel. Slide your hands between dough and tea-towel. Lift and stretch dough till thin enough to see pattern of tea-towel through. The rectangle should eventually measure about 20x16 inches (50x40 cm).

Preheat the oven to 400°F (200°C) Gas 6.

Brush dough with half remaining melted butter. Sprinkle with remaining breadcrumbs, leaving a 1 inch (2.5 cm) border all round. Spread almond mixture evenly over dough. Arrange apple slices on top. Fold border over filling, then roll up. Place on greased baking tray, curving to fit.

Brush with remaining butter and bake for 10 minutes. Reduce heat to 375°F (190°C) Gas 5 and bake for a further 30 minutes. Sprinkle with icing sugar and serve warm.

Banana pudding with rum sauce

Overall timing 1¼ hours

Freezing Suitable: reheat in 350°F (180°C) Gas 4 oven

To serve 6

2 lb	Bananas	900 g
3½ oz	Caster sugar	100 g
2 oz	Softened butter	50 g
2 oz	Plain flour	50 g
	Grated nutmeg	
2	Eggs	2
2 tbsp	Icing sugar	2x15 ml
1 tbsp	Rum or rum flavouring	15 ml
¼ pint	Carton of single cream	150 ml

Preheat the oven to 350°F (180°C) Gas 4.

Reserve half a large or 1 medium-sized banana for decoration. Peel the rest. Mash them with a fork in a bowl with sugar, butter, flour and a pinch of nutmeg.

Separate the eggs. Add yolks to banana mixture and beat well with a wooden spoon until smooth and creamy. Beat the egg whites till very stiff, then gently fold into the banana mixture.

Lightly grease and flour a pudding basin. Fill with the banana mixture and bake for 1 hour.

Remove from oven. Leave to cool slightly then turn out on to a warmed serving plate. Sprinkle with icing sugar and decorate with the reserved banana, sliced. Mix rum or rum flavouring into single cream and serve separately.

Irish lemon pudding

Overall timing 1 hour

Freezing Not suitable

To serve 4–6

4 oz	Butter	125 g
6 oz	Caster sugar	175 g
4	Eggs	4
1	Lemon	1
3 tbsp	Plain flour	3x15 ml
½ pint	Milk	300 ml
1 tbsp	Icing sugar	15 ml

Preheat the oven to 400°F (200°C) Gas 6.

Cream the butter and caster sugar in a bowl till light and fluffy. Separate the eggs and add the yolks to the creamed mixture. Beat well. Grate rind from lemon and squeeze out juice. Beat into the creamed mixture. Gradually stir in the flour, then the milk.

Beat egg whites till stiff, then carefully fold into mixture. Turn into a greased 7 inch (18 cm) soufflé dish and sift icing sugar over. Place dish in roasting tin containing 1 inch (2.5 cm) hot water. Bake for 40–50 minutes till the pudding has risen and the top is golden. Serve hot or cold.

Blackberry and pear meringue

Overall timing 50 minutes

Freezing Not suitable

To serve 6–8

12 oz	Ripe blackberries	350 g
2 oz	Caster sugar	50 g
3 tbsp	Ground almonds	3 x 15 ml
4	Large ripe pears	4
3	Egg whites	3
7 oz	Icing sugar	200 g

Preheat the oven to 350°F (180°C) Gas 4.

Hull the berries and arrange over the bottom of a shallow ovenproof dish. Mix the caster sugar and 2 tbsp (2x15 ml) of the almonds together and sprinkle over the berries.

Peel and halve the pears lengthways. Remove the cores. Arrange cut sides down in a single layer on the berries. Bake on the centre shelf of the oven for 20 minutes.

Put the egg whites and sifted icing sugar into a large heatproof bowl over a pan of simmering water. Whisk till the meringue is stiff and glossy. Spoon or pipe the meringue over the pears and sprinkle with the reserved almonds.

Return to the oven and bake for a further 10 minutes till lightly browned. Serve immediately.

Walnut pear pie

Overall timing 1 hour plus chilling

Freezing Suitable: decorate with cream after thawing

To serve 6–8

6 oz	Plain flour	175 g
4 oz	Butter	125 g
2 oz	Caster sugar	50 g
2 oz	Walnuts	50 g
2 teasp	Ground cinnamon	2x5 ml
1	Egg	1
Filling		
4	Ripe dessert pears	4
1½ oz	Caster sugar	40 g
¼ pint	Whipping cream	150 ml

Sift flour into a large bowl and rub in butter. Stir in sugar, finely chopped walnuts and cinnamon. Add egg with enough water to bind to a firm dough. Chill for 1 hour.

Preheat the oven to 375°F (190°C) Gas 5.

Roll out two-thirds of dough and use to line an 8 inch (20 cm) fluted flan dish. Peel, core and quarter pears. Arrange over pastry in a circle, core-side downwards and with the stem ends pointing towards the centre but not joining up. Sprinkle with 1 oz (25 g) caster sugar.

Roll out remaining dough and place over pears. Trim edges and pinch together to seal. Using a 3 inch (7.5 cm) pastry cutter, cut a circle out of the centre of the pastry lid. Brush pastry with egg white (from egg shell) and dredge with remaining caster sugar. Bake for 15 minutes, then reduce oven temperature to 350°F (180°C) Gas 4 and bake for a further 25 minutes. Cool in tin.

Whip cream and spoon or pipe into centre of pie before serving.

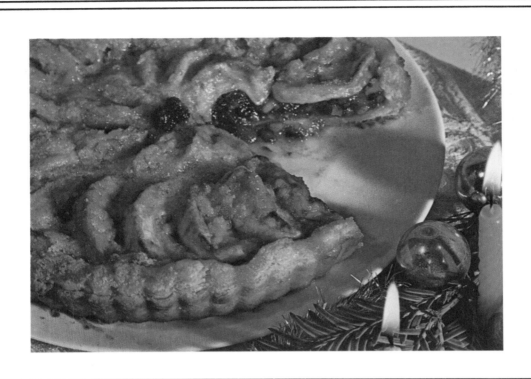

Apple and mincemeat tart

Overall timing 1 hour

Freezing Suitable: reheat in 350°F (180°C) Gas 4 oven for 40 minutes

To serve 6

8 oz	Shortcrust pastry	225 g
14½ oz	Jar of mincemeat	411 g
1 lb	Bramley apples	450 g
3 oz	Caster sugar	75 g
½ teasp	Ground allspice	2.5 ml
2 oz	Butter	50 g
1 tbsp	Plain flour	15 ml

Preheat the oven to 425°F (220°C) Gas 7. Roll out the dough and line a 9½ inch (24 cm) fluted loose-bottomed flan tin. Spread mincemeat evenly over pastry.

Peel, core and finely slice the apples. Mix with 2 oz (50 g) of sugar and the allspice. Arrange in circles on mincemeat.

In a bowl, cut and fold the butter with remaining 1 oz (25 g) sugar and flour until the mixture resembles fine breadcrumbs. Sprinkle evenly over the apples. Place flan on a baking tray.

Bake in oven for 15 minutes, then reduce to 375°F (190°C) Gas 5 and bake for a further 30 minutes. Remove from oven and allow to cool.

Lift tart from flan tin and place on serving plate. Spoon any topping from baking tray on to tart. Serve warm or cold, with whipped cream or vanilla ice cream.

Canadian cherry pie

Overall timing 1¼ hours

Freezing Not suitable

To serve 6

8 oz	Shortcrust pastry	225 g
2 lb	Fresh cherries *or*	900 g
2x15 oz	Cans of cherries	2x425 g
1 oz	Ground rice	25 g
2 oz	Caster sugar	50 g
1	Lemon	1
1	Egg white	1
	Caster sugar	

Preheat the oven to 450°F (230°C) Gas 8.

Roll out two-thirds of dough and use to line 7½ inch (19 cm) fluted loose-bottomed flan tin.

Stone cherries (drain first if canned) and put into saucepan with rice and sugar. Grate rind from lemon and squeeze out juice. Add both to pan and bring to the boil, stirring. Simmer for 2 minutes. Cool.

Spread cherry mixture in pastry case. Roll out remaining dough and lay over filling. Moisten edges and press together to seal. Brush with lightly beaten egg white and dredge with caster sugar.

Bake for 10 minutes, then reduce heat to 350°F (180°C) Gas 4. Bake for a further 40–45 minutes till top is golden.

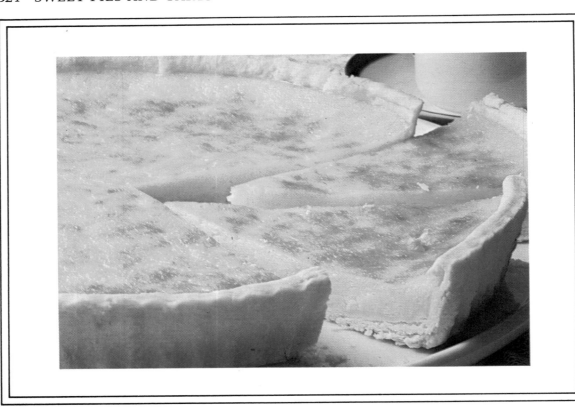

Custard tart

Overall timing 1½ hours plus cooling

Freezing Not suitable

To serve 4–6

8 oz	Plain flour	225 g
2 oz	Lard	50 g
2 oz	Butter	50 g
2–3 tbsp	Water	2–3 x 15 ml
Filling		
1 pint	Milk	560 ml
1	Vanilla pod	1
	Strip of lemon rind	
4	Eggs	4
2 oz	Caster sugar	50 g
	Grated nutmeg	

Preheat the oven to 400°F (200°C) Gas 6.

Put the flour into a bowl and rub in the fat till the mixture resembles fine breadcrumbs. Gradually add the water and mix to a smooth dough.

Roll out the dough on a lightly floured surface and use to line a 9 inch (23 cm) flan tin or ring. Bake blind for 10 minutes. Remove from oven and reduce temperature to 350°F (180°C) Gas 4.

Put milk, vanilla pod and lemon rind into a pan and bring almost to the boil. Remove from heat and leave to infuse for 10 minutes. Remove vanilla pod and lemon rind.

Beat eggs and sugar in bowl. Pour in milk, stirring. Strain into flan case and sprinkle with nutmeg. Bake for 35 minutes or till just set. Cool.

Marmalade and ginger tart

Overall timing 1¼ hours

Freezing Not suitable

To serve 6–8

8 oz	Plain flour	225 g
1 teasp	Ground ginger	5 ml
4 oz	Butter	125 g
2 tbsp	Caster sugar	2x15 ml
1	Egg yolk	1
8 tbsp	Marmalade	8x15 ml

Sift flour and ginger into a bowl. Rub in the butter till the mixture resembles breadcrumbs. Add sugar and mix to a dough with the egg yolk and a little water. Knead lightly till smooth, then chill for 30 minutes.

Preheat the oven to 375°F (190°C) Gas 5.

Roll out about three-quarters of the dough on a floured surface and use to line a 9 inch (23 cm) pie plate or flan tin. Crimp the edges and prick base.

Spread a thick layer of marmalade over the tart base. Roll out the remaining dough and cut into strips with a pastry wheel. Make a lattice over the marmalade filling, pressing the joins to seal. Bake for about 40 minutes, till golden. Remove from tin and serve hot or cold with custard or ice cream.

Nectarine almond tart

Overall timing 50 minutes plus chilling

Freezing Suitable

To serve 4

8 oz	Plain flour	225 g
	Pinch of salt	
4 oz	Butter	125 g
2 oz	Caster sugar	50 g
1	Egg	1
Filling		
1 tbsp	Semolina	15 ml
1 tbsp	Ground almonds	15 ml
4 oz	Caster sugar	125 g
1¾ lb	Nectarines	800 g
½ oz	Split almonds	15 g

Sift the flour and salt into a bowl. Add butter, cut into flakes, sugar and egg and work into a dough. Chill for 30 minutes.

Preheat the oven to 425°F (220°C) Gas 7.

Roll out dough on a floured surface and use to line 9 inch (23 cm) loose-bottomed flan tin. Mix together the semolina, ground almonds and half the caster sugar. Sprinkle over the pastry.

Halve the nectarines and remove the stones. Arrange the fruit in the pastry case, cut sides down, and sprinkle with the remaining sugar and split almonds. Bake for 35–40 minutes.

Allow to cool slightly, then remove from tin and serve warm or cold with pouring cream.

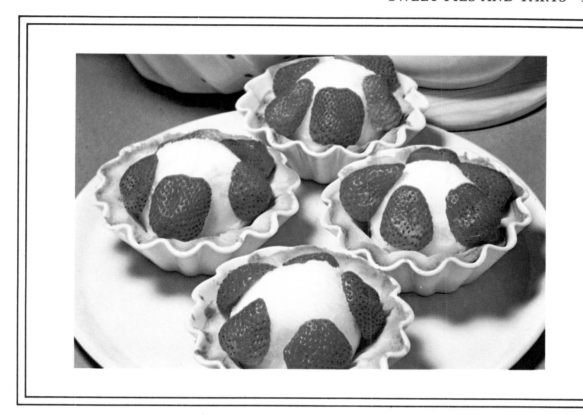

Iced strawberry tartlets

Overall timing 40 minutes

Freezing Not suitable

Makes 4

6 oz	Rich shortcrust pastry	175 g
4 oz	Gooseberry jam	125 g
2 tbsp	Sherry	2x15 ml
12 oz	Strawberries	350 g
1 pint	Vanilla ice cream or lemon sorbet	560 ml

Preheat the oven to 375°F (190°C) Gas 5. Put baking tray in oven to heat.

Divide dough into four. Put one-quarter into each of four 3 inch (7.5 cm) tartlet dishes and press into shape. Prick bottoms with a fork and place on heated baking tray. Bake for about 25 minutes till crisp and golden. Remove from the oven and leave to cool completely.

Meanwhile, put the jam and sherry into a saucepan and heat gently till melted. Sieve into a sauceboat and leave to cool.

Hull the strawberries. Cut a quarter of them in half lengthways and put the rest into a serving dish.

Arrange the tartlets on a serving dish. Put a scoop of ice cream or sorbet into each and decorate with halved strawberries. Serve immediately with remaining strawberries and gooseberry sauce.

Lime tart

Overall timing 50 minutes plus chilling

Freezing Suitable

To serve 8

6 oz	Shortcrust pastry	175 g
4 teasp	Powdered gelatine	4x5 ml
4 tbsp	Water	4x15 ml
4	Eggs	4
4 oz	Caster sugar	125 g
3	Limes	3
¼ pint	Carton of double cream	150 ml

Preheat the oven to 400°F (200°C) Gas 6.

Roll out dough on a lightly floured surface and use to line an 8 inch (20 cm) flan tin. Bake blind for 10 minutes, then remove beans and foil and bake for a further 10 minutes till golden. Allow to cool, then carefully remove from the tin.

To make the filling, dissolve the gelatine in the water. Separate eggs. Whisk the yolks and sugar together till pale and creamy. Grate rind from limes and squeeze out the juice. Stir two-thirds of the rind and all the juice into the egg mixture. Stir in the gelatine.

Whip cream till stiff. In another bowl, whisk the egg whites till stiff peaks form. Carefully fold cream, then whisked whites into lime mixture. Spoon into pastry case and fluff up the surface.

Sprinkle with the remaining grated lime rind and chill for at least 3 hours or overnight before serving.

French cherry tart

Overall timing 1 hour plus chilling

Freezing Not suitable

To serve 8

8 oz	Plain flour	225 g
	Pinch of salt	
3½ oz	Icing sugar	100 g
4 oz	Butter	125 g
1	Lemon	1
1	Egg	1
Filling		
4 teasp	Dried breadcrumbs	4x5 ml
13½ oz	Jar of cherry pie filling	382 g
3	Eggs	3
3 oz	Caster sugar	75 g
1 tbsp	Cornflour	15 ml
	Ground cinnamon	
1 oz	Cream cheese	25 g

Put the flour, salt and icing sugar into a bowl. Rub in butter. Grate rind and squeeze juice from lemon. Add rind to bowl with egg and mix to a dough. Chill for 30 minutes.

Preheat the oven to 425°F (220°C) Gas 7.

Roll out dough and use to line 10 inch (25 cm) flan ring placed on baking tray. Bake blind for about 15 minutes.

Remove flan case from oven and reduce heat to 375°F (190°C) Gas 5. Sprinkle breadcrumbs over bottom of flan case. Spread cherry pie filling on top.

Separate eggs. Whisk egg yolks with 2 tbsp (2x15 ml) lemon juice, the caster sugar and cornflour until creamy. Beat in cinnamon and cream cheese until smooth.

Beat egg whites until soft peaks form. Fold into yolk mixture. Pour over cherries. Bake for 30–40 minutes. Carefully remove tart from ring and place on a serving dish. Dredge with more icing sugar and serve warm with cream or ice cream.

Linzertorte

Overall timing 50 minutes

Freezing Suitable

To serve 12

8 oz	Plain flour	225 g
½ teasp	Ground cinnamon	2.5 ml
5 oz	Butter	150 g
3 oz	Ground almonds	75 g
3 oz	Caster sugar	75 g
½	Lemon	½
2	Egg yolks	2
8 oz	Raspberry jam	225 g

Sift flour and cinnamon into a large bowl. Rub in butter. Stir in almonds and caster sugar. Grate rind from lemon and squeeze out juice. Add both to bowl with egg yolks and mix to a soft dough. Knead lightly, then chill for 1 hour.

Preheat the oven to 375°F (190°C) Gas 5.

Roll out two-thirds of the dough on a floured surface and use to line an 8 inch (20 cm) flan tin. Don't trim away excess dough.

Spread jam over the pastry case. Roll out remaining dough and cut into strips. Arrange in a lattice pattern across the jam. Fold dough edges in, crimping to make a decorative border.

Bake for 30–35 minutes. Leave to cool in tin. Serve with pouring cream.

Plum tart

Overall timing 1¾ hours

Freezing Not suitable

To serve 6–8

12 oz	Self-raising flour	350 g
8 oz	Butter	225 g
3 tbsp	Caster sugar	3×15 ml
1	Egg	1
3–4 tbsp	Milk to mix	3–4x 15 ml
Filling		
1 pint	Milk	560 ml
1 teasp	Vanilla essence	5 ml
1½ lb	Ripe yellow plums	700 g
4	Egg yolks	4
6 oz	Caster sugar	175 g
3 oz	Plain flour	75 g

To make filling, put milk and vanilla essence into saucepan and bring to the boil. Remove from heat, cover and leave to infuse for 10 minutes.

Meanwhile halve and stone plums. Beat egg yolks with sugar till pale and thick. Beat in sifted flour, then gradually stir in milk. Pour back into saucepan and cook gently, stirring, till thick. Leave to cool.

Preheat the oven to 400°F (200°C) Gas 6.

Sift flour into a bowl and rub in 6 oz (175 g) butter. Stir in sugar, and add egg and enough milk to give a soft dough. Roll out and use to line greased 8 inch (20 cm) square deep cake tin, moulding it into the corners. Rest in refrigerator for 15 minutes.

Pour filling into pastry-lined tin and arrange plums on top, pressing them in lightly. Bake for 30 minutes.

Meanwhile, melt remaining butter in a saucepan. Remove tart from tin and place on a baking tray. Brush sides and top edge of pastry with butter and bake for a further 10 minutes till pastry is crisp and golden. Serve hot or cold.

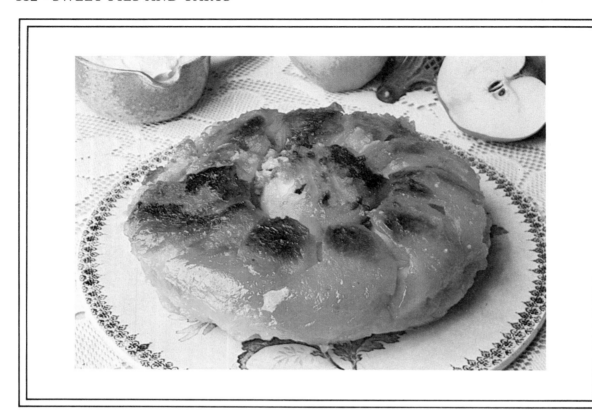

Tarte Tatin

Overall timing 1¼ hours

Freezing Not suitable

To serve 8–10

7 oz	Frozen puff pastry	212 g
3 oz	Unsalted butter	75 g
3 oz	Caster sugar	75 g
7	Large dessert apples	7

Thaw the pastry. Preheat the oven to 425°F (220°C) Gas 7.

Cut the butter into pieces and put into a 9 inch (23 cm) round cake tin with the sugar. Peel and core the apples; cut six of them in half. Arrange the apple halves on end around the side of the tin and place the whole apple in the centre.

Place the tin over a low heat and heat till the butter melts. Increase the heat and cook, shaking the tin occasionally, till the sugar caramelizes and is golden. Remove from the heat. Brush a little water round the edge of the tin.

Roll out the dough on a floured surface to a 9 inch (23 cm) round and place over the apples. Press down lightly.

Bake for 25–30 minutes till the pastry is well risen and golden brown. Leave to cool in the tin for 5 minutes.

Run a knife round the edge of the tart and turn out on to a serving dish so that the caramelized apples are on top. Serve hot or cold with whipped cream or scoops of vanilla ice cream.

Brioche

Overall timing 1¼ hours plus proving

Freezing Suitable: shape dough and bake after thawing

Makes 1 large or 12 small

2 teasp	Caster sugar	2x5 ml
2 tbsp	Lukewarm water	2x15 ml
2 teasp	Dried yeast	2x5 ml
8 oz	Strong plain flour	225 g
	Salt	
2 oz	Butter	50 g
2	Eggs	2
	Milk for glazing	

Dissolve ½ teasp (2.5 ml) sugar in water and sprinkle yeast on top. Leave till frothy.

Sift flour, a pinch of salt and remaining sugar into a large bowl. Add yeast mixture, melted butter and eggs and mix to a soft dough. Knead till smooth and glossy. Leave to rise in a warm place till doubled in size.

Knock back dough and knead for 3–4 minutes till smooth. To make one large brioche, cut off one-quarter of the dough and shape both pieces into balls. Place large one in lightly greased 8 inch (20 cm) brioche tin and push a finger down through centre to base. Place smaller ball in indentation and press down lightly.

To make 12 small brioches, divide dough into 12 pieces and remove one-quarter from each. Shape all pieces into balls. Place each large ball in a 3 inch (7.5 cm) brioche tin, push a finger down through centre, then top with small balls, pressing down lightly. Leave to rise till doubled in size.

Preheat the oven to 450°F (230°C) Gas 8. Brush each brioche with milk and bake for 8–10 minutes (small) or 15–20 minutes (large) till well risen and golden. Serve warm.

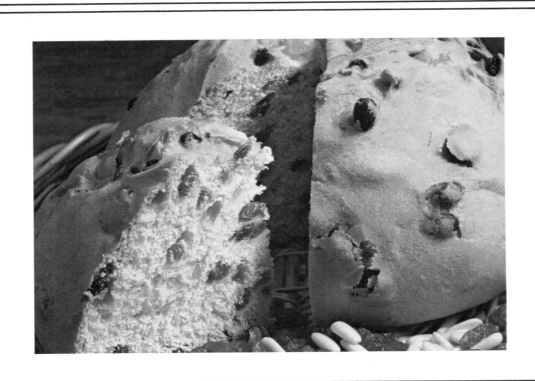

Italian fruit bread

Overall timing 1½ hours plus proving

Freezing Suitable: reheat in 350°F (180°C) Gas 4 oven for 10 minutes

To serve 5

12 oz	Strong plain flour	350 g
4 teasp	Dried yeast	4x5 ml
2 oz	Caster sugar	50 g
¼ pint	Lukewarm milk	150 ml
¼ teasp	Salt	1.25 ml
2 oz	Pine nuts	50 g
2 oz	Candied peel	50 g
2 oz	Seedless raisins	50 g
2 oz	Butter	50 g
1	Egg	1
1 tbsp	Marsala	15 ml

Mix together 4 oz (125 g) flour, the yeast, 1 teasp (5 ml) sugar and the milk to a smooth batter. Leave till frothy.

Sift remaining flour and the salt into a large bowl. Add remaining sugar, the pine nuts, candied peel and raisins. Stir melted butter, beaten egg and Marsala into frothy batter, then add to fruit mixture. Mix to a soft dough. Turn out on to a lightly floured surface and knead till smooth and glossy. Cover with oiled polythene and leave to rise till doubled in size.

Knock back dough and knead till smooth. Shape into a smooth ball and place on greased baking tray. Leave to prove till doubled in size.

Preheat the oven to 400°F (200°C) Gas 6. Score a cross on top of the ball and bake for 10 minutes. Reduce the heat to 350°F (180°C) Gas 4 and bake for a further 25 minutes. Cool on a wire rack.

Caraway seed bread

Overall timing 1½ hours plus proving

Freezing Suitable: refresh in hot oven for 10 minutes

Makes 2 small or 1 large loaf

1 lb	Strong plain flour	450 g
1½ oz	Caster sugar	40 g
2 teasp	Dried yeast	2x5 ml
5 tbsp	Lukewarm water	5x15 ml
4 fl oz	Lukewarm milk	120 ml
1 teasp	Salt	5 ml
2 tbsp	Caraway seeds	2x15 ml
4 oz	Softened butter	125 g
2	Eggs	2
1 tbsp	Milk	15 ml

Mix together 4 oz (125 g) flour, 1 teasp (5 ml) sugar, the yeast, water and milk in a large bowl. Cover and leave in a warm place for about 20 minutes till frothy.

Mix remaining flour with salt, remaining sugar and caraway seeds. Add to yeast mixture with butter and beaten eggs. Mix well to a soft dough. Turn on to a lightly floured surface and knead till smooth and elastic. Cover and leave to rise until doubled in size.

Turn dough on to a lightly floured surface and knead till dough is firm again. Shape into two rolls about 6 inches (15 cm) long. Place on greased and floured baking tray. Make three cuts across top of each loaf. Brush with milk. Cover with polythene bag and leave to rise until loaves double in size.

Preheat the oven to 400°F (200°C) Gas 6. Bake the loaves for 30–35 minutes. Cool on a wire rack.

Milk buns

Overall timing About 3 hours

Freezing Suitable

Makes about 15

2 teasp	Dried yeast	2x5 ml
¼ pint	Lukewarm milk	150 ml
9 oz	Plain flour	250 g
4 teasp	Caster sugar	4x5 ml
½ teasp	Salt	2.5 ml
3½ oz	Butter	100 g

Mix yeast, all but 2 tbsp (2x15 ml) milk, 2 oz (50 g) flour and 3 teasp (3x5 ml) sugar to make a batter. Leave till frothy.

Add rest of flour and salt to batter. Mix by hand to soft dough that leaves bowl clean. Knead till smooth and no longer sticky. Leave to rise for 1 hour in warm place.

Cut butter into small pieces. Make a hollow in dough and drop in a few pieces of butter. Knead or squeeze into dough. Continue adding butter in this way till dough becomes silky and smooth. Divide into egg-size pieces and shape into rolls. Place on greased baking tray. Lightly mark a cross on each. Leave to rise till doubled in size.

Preheat the oven to 375°F (190°C) Gas 5.

Heat remaining milk and sugar and brush over rolls. Bake for 30 minutes till golden brown. Cool on wire rack.

Fruit and nut bread

Overall timing 35 minutes plus rising

Freezing Suitable

Makes 1 loaf

7 fl oz	Lukewarm milk	200 ml
4 teasp	Dried yeast	4x5 ml
2½ oz	Caster sugar	65 g
1 lb	Strong plain flour	450 g
1 teasp	Salt	5 ml
4 oz	Butter	125 g
2 oz	Stoned prunes	50 g
2 oz	Dried figs	50 g
2 oz	Sultanas	50 g
4 oz	Mixed nuts	125 g
1	Egg	1
1 tbsp	Icing sugar	15 ml

Mix ¼ pint (150 ml) milk with yeast and 1 teasp (5 ml) sugar. Leave till frothy.

Sift flour and salt into a large bowl. Add yeast mixture, melted butter, remaining sugar, chopped fruit and nuts and remaining milk. Mix to a soft dough. Leave to rise till doubled in size.

Knead until smooth. Shape into a rectangle and place in 2 lb (900 g) loaf tin. Leave to prove until doubled in size.

Preheat the oven to 425°F (225°C) Gas 7. Brush top of loaf with lightly beaten egg and bake for 15 minutes. Cover top with grease-proof paper and reduce heat to 400°F (200°C) Gas 6. Bake for further 20–30 minutes. Dredge with icing sugar and serve warm.

Sesame bread

Overall timing 2 hours plus proving

Freezing Suitable

Makes 2 loaves

6	Saffron strands	6
¼ pint	Lukewarm milk	150 ml
4 fl oz	Lukewarm water	120 ml
1 tbsp	Dried yeast	15 ml
4 teasp	Caster sugar	4x5 ml
1 lb	Strong plain flour	450 g
2 oz	Butter	50 g
2	Eggs	2
½ teasp	Salt	2.5 ml
2 tbsp	Sesame seeds	2x15 ml

Mix together saffron, all but 2 tbsp (2x15 ml) milk, the water, yeast, 1 teasp (5 ml) sugar and 2 tbsp (2x15 ml) flour. Leave in a warm place till frothy.

Melt butter and cool, then beat into batter with one egg and the remaining milk and sugar. Sift remaining flour and the salt over batter and mix to a soft dough. Knead till smooth. Leave to rise till doubled in size.

Knock back the dough. Knead till smooth and divide into six pieces. Roll into sausages about 9 inches (23 cm) long. Moisten ends of sausages with beaten egg. Plait three together, pinching together at both ends to seal. Repeat with remaining three sausages and arrange on greased baking tray. Leave to rise till doubled in size.

Preheat the oven to 375°F (190°C) Gas 5. Brush plaits carefully with beaten egg, then sprinkle with sesame seeds. Bake for about 35 minutes. Cool on wire rack.

Quick cottage loaf

Overall timing 1½ hours

Freezing Suitable

Makes 1 loaf

1 oz	Fresh yeast	25 g
12 fl oz	Lukewarm water	350 ml
1 tablet	Vitamin C	25 mg
1¼ lb	Strong plain flour	600 g
2 teasp	Salt	2x5 ml
1 teasp	Sugar	5 ml
½ oz	Lard	15 g

Blend the fresh yeast with the warm water. Crush vitamin tablet and add to the yeast liquid.

Sift the flour, salt and sugar into a bowl and rub in lard. Add the yeast liquid and mix to a dough that leaves the bowl clean. Turn the dough on to a lightly floured surface and knead till smooth and elastic.

To shape dough into a cottage loaf, divide it into two pieces with one about a third bigger than the other. Shape both into rounds and place smaller one on top. Press handle of wooden spoon through centre of both pieces. Place on baking tray and cover with oiled polythene. Leave to rise for 40–50 minutes.

Preheat the oven to 450°F (230°C) Gas 8. Dust loaf with flour and bake for 30–35 minutes.

Soda bread

Overall timing 1 hour

Freezing Suitable: bake after thawing

Makes 1 loaf

1 lb	Strong white or white and wholemeal flour	450 g
1 teasp	Salt	5 ml
2 teasp	Bicarbonate of soda	2x5 ml
4 teasp	Cream of tartar	4x5 ml
1 oz	Fat	25 g
9 fl oz	Milk	250 ml

Preheat the oven to 425°F (220°C) Gas 7.

Sift the flour, salt, soda and cream of tartar into a bowl. Rub in the fat and add enough milk to make a soft dough. Knead for 1 minute, then shape into a ball and place on a greased baking tray. Mark with a cross, cutting almost to the base of the dough.

Bake for 40–50 minutes till well risen, lightly browned and firm underneath.

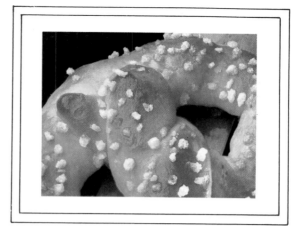

Chelsea buns

Overall timing 1 hour plus proving

Freezing Suitable

Makes 6

1 lb	Strong plain flour	450 g
7 tbsp	Caster sugar	7x15 ml
8 fl oz	Lukewarm milk	225 ml
4 teasp	Dried yeast	4x5 ml
4 oz	Butter	125 g
1	Egg	1
4 oz	Mixed dried fruit	125 g
1 teasp	Mixed spice	5 ml

Mix 4 oz (125 g) flour with 1 teasp (5 ml) sugar, 7 fl oz (200 ml) milk and the yeast to a smooth batter. Leave till frothy.

Sift remaining flour and 4 teasp (4x5 ml) sugar into a bowl and rub in 3 oz (75 g) butter. Add egg and yeast mixture and mix to a soft dough. Knead till smooth and glossy. Leave to rise till doubled in size.

Knock back dough and knead till smooth. Roll out to a 9 inch (23 cm) square. Brush remaining butter, melted, over dough. Mix all but 1 tbsp (15 ml) of remaining sugar with fruit and spice and sprinkle over dough. Roll up, then cut across into six thick slices. Arrange, cut sides up, in greased 9x6 inch (23x15 cm) roasting tin, leaving equal space between. Prove till slices join together.

Preheat oven to 375°F (190°C) Gas 5. Brush buns with remaining milk and sprinkle with remaining sugar. Bake for about 35 minutes till golden. Cool on wire rack.

Pretzels

Overall timing 1 hour plus proving

Freezing Suitable: reheat in 375°F (190°C) Gas 5 oven for 5–10 minutes

Makes about 30

½ teasp	Caster sugar	2.5 ml
7 fl oz	Lukewarm water	200 ml
2 teasp	Dried yeast	2x5 ml
10 oz	Strong plain flour	275 g
1 teasp	Salt	5 ml
1 teasp	Poppy seeds	5 ml
1 oz	Butter	25 g
2	Eggs	2
2 tbsp	Coarse salt	2x15 ml

Dissolve sugar in water and sprinkle yeast on top. Leave in warm place till frothy.

Sift flour and salt into a bowl and stir in poppy seeds, yeast mixture, melted butter and one egg. Mix to soft dough. Leave to rise till doubled in size.

Knead till smooth. Break off small pieces and tie into loose knots, tucking ends in. Arrange pretzels on greased baking trays. Leave to prove till doubled in size.

Preheat the oven to 400°F (200°C) Gas 6. Beat remaining egg and brush over pretzels. Sprinkle with coarse salt and bake for about 10 minutes till crisp and golden. Cool on wire rack.

MICROWAVE COOKING

Fast-food need not be junk food. A quick glance through the following recipes will show you there is more to microwaving than defrosting and reheating. A selection of recipes have been included to help you realize the full potential of your microwave by creating tasty and nutritious meals for the family in a fraction of the conventional time.

How Microwaves Work

Microwaves are a form of high frequency radio waves similar to those used by radio, including AM, FM and CB. They are, however, much shorter than radio waves. A microwave oven plugs into a standard socket and the electricity flows into the oven to a transformer. This boosts the power and takes the electricity to the magnetron tube which converts it into microwaves. The microwaves then go via a wave guide into the oven cavity.

Waveguide

Magnetron

Turntable

Oven Cavity

Microwaves have three properties; firstly they are reflected from metal and the whole of the interior of a microwave is like a metal bowl. Some ovens have a stainless steel finish, others have a plastic coating over the metal. Both, however, do the same job; they reflect the microwave energy just like a ball bouncing off a wall. The microwave energy is reflected in all directions from the top, back front, sides and base.

The second property of microwaves is that they will pass through some materials, such as glass, plastics and paper, just like sunlight passing through a pane of glass. As the substances do not reflect or absorb microwave energy, they make ideal cooking containers.

The third property of microwaves is that they are absorbed by the food. They penetrate the food to a depth of ¾–1½ inches (2–4 cm) all the way round. They cause the water molecules to vibrate at speed – 245,000,000 times per second. This intense vibration causes friction which produces heat in the food and not in the oven cavity. This means that the oven cavity stays cool, so any splashes can be wiped off with a damp soapy cloth – goodbye to the days of scouring the traditional cooker. It also means that as heat is only produced in the food a microwave oven needs no preheating and there is no wasted energy at the end of cooking. This adds up to greater fuel savings.

Using a Microwave

As microwaving is such a safe method of cooking (no hot heavy pans to lift, cool oven walls, and cool handles on cups, dishes and jugs), it is ideal for single people, couples, children, families and the elderly. Meals can be prepared in a fraction of the time; snacks are instant and food no longer stays inaccessibly frozen in the deep-freeze.

Convenience foods and the microwave are made for each other and the busy consumer. There is a huge range of frozen convenience foods, speciality dishes and dinners available that can usually be cooked in their shallow container; just remove the outside wrapper and the lid.

Reflected

Microwaves reflect off metal. Therefore, food will not become heated if contained in metal utensils.

Transmitted

Microwaves pass through paper, glass, china, and plastics; microwaves do not affect these materials at all.

Absorbed

Microwaves are absorbed by the food and are converted to heat energy.

Microwave Cooking Utensils

As microwaves will pass through items that do not contain moisture, it opens up a whole range of substances that can be used in a microwave. Heat-resistant glass is invaluable; many of these items will be readily available in kitchen cupboards; measuring jugs, mixing bowls, basins, covered casserole dishes, round, oblong or square baking dishes and pie plates, and custard dishes. There are numerous shapes and designs made by Pyrex, Corningware by Corning, Fireking by Anchor Hocking and Glassbake by Jeannette glass. Some dinnerware sets can also be used. However, do avoid those with a silver or gold trim as these can cause "arcing" (this is a static discharge of electricity and is seen by sparks inside the oven and a crackling noise will be heard). If arcing occurs, switch off the oven and put the food in a suitable container.

There is a wide range of specialist microwave ware available in all sorts of shapes and sizes. Usually these are plastic dishes, some of which are suitable for a conventional cooker up to about 400°F/200°C/Gas Mark 6. One of the most comprehensive ranges is Nordicware: this is made by Nordic and has a special Silverstone non stick finish.

Most other plastic ware is suitable for microwave use. Look for statements such as "For microwave use only" or "suitable for conventional or microwave cooking" on packaging or in brochures. Waveware products have specially designed dishes suitable for every type of food. Most microwave-safe plastic containers are suitable for any kind of cooking. Some, however, should not be used for cooking foods with a high fat or sugar content; these are usually the semi-disposable, softer, plastic dishes. Do not use plastic food storage containers as these can become distorted from the heat of the food.

Other plastic items such as cooking bags designed to withstand boiling or roasting are ideal in the microwave: follow manufacturer's instructions for use. Microwave-safe cling film can be used to cover most dishes, but should be pierced or a small section folded back to allow the steam to escape. When removing cling film "covers" and glass lids, remove them away from you to avoid steam burns. After cooking, loosen the cling film by piercing, but leave the dish covered for the stand time. For ovens with "autosensor" features, refer to manufacturer's instructions. Usually for these ovens the cling film is unpierced.

Language of Microwaves

All cooking methods have their own terminology and microwaving is no exception. In the following chapters, the recipes will include various phrases, so here to help you is a dictionary of useful terms.

Arranging food Arrange denser or thicker parts of the food towards the outside of the dish, with thinner parts towards centre.

Browning Meats and poultry cooked for 10–15 minutes brown naturally from their own fat. Foods cooked for a shorter time can be aided with special microwave seasonings. Paprika pepper, soy sauce etc., can be sprinkled or "painted" onto the food with a pastry brush. Cakes and teabreads can be made with brown sugar, or the surface of the food can be sprinkled with a topping such as chopped nuts, brown sugar and cinnamon.

Browning skillets or dishes These are special dishes that can be used in the microwave only. They are first preheated empty on HIGH power for 6 minutes and, when the food is placed into them, it is seared. Food will need to be turned after half the recommended cooking times. Do take care to lift the browning dish by its handles; never touch the base as it is extremely hot. Do not place the dish directly onto a work top or cloth-covered surface.

Covering As with conventional methods, moisture evaporates during cooking. Since microwave cooking is done by time and not by direct heat, the rate of evaporation cannot be easily controlled. Unless specified, a recipe is heated uncovered. Foods normally covered are vegetables, fish, meat, casseroles, and covers should be used when reheating. Items such as cakes, gravies, sauces and drinks are heated uncovered.
Casserole lids or cling film can be used for covering. However, cling film must be pierced or a corner should be folded back.

Defrosting Defrosting frozen foods is one of the benefits of owning a microwave oven. The lower power settings will defrost the ice without cooking the food.

Piercing	The skin or membrane on some foods will cause steam to build up during cooking. Foods must be pierced, scored or have a strip of skin peeled off before cooking to allow steam to escape. *Eggs* Pierce yolk twice and the white several times with a toothpick. *Clams and oysters* Pierce several times. *Whole potatoes and vegetables* Pierce with a fork before cooking. *Frankfurters and sausages* Score smoked Polish sausage. Pierce fresh or brown sausages and serve with a fork.
Programme cooking	On some models of microwave you are able to set a selection of cooking commands. These are fed into the memory at the beginning of the cooking sequence.
Reheating	To bring already cooked foods to serving temperature, reheat covered on HIGH or MEDIUM HIGH.
Shielding	Aluminium foil can be used if certain guidelines are followed. As aluminium foil will reflect microwave energy, it can be used to prevent overcooking. Small pieces of foil are used to cover wings on chickens, tips of roasts, or other thin parts that cook before the rest of the dish is cooked. Foil is thus used to slow or stop the cooking process.
Spacing	Individual foods, such as baked potatoes, cup cakes and appetisers, will heat more evenly if placed in the oven at equal distances apart. When possible, arrange food in a circular pattern. Similarly, when placing foods in a baking dish, arrange around the outside of the dish and not lined up against each other. Never stack foods one on top of the other.
Standing times	Most foods will continue to cook by conduction after the microwave is switched off. In meat cookery, a standing time of 15–20 minutes is needed to allow the heat to carry on cooking through to the centre by conduction. Standing time is outside of the oven. Food will not go cold in this time: in fact the temperature of meat will rise 5–15 degrees during this time. Always stand meat wrapped in foil, shiny side in, for its full standing time and do not test for doneness until after the standing time.
Starting Temperature	This is the temperature of the food before cooking begins. The lower the initial temperature, the longer the food will take to cook.
Stirring	Stirring is usually necessary in microwave cooking; the recipes note when stirring is helpful using the words "once", "twice", "frequently" or "occasionally" to describe the amount of stirring necessary. Always bring the outside edges towards the centre and the less cooked centre to the outside.
Turning and rearranging	It is not possible to stir some foods to redistribute the heat. At times, microwave energy will concentrate in an area of food. To help ensure even cooking, some foods need to be turned over or around 90–180 degrees. Uneven shapes, such as chicken pieces, will need rearranging.

Variable power Most microwave ovens have multiple power settings. For foods such as vegetables, fish, sauces and cakes, reheating can be done on HIGH. Meat and poultry benefit from cooking on MEDIUM. LOW power can be used for pot roasts and custards, while SIMMER is ideal for long slow cooking of stews and casseroles. Variable power settings give a microwave the flexibility to cook a whole range of foods, just as a thermostat on a conventional cooker gives different heat settings suitable for various foods.

Increasing and Decreasing Recipe Servings

The recipes in the following pages all give an indication of serving numbers. However, your microwave can easily cope with cooking smaller or larger quantities of food. Follow the basic guidelines which are based on three principles:
1   The weight of the food
2   The density of the food
3   The initial temperature of the food.
  If you decrease the recipe quantities, you therefore decrease the cooking time and, likewise, if you increase the quantities, you should also allow extra time. Remember, it is always better to undercook as you can always add extra time; you can never take time away and it is very difficult to rectify overcooked results.

Decreasing a recipe
1   For one serving, divide all ingredients by the total number of servings. For two servings, halve quantities or divide all the quantities by two.
2   Choose a dish that is proportionally smaller to the one recommended in the recipe, but do make sure it is deep enough to prevent foods from boiling over. Foods cooked in a larger, flatter dish cook faster than those cooked in a smaller, deeper dish.
3   Use the cooking power recommended in the original recipe. For one serving, allow one-quarter to half the original time given. For two portions, allow half to two-thirds the time. Start checking the results after the minimum time. You can open the door at any time as the oven will automatically switch off.
4   Always follow the directions in the recipe for covering, stirring or rearranging. If a recipe states stir frequently, two stirrings will be enough.
5   Always let food stand at the end of cooking. Meat and poultry need a minimum of 5 minutes per pound (450 g), although a small piece is best left for 10 minutes.
  Foods with a high fat or sugar content tend to cook quickly as do delicate items such as eggs, cheese and fish dishes. It is always best to check these items after the minimum expected cooking time.

Increasing recipe quantities
1   To increase a recipe from four to six servings, increase each ingredient by half. To double the number of servings, simply double the quantities of every listed ingredient.
2   Remember that the larger quantities will need a larger cooking dish, both in depth and width.
3   Cover as directed in the recipe. Stir and rearrange as recommended.
4   Increase stand times. Allow 5 minutes per pound (450 g) for meat and poultry.
5   Check the recipe during cooking. When adding half the amounts again, allow one-third extra cooking time; when doubling the quantities, add half the original time again.

6   When cooking pieces of meat and whole poultry, always work the time out based on minutes per pound (450 g).

All the timings given are based on a 600 watt oven. For 700 watt ovens, decrease the timings by 20 seconds per minute. For 500 watt ovens, increase the timings by 15 seconds per minute. Always check the food before the recommended cooking time.

Preparing Soups in the Microwave

Canned soups Empty the contents of the can into a casserole dish. Dilute according to label directions with water or milk. Cover the dish with a lid or cling film and heat. A 10½ oz (310 g) can of condensed soup diluted with milk should be heated on MEDIUM for 4–6 minutes; those diluted with water can be heated on HIGH for 3–5 minutes. Stir twice during heating.

Dry packet soups Select a casserole that contains twice the volume of the water recommended on the soup packet. Add boiling water to the dish and stir in the soup mix. Cover the dish with a lid and heat on MEDIUM for 3–4 minutes for soups with narrow noodles, or 7–8 minutes for soups with broad noodles. Stir the soup once during heating and let stand for 5 minutes before serving.

To defrost frozen soups

Remove from original wrapping and place in a large casserole dish. Heat on HIGH for 10 minutes, stirring frequently to break up the ice. When defrosted, cover the dish with cling film and reheat on HIGH for 5–8 minutes, stirring once.

Cooking Eggs in the Microwave

As eggs cook very quickly in the microwave, care is needed to achieve the best results. Most types of egg dishes can be cooked. However, eggs should not be cooked in their shells: they will explode, cause injury and damage the oven.

If a recipe calls for a chopped or sieved egg for garnish, or if you are making sandwich fillings, eggs can be easily and quickly hard-cooked in the microwave. Grease a 6 ounce (175 g) ramekin for each egg. Break the egg into the ramekin and pierce the egg white and egg yolk several times with a toothpick. Cover with cling film and cook on MEDIUM power. One egg will take 1–1½ minutes: 2 eggs will take 2–2½ minutes. After cooking, let the egg stand before slicing, chopping or sieving.

Many recipes call for eggs to be added whole towards the end of cooking so they can be baked. To do this, make a dip in the mixture so the egg can sit in it. Break the egg into the dish. Using a toothpick, pierce the egg yolk twice and the white several times. Top with 1 tsp (1x5 ml) of milk. If possible, cover with cling film. Cook on MEDIUM allowing 1 minute for 1 egg, 1½ minutes for 2 eggs, 2½ minutes for 4 eggs and leave to stand for 3 minutes at the end of cooking. The eggs will look slightly underdone at the end of cooking, but they will continue to cook during the stand time.

Cooking Fish in the Microwave

Fish is one food that benefits greatly from being cooked in the microwave. The moist method of cooking ensures flaky, moist and flavoursome results every time, without cooking smells wafting around the house. For best results, always weigh fish and allow 5 minutes per pound (450 g) for white fish such as cod, halibut, haddock, etc. For whole fish, also allow 5 minutes per pound (450 g). Delicate fish fillets, such as plaice or sole, need only 4 minutes per pound (450 g). Fold or roll fillets to protect the thinner ends; small pieces of foil can also be used to shield thin areas. For the simplest cooking method, sprinkle fish with lemon juice, cover with cling film and cook on HIGH for the calculated time. Stand for 5 minutes before serving.

Shellfish cook well in the microwave, their shells acting as the cooking container. Allow 4 minutes per pound (450 g) for prawns. Mussels should be cooked in wine or bouillon; 4 pounds (2 kg) of mussels will take 15 minutes on HIGH. Shake or stir every 5 minutes and remove cooked open mussels. Any that have not opened after the 15 minutes should be discarded.

Provençal cod soup

Overall timing 18–22 minutes

Freezing Not suitable

To Serve 4

1¾ lb	Potatoes	750 g
1	Large onion	1
1	Leek	1
1	Large tomato	1
2 tbsp	Oil	2x15 ml
2	Garlic cloves	2
2½ pints	Hot water	1.4 litres
	Bouquet garni	
	Orange rind	
¼ tsp	Saffron	½x2.5 ml
	Salt and pepper	
1 lb	Cod fillet	450 g
4	Thick slices of bread	4
1 tbsp	Chopped parsley	1x15 ml

Peel and finely dice the potatoes. Peel and slice the onion. Trim and finely chop the leek. Skin and chop the tomato. Put the potatoes, onion, leek and tomato in a large casserole dish with the oil and the peeled and crushed garlic. Heat on HIGH for 10-12 minutes.

Add the water, bouquet garni, a strip of orange rind, saffron and seasoning. Chop the cod into pieces and stir into the liquid. Heat on HIGH for a further 8–10 minutes.

To serve, put a slice of bread into each serving bowl, sprinkle with chopped parsley and spoon over the soup.

TIP

To skin a tomato by microwave, prick the skin of the tomato with a fork. Put tomato onto a plate and heat on HIGH for 30–40 seconds. Cool for a few minutes before peeling off the skin.

American Fish chowder

Overall timing 30–35 minutes

Freezing Not suitable

To serve 4

2 lb	Mixed white fish	900 g
1	Large onion	1
4	Medium-size potatoes	4
4	Carrots	4
4	Stalks of celery	4
4 oz	Diced bacon	100 g
1 tbsp	Chopped parsley	1x15 ml
14 oz	Can of tomatoes	397 g
2 pints	Hot fish stock or water	1 litre
2 tbsp	Tomato ketchup	2x15 ml
2 tbsp	Worcestershire sauce	2x15 ml
	Dried thyme	
	Salt and pepper	

Skin and bone the fish and cut into even bite-size pieces. Peel and finely chop the onion. Peel and finely dice the potatoes and carrots. Finely chop the celery. Put the vegetables in a large casserole dish with the bacon, cook on HIGH for 10–12 minutes or till soft.

Stir in the parsley, tomatoes and their juice, hot stock or water, tomato ketchup, Worcestershire sauce, a pinch of thyme and seasoning. Add the fish pieces, stir well. Cover the casserole with a lid and cook on HIGH for 10 minutes, then LOW for 10 minutes.

If a thicker soup is required, stir in 3 tsp (3x5 ml) cornflour mixed to a paste with a little water. Heat on HIGH for 2–3 minutes to thicken.

Creamy cauliflower soup

Overall timing 19–21 minutes

Freezing Not suitable

To serve 4

1	Large cauliflower	1
1	Small onion	1
2 oz	Butter	50 g
1 oz	Flour	25 g
¾ pint	Milk	450 ml
½ tsp	Turmeric	1x2.5 ml
½ tsp	Dried mixed herbs	1x2.5 ml
	Salt and pepper	
¼ tsp	Grated nutmeg	½x2.5 ml
1	Egg yolk	1
4 tbsp	Single cream	4x15 ml
	Fresh dill	

Trim cauliflower, separate into florets and wash. Peel and finely chop onion. Put the cauliflower and onion into a casserole dish with 8 fl oz (200 ml) water, cover and cook on HIGH for 8 minutes. Drain, reserving liquid. Reserve half the cauliflower and purée the remainder.

In a large bowl, heat the butter on HIGH for ½–1 minute, stir in the flour and gradually blend in the milk and reserved liquid. Add the turmeric, herbs, salt, pepper and nutmeg. Heat on HIGH for 5 minutes, stirring twice. Stir in the puréed cauliflower and the reserved florets. Heat on HIGH for 3–5 minutes, stirring once. Taste and adjust seasoning; add extra liquid if the soup is too thick.

Lightly mix together the egg yolk and cream and add to the soup, stirring continuously. Reheat on HIGH for 2 minutes and then serve garnished with chopped dill.

Pea and ham soup

Overall timing 15 minutes

Freezing Suitable

To serve 4

1¼ pints	Chicken stock	750 ml
1 lb	Frozen peas	450 g
2 tbsp	Single cream	2x15 ml
	Pinch of sugar	
	Salt and pepper	
4 oz	Cooked ham	100 g

Put the stock and the peas in a large bowl, cover and cook on HIGH for 10 minutes. Reserve one-third of the peas. Purée the remaining peas in a blender or by passing through a sieve.

Return the puréed peas and the reserved peas to a bowl, stir in the cream, sugar, salt and pepper. Dice the ham and add. Cook on HIGH for 5 minutes, then serve hot.

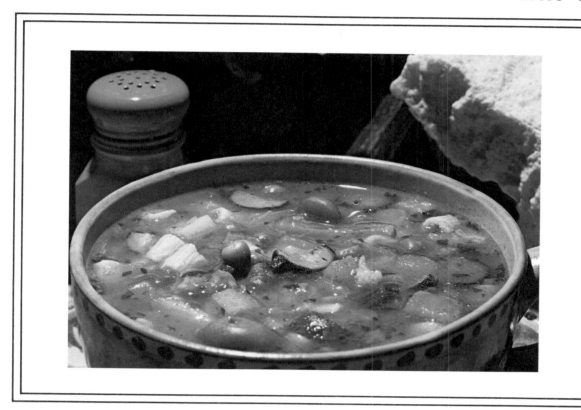

Minestrone

Overall timing 35–39 minutes

Freezing Not suitable

To serve 6

1	Onion	1
1	Small leek	1
1 tbsp	Olive oil	1x15 ml
1	Garlic clove	1
1 tbsp	Chopped parsley	1x15 ml
2	Sage leaves	2
2	Carrots	2
2	Potatoes	2
2	Stalks of celery	2
1	Courgette	1
8 oz	Savoy cabbage	225 g
4 oz	Chopped bacon	100 g
3	Basil leaves	3
1 tbsp	Tomato purée	1x15 ml
14 oz	Can of tomatoes	397 g
	Salt and pepper	
1¾ pints	Hot beef stock	1 litre
14 oz	Can of cannellini beans	397 g
2 oz	Short-cut macaroni	50 g
	Grated Parmesan cheese	

Peel and finely chop the onion. Trim and chop the leek. Put the onion and leek in a large casserole dish with the olive oil, peeled and crushed garlic, parsley and sage. Cover and cook on HIGH for 5 minutes.

Meanwhile, peel and finely dice the carrots and potatoes. Slice the celery and courgette. Finely shred the cabbage. Add to the casserole dish with the bacon and chopped basil. Re-cover and continue to cook on HIGH for 10–12 minutes, stirring twice.

Stir in the tomato purée, tomatoes, salt, pepper and the stock. Drain the cannellini beans and add with the macaroni. Re-cover and cook for 10–12 minutes. Leave to stand for 10 minutes before serving.

Serve sprinkled with Parmesan cheese.

Pipérade

Overall timing 11–15 minutes

Freezing Not suitable

To serve 4

1 lb	Ripe tomatoes	450 g
2	Green peppers	2
2	Onions	2
1	Garlic clove	1
1 tbsp	Oil	1x15 ml
	Salt and pepper	
¼ tsp	Dried marjoram	½x2.5 ml
	Tabasco sauce	
8	Eggs	8

Cut the tomatoes in half and arrange on a plate. Heat on HIGH for 2 minutes, leave to cool, then peel off skins and chop the flesh. Seed and chop the peppers. Peel and slice onions. Peel and crush garlic.

Put the onions, peppers, tomatoes and garlic in a large casserole dish with the oil. Heat on HIGH for 6–8 minutes or until the peppers are soft. Season with salt and pepper, marjoram and Tabasco.

Lightly beat the eggs in a bowl and season. Pour over the vegetable mixture. Continue to cook on HIGH for 3–5 minutes, stirring every minute; the mixture should be creamy. Serve with buttered toast and a green salad.

Egg *and pea scramble*

Overall timing 14–18 minutes

Freezing Not suitable

To serve 2–4

2 lb	Fresh peas	900 g
1	Onion	1
2 oz	Bacon rashers	50 g
2 oz	Butter	50 g
4 oz	Soft breadcrumbs	100 g
2 oz	Grated cheese	50 g
4	Eggs	4
	Salt and pepper	

Shell peas. Peel and thinly slice the onion; dice the bacon. Put the peas in a dish with 4 tbsp (4x15 ml) water. Cover the dish with a lid or with cling film; pierce cling film twice. Heat on HIGH for 8–10 minutes, then leave to stand for 5 minutes.

Put the bacon, onion and butter in a casserole dish and heat on HIGH for 4 minutes. Stir in the peas, breadcrumbs and cheese. Lightly beat the eggs and season, pour over the pea mixture. Cook on HIGH for 2–4 minutes, stirring every minute, till the mixture is creamy. Serve immediately.

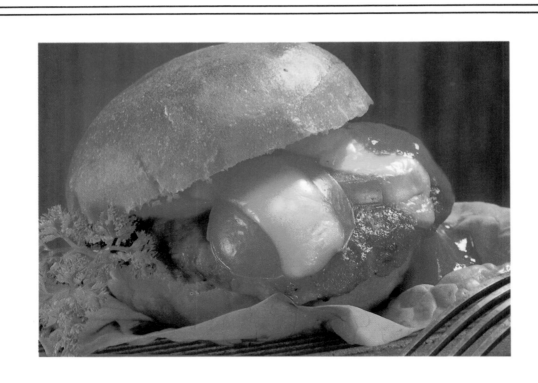

Cheeseburgers

Overall timing 6–8 minutes

Freezing Suitable: cook patties from frozen, then top with cheese

To serve 4

1	Small onion	1
1 lb	Minced beef	450 g
2 oz	Soft breadcrumbs	50 g
2 tbsp	Milk	2x15 ml
	Salt	
	Paprika	
1 tsp	Powdered mustard	1x5 ml
4	Small tomatoes	4
4	Slices of Cheddar cheese	4
4	Buns	4

Peel and chop the onion finely. In a bowl, combine the minced beef, onion, breadcrumbs, milk, salt, paprika and mustard powder. Shape into four patties. Put on a plate and cook on HIGH for 5–7 minutes. Slice the tomatoes and arrange on top of each burger. Put a slice of cheese over the top and heat for 1-2 minutes or till the cheese has melted. Serve in buns.

Tomato marjoram pizza

Overall timing 15 minutes plus 20 minutes proving

Freezing Suitable: defrost and reheat on HIGH for 5 minutes

To serve 4

1½ lb	Ripe tomatoes	675 g
1	Large onion	1
2	Garlic cloves	2
1 tbsp	Oil	1x15 ml
2 tsp	Dried marjoram	2x5 ml
6	Basil leaves	6
1 tsp	Sugar	1x5 ml
	Salt and pepper	
Base		
10 oz	Packet of bread mix	275 g
4 oz	Grated Cheddar cheese	100 g
¼ tsp	Powdered mustard	½x2.5 ml

Cut the tomatoes in half and place cut side down on a plate. Heat on HIGH for 2–3 minutes. Cool, then remove skins and chop the flesh. Peel and thinly slice the onion; peel and crush the garlic. Put them in a bowl with the oil and heat on HIGH for 3 minutes. Add the tomatoes, 1 tsp (1x5 ml) marjoram, basil leaves, sugar and seasoning. Cover and cook on HIGH for 5 minutes.

In a bowl, mix together the bread mix, cheese and mustard powder. Add hot water (according to the packet instructions) and mix to a soft but not sticky dough. Knead for 5 minutes, then roll out on a floured surface to a round 10 inches (25 cm) in diameter. Place on a lightly greased plate and pinch up the edge to form a lip. Spread the tomato mixture over the dough and sprinkle with the remainder of the marjoram. Put the pizza in the microwave and heat on HIGH for 10 seconds, then leave to stand for 10 minutes. Repeat this process until the pizza has almost doubled in size. (Twice is usually sufficient.)

When the pizza has doubled in size, cook on HIGH for 5 minutes. Serve hot with a tossed salad.

Coley with spicy sauce

Overall timing 13–15 minutes

Freezing Not suitable

To serve 4

4	Onions	4
4–6	Garlic cloves	4–6
1 lb	Tomatoes	450 g
1	Lemon	1
1 tbsp	Oil	1x15 ml
¼ tsp	Cayenne	½x2.5 ml
4	Coley steaks	4
	Chopped parsley	

Peel and thinly slice onions. Peel and crush garlic. Cut tomatoes into quarters and place on a plate. Heat on HIGH for 2 minutes, remove tomato skins and chop flesh. Cut four thin slices from the lemon and reserve; squeeze the juice from the remainder.

Put the onions, garlic, tomatoes and oil in a shallow baking dish (large enough to take the fish in a single layer). Heat the onion mixture on HIGH for 5 minutes. Add the cayenne and mix well. Arrange the fish over the onion mixture, sprinkle with lemon juice. Cover the dish with a piece of cling film pierced twice. Cook on HIGH for 6-8 minutes, when the fish should be opaque and flake easily.

To serve, arrange fish on a bed of boiled rice with the tomato sauce spooned over. Garnish with parsley and reserved lemon slices.

Trout with almonds

Overall timing 8–12 minutes

Freezing Not suitable

To serve 2

2 oz	Butter	50 g
2 oz	Almonds	50 g
2	Trout, cleaned	2
	Salt and pepper	
1–2 tbsp	Lemon juice	1–2 x15 ml
2	Lemon slices	2
1–2 tbsp	Chopped parsley	1–2 x15 ml

Put the butter and almonds in a heatproof casserole dish, cook on HIGH for 3–5 minutes, stirring once. The almonds should be golden brown: if not brown enough, cook for a further minute.

Arrange the trout in a shallow oblong dish, cut sides to the centre and heads at opposite ends to each other. Season the cavities with a little salt and pepper and sprinkle with lemon juice. Cover the dish with cling film and pierce twice. Cook on HIGH for 5–7 minutes.

Remove cling film, drain off liquid, then sprinkle over almonds. Garnish with lemon slices and chopped parsley. Serve with boiled potatoes and a mixed salad.

Baked fish steaks

Overall timing 4–6 minutes

Freezing Not suitable

To serve 4

4	Cod steaks	4
	Salt and pepper	
¼ pint	Dry white wine or hard cider	150 ml
2 tbsp	Lemon or lime juice	2x15 ml
2 oz	Butter	50 g
2 tbsp	Chopped fresh coriander (optional)	2x15 ml
	Lemon or lime slices	

Wash and dry cod steaks. Arrange in a single layer in a shallow dish, meatier parts to the outside. Sprinkle with a little salt and pepper. Add the wine or cider and lemon or lime juice and dot with butter. Cover the dish with a piece of cling film turned back at one corner. Cook on HIGH for 4–6 minutes.

To serve, sprinkle with freshly chopped coriander and lemon or lime slices. Serve with mashed potatoes and a green vegetable.

Mustard-topped cod

Overall timing 10 minutes

Freezing Not suitable

To serve 4

1¾ lb	Cod fillets	825 g
1 tbsp	Vinegar	1x15 ml
1	Onion	1
1	Bay leaf	1
6	Peppercorns	6
4 oz	Butter	100 g
2 tbsp	Powdered English mustard	2x15 ml
1 tsp	Sea salt	1x5 ml
	Sprigs of parsley	
	Lemon slices	

Cut the cod into large pieces and arrange in the base of a shallow dish. Mix the vinegar with 4 fl oz (100 ml) water. Pour over the cod. Peel and thinly slice the onion, scatter over the cod. Add the bay leaf and peppercorns, cover the dish with cling film and pierce twice. Cook on HIGH for 8 minutes.

Put the butter in a jug and heat on MEDIUM for 1½ minutes. Stir in the mustard powder and salt and heat for a further 30 seconds. Drain the liquid from the fish. Spoon a little of the mustard butter over each piece of fish and garnish with parsley sprigs and lemon slices.

PORK

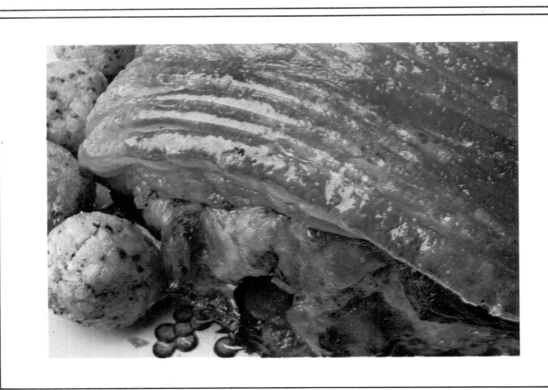

Roast pork with stuffing balls

Overall timing 45 minutes

Freezing Not suitable

To serve 6

2½ lb	Rolled boneless pork loin roast	1.1 kg
	Oil	
	Salt	
Stuffing		
1	Onion	1
2 oz	Butter	50 g
8 oz	Soft breadcrumbs	225 g
2 tsp	Dried sage	2×5 ml
	Salt and pepper	
2	Eggs	2

Weigh the roast and calculate the cooking time, allowing 12–13 minutes per lb (450 g). Score the skin on the roast and brush with oil. Taking care not to salt the flesh, sprinkle the skin with a little salt. (This will draw the fat out and cause it to "crackle".) Place the meat on a roasting rack and cover with either the roasting set lid or a roaster bag split up one side and tented over the joint. Cook on MEDIUM for the calculated time. At the end of cooking, wrap the meat in foil, shiny side in, and leave to stand for 15–20 minutes, while the stuffing and vegetables are cooked.

To make the stuffing balls, peel and finely chop the onion, put in a bowl with the butter. Cook on HIGH for 2–3 minutes. Add the breadcrumbs, sage and seasoning and bind with the eggs. Shape into small balls and arrange in a circular pattern on a plate or shallow dish. Heat on HIGH for 3–5 minutes.

Sweet and sour pork

Overall timing 22–23 minutes

Freezing Not suitable

To serve 4

1 lb	Lean boneless pork	450 g
1	Onion	1
1	Carrot	1
1 tbsp	Oil	1x15 ml
1	Cucumber	1
2	Garlic cloves	2
4 tbsp	Tomato ketchup	4x15 ml
2 tsp	Soy sauce	2x5 ml
2 tbsp	Vinegar	2x15 ml
1 tbsp	Brown sugar	1x15 ml
1 tbsp	Cornflour	1x15 ml
½ pint	Water	300 ml

Cut the pork into bite-size pieces. Peel and chop the onion; peel and chop the carrot. Put the onion and carrot in a casserole dish with the oil and heat on HIGH for 2–3 minutes. Stir in the pork. Peel and chop the cucumber; peel and crush the garlic. Add to the pork with the remaining ingredients, blending the cornflour to a paste with a little of the water to make it easy to mix in. Stir all the ingredients together, cover the dish with a lid and cook on MEDIUM for 20 minutes, stirring once.

Serve with boiled rice and side dishes of cucumber slices and tomato wedges.

Chinese spare ribs

Overall timing 20–23 minutes plus marinating

Freezing Not suitable

To serve 4

1½ lb	Pork spareribs	675 g
2	Garlic cloves	2
½ inch	Piece of ginger root	1.5 cm
2 tbsp	Oil	2x15 ml
1 tbsp	Soy sauce	1x15 ml
2 tbsp	Dry sherry	2x15 ml
2 tbsp	Tomato purée	2x15 ml
2 tbsp	Vinegar	2x15 ml
2 tbsp	Brown sugar	2x15 ml
4 tbsp	Pineapple juice	4x15 ml
½ pint	Water	300 ml
1–2 tbsp	Cornflour	1–2 x15 ml

Separate the pork into ribs and place in a deep casserole dish. Peel and crush the garlic; peel and finely chop the ginger. Put the garlic, ginger, oil, soy sauce, sherry, tomato purée, vinegar and sugar in a jug. Gradually mix in the pineapple juice and the water, pour over the ribs and leave to marinate for 3 hours, or overnight, turning the ribs occasionally.

To cook, drain the ribs from the marinade and place on a roasting rack. Cook on MEDIUM for 15–18 minutes, then leave to stand for 5 minutes.

To make the sauce, blend the cornflour to a paste with a little of the sauce and then stir into the sauce mix. Heat the sauce on HIGH for 5 minutes, stirring twice.

To serve, arrange the ribs on a serving dish and pour over the sauce. Accompany with boiled rice.

445

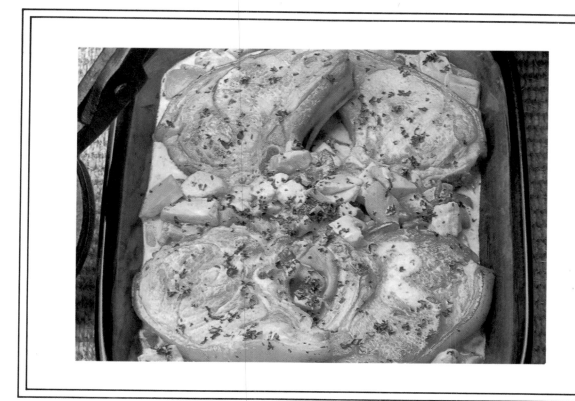

Russian pork chop casserole

Overall timing 28 minutes

Freezing Not suitable

To serve 4

1 lb	Potatoes	450 g
1	Onion	1
4 oz	Button mushrooms	100 g
1 tbsp	Butter	1x15 ml
1 tsp	Garlic salt	1x5 ml
4	Pork loin chops	4
¼ pint	Soured cream	150 ml
	Salt and pepper	
2 tbsp	Chopped parsley	2x15 ml

Peel the potatoes and dice very finely. Peel and chop onion. Slice the mushrooms. Put the potatoes, onion and mushrooms in a bowl with the butter and cook on HIGH for 8 minutes, stirring twice. Season with the garlic salt.

Heat the empty browning dish on HIGH for 6 minutes, then immediately add the chops. Cook on HIGH for 4 minutes, turn over and cook for a further 4 minutes.

Pour over the potato mixture and the cream. Cover the browning dish with its lid. Heat on high for 5–6 minutes. Taste and adjust seasoning, sprinkle with the parsley and serve.

Pork with bananas and peanuts

Overall timing 27–28 minutes

Freezing Not suitable

To serve 6

12 oz	Onions	375 g
2	Garlic cloves	2
1 tbsp	Oil	1x15 ml
2 lb	Boneless pork	900 g
8 oz	Long grain rice	225 g
14 oz	Can of tomatoes	397 g
1	Chicken stock cube	1
¼ tsp	Paprika	½x2.5 ml
¼ tsp	Ground cinnamon	½x2.5 ml
	Salt and pepper	
2	Bananas	2
4 oz	Salted peanuts	100 g

Peel and chop the onions; peel and crush the garlic. Put the onions and garlic in a casserole dish with the oil and heat on HIGH for 2–3 minutes.

Cut the pork into bite-size pieces and add to the onions along with the rice. Pour the juice from the can of tomatoes into a measuring cup, crumble in the stock cube and add enough water to make ¾ pint (450 ml). Add to the rice. Chop the tomatoes and add along with the paprika, cinnamon, salt and pepper. Cover the dish with a lid and cook on MEDIUM for 20 minutes. Leave to stand for 5 minutes, so the rice absorbs the last of the liquid. Peel and slice the bananas and stir into the stew with the peanuts, fluff up rice with a fork and serve.

Meatballs and spinach

Overall timing 18–20 minutes

Freezing Not suitable

To serve 4

1 lb	Minced pork	450 g
1 tbsp	Chopped chives	1x15 ml
1	Egg	1
2 tbsp	Soy sauce	2x15 ml
	Salt and pepper	
2 lb	Leaf spinach	900 g
2 tbsp	Dry sherry	2x15 ml
1 tsp	Cornflour	1x5 ml

In a mixing bowl, combine the minced pork, chives, egg and half the soy sauce. Season with salt and pepper. Shape into eight balls. Arrange in a circle on a large plate. Heat on HIGH for 8–10 minutes, then leave to stand for 5 minutes.

Shred and wash the spinach. Drain well and put it in a large bowl. Cover and cook on HIGH for 8 minutes.

Meanwhile, combine the remaining soy sauce, sherry and cornflour in a jug, then stir in 2 tbsp (2x15 ml) cold water. When the spinach has cooked, heat the sauce on HIGH for 1½ minutes, stirring once.

Drain and chop spinach, arrange on a warm serving plate. Place meatballs on top and pour over the sauce. Serve with a dish of soy sauce.

BEEF

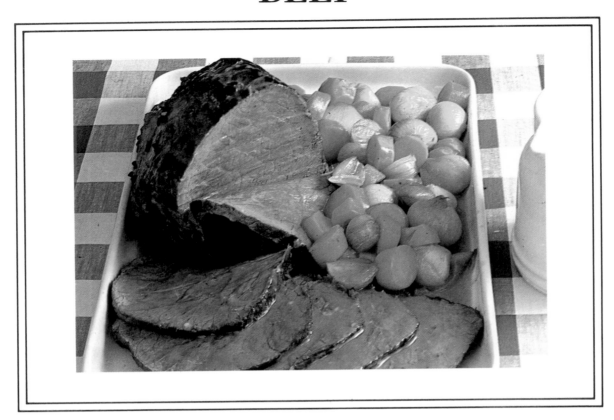

Beef pot roast

Overall timing 75–85 minutes plus marination

Freezing Not suitable

To serve 6

3 lb	Braising beef	1.4 kg
1	Large onion	1
2	Carrots	2
2	Stalks of celery	2
1	Garlic clove	1
	Sprigs of parsley	
2	Bay leaves	2
	Sprigs of thyme	
	Salt and pepper	
½ pint	Red wine	300 ml
¾ pint	Hot beef stock	450 ml
2 tsp	Cornflour	2x5 ml

Put the beef in a large casserole dish. Peel and slice the onion, carrots and celery; peel and crush the garlic. Add to the beef with the herbs, salt, pepper, wine and stock. Cover the dish with a lid and leave to marinate for 2–3 hours or overnight.

To cook, heat on HIGH for 10 minutes then on SIMMER for 60–70 minutes. Turn the beef over every 20 minutes.

To serve, remove the beef from the juices and strain the vegetables. Wrap the beef and vegetables in foil, shiny side in. Mix the cornflour with a little cold water and add to the juices. Cook on HIGH for 5 minutes, stirring once. Slice the beef onto a serving plate and serve with the vegetables. Put the gravy in a sauceboat and serve separately.

Beef with onions

Overall timing 1 hour

Freezing Suitable: defrost and reheat on HIGH for 15 minutes, stirring every 5 minutes

To serve 4

1½ lb	Chuck steak	675 g
12 oz	Onions	375 g
1½ oz	Butter	40 g
¾ pint	Beef stock	450 ml
1	Garlic clove	1
½ tsp	Ground cumin	1x2.5 ml
	Pinch of dried marjoram	
2 tbsp	Wine vinegar	2x15 ml
	Salt and pepper	
1–2 tbsp	Cornflour	1–2 x15 ml

Cut the meat across the grain into finger-length strips. Peel onions, slice crosswise and separate rings. Put the onions and butter in a casserole dish and heat on HIGH for 5 minutes. Add the beef, stock, peeled and crushed garlic, cumin, marjoram, wine vinegar and seasoning. Place a small plate on top of the meat to keep it under the juices and cover the dish with a lid. Heat on HIGH for 10 minutes, then on LOW for 40 minutes.

Remove the cover and plate, mix the cornflour to a paste with a little cold water and mix into the beef. Cook on HIGH for 5 minutes until thickened. Serve with mashed potatoes or savoury rice.

Beef and bean casserole

Overall timing 1 hour 25 minutes

Freezing Suitable: reheat from frozen on HIGH for 12–15 minutes, stirring every 5 minutes

To serve 4–6

2	Onions	2
1 tbsp	Oil	1x15 ml
1 lb	Stewing beef	450 g
¼ tsp	Chilli powder	½x2.5 ml
1 tsp	Curry powder	1x5 ml
2 tbsp	Flour	2x15 ml
½ pint	Beef-stock	300 ml
14 oz	Can of tomatoes	397 g
2 tbsp	Tomato purée	2x15 ml
2 tsp	Sugar	2x5 ml
1	Large cooking apple	1
2 oz	Sultanas	50 g
14 oz	Can of cannellini beans, drained	397 g

Peel and chop the onions and put in a large casserole dish with the oil. Heat on HIGH for 5 minutes. Stir in the meat and the remaining ingredients, except the apple, sultanas and beans. Place a small plate on top of the meat to keep it under the juices and cover the casserole with a lid. Cook on HIGH for 10 minutes, then SIMMER for 45 minutes.

Uncover and remove the plate. Peel, core and chop the apple. Add the apple, sultanas and cannellini beans to the casserole and top up with stock if necessary. Replace lid and continue to cook on SIMMER for a further 15 minutes. Leave to stand for 10 minutes, then taste and adjust seasoning. Serve with hot crusty bread.

Hamburgers

Overall timing 5–6 minutes

Freezing Suitable

To serve 4

1 lb	Minced beef	450 g
1	Onion	1
	Salt and pepper	
4	Hamburger rolls	4
1 tbsp	Dijon-style mustard	1x15 ml

Put the beef in a mixing bowl. Peel and finely chop the onion and add to the beef with plenty of seasoning. Divide and shape the mixture into four patties and place on a meat roasting rack. Cook on HIGH for 5–6 minutes, turning them over once.

Meanwhile, halve and lightly toast the rolls, then spread with the mustard.

To serve, place a hamburger in each roll, top with onions and ketchup or cheese, if desired.

Texan stew

Overall timing 1 hour 25 minutes

Freezing Not suitable

To serve 4

1 lb	Stewing beef	450 g
2	Onions	2
1	Green pepper	1
1	Red pepper	1
1 oz	Butter	25 g
14 oz	Can of tomatoes	397 g
½ pint	Hot beef stock	300 ml
	Salt and pepper	
11½ oz	Can of sweetcorn	337 g
10 oz	Can of peas and carrots	285 g
2 tsp	Cornflour	2x5 ml

Cut the meat into 1 inch (2.5 cm) cubes. Peel and chop the onions. Seed and slice the peppers. Put them in a casserole dish with the butter and cook on HIGH for 5 minutes. Add the meat, chopped tomatoes and their juice, stock and seasoning. Cover and cook on HIGH for 10 minutes, then LOW for 60 minutes, stirring once and topping up stock if necessary.

Drain the corn and the peas and carrots. Mix the cornflour to a paste with a little cold water. Add them all to the stew and stir well. Re-cover and cook on HIGH for 7–10 minutes. Serve stew in warm bowls.

Beef and horseradish loaf

Overall timing 22–23 minutes

Freezing Suitable: defrost for 10 minutes, then heat on HIGH for 7 minutes

To serve 4

¼ pint	**Strong beef stock**	150 ml
8 oz	**Soft breadcrumbs**	225 g
1	**Large onion**	1
1 lb	**Minced beef**	450 g
1 tbsp	**Grated horseradish**	1x15 ml
3	**Eggs**	3
2 tbsp	**Cream sherry**	2x15 ml
	Salt and pepper	

Put the stock in a bowl with the breadcrumbs and heat on HIGH for 2 minutes. Peel and finely chop the onion. Add the beef, onion, horseradish, eggs and sherry to the breadcrumbs, season well. Mix with a wooden spoon till all the ingredients are blended.

Press the mixture into an oblong loaf or casserole dish. Cover the dish and cook on HIGH for 15–16 minutes. Leave to stand for 5 minutes. Drain off excess juices and serve with boiled potatoes and buttered carrots.

Beef carbonnade

Overall timing 1½ hours

Freezing Suitable: defrost and reheat on HIGH for 15 minutes, stirring every 5 minutes

To serve 4

1½ lb	Braising steak	675 g
4 oz	Bacon rashers	100 g
8 oz	Onions	225 g
2	Garlic cloves	2
1 tbsp	Butter	1x15 ml
1 tbsp	Brown sugar	1x15 ml
1 tbsp	Wine vinegar	1x15 ml
¾ pint	Stout or beer	450 ml
¾ pint	Hot beef stock	450 ml
1	Bouquet garni	1
	Salt and pepper	
2 tbsp	Cornflour	2x15 ml

Cut the meat into bite-size pieces. Chop the bacon into 1 inch (2.5 cm) pieces. Peel and chop the onions; peel and crush the garlic. Put the bacon, onions and garlic in a large casserole dish with the butter and heat on HIGH for 5 minutes. Add the beef, sugar, vinegar, beer, stock and bouquet garni and season well with salt and pepper. Put a small plate over the meat so it is kept under the juices. Cover the casserole dish with a lid. Cook on HIGH for 10 minutes, then SIMMER for 70 minutes.

Remove the plate and discard the bouquet garni. Mix the cornflour to a paste with a little water, then stir into the stew. Heat on HIGH for 5 minutes. Serve with mashed potatoes and a green salad.

Beef paprika

Overall timing 1½ hours

Freezing Suitable: defrost and reheat on HIGH for 15 minutes, stirring every 5 minutes

To serve 6

2 lb	Stewing beef	900 g
8 oz	Onions	225 g
1 oz	Butter	25 g
2	Garlic cloves	2
1¼ pints	Beef stock	1.1 litres
½ tsp	Dried marjoram	1x2.5 ml
½ tsp	Caraway seeds	1x2.5 ml
	Brown sugar	
2 tsp	Paprika	2x5 ml
	Salt and pepper	
2 tbsp	Cornflour	2x15 ml

Cube the beef. Peel and slice the onions and put them in a casserole dish with the butter. Heat on HIGH for 3–5 minutes. Add the beef, peeled and crushed garlic, stock, marjoram, caraway seeds, pinch of brown sugar, paprika and seasoning. Put a small plate on top of the meat to keep it under the juices and cover the casserole with a lid. Cook on HIGH for 10 minutes, then SIMMER for 75 minutes.

Remove the cover and plate. Mix the cornflour to a paste with a little cold water and stir into the stew. Heat on HIGH for 5 minutes until thickened.

LAMB

Roast lamb with garlic

Overall timing 1 hour

Freezing Not suitable

To serve 6

2–3	Garlic cloves	2–3
3½ lb	Leg of lamb	1.5 kg
1½ oz	Butter	40 g
	Microwave browning	

Peel the garlic cloves and slice into thin slivers. Weigh lamb and place, thickest fat uppermost, on a roasting rack. With a sharp thin knife, make incisions about 1 inch (2.5 cm) deep in the meat. Insert a sliver of garlic into each incision, pressing it down so it is level with the surface of the meat. Spread the butter over the lamb and sprinkle with microwave browning. Cook on MEDIUM for 42 minutes (12 minutes per lb (450 g)).

At the end of cooking, wrap the meat in foil, shiny side in, and leave to stand for 20 minutes. In the meantime, cook the vegetables to serve with the roast.

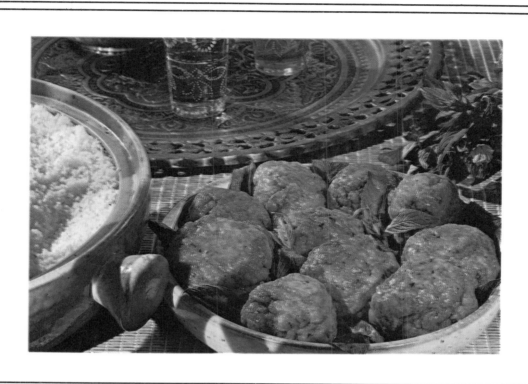

Minted lamb meatballs

Overall timing 5–7 minutes

Freezing Suitable: defrost for 10 minutes, then reheat on HIGH for 5 minutes

To serve 4

1 lb	Minced lamb	450 g
2	Garlic cloves	2
2 tbsp	Fresh mint	2x15 ml
1	Egg	1
	Salt and pepper	
1 tsp	Ground coriander	1x5 ml
	Plain flour	
	Oil	
	Mint or coriander leaves	

Place the lamb in a bowl with peeled and crushed garlic, chopped mint, egg, salt, pepper and coriander. Mix with a wooden spoon until well combined. Make the mixture into 16 little balls, flouring your hands so the mixture does not stick. Arrange them in a circle on a plate and brush with oil.

Cook on HIGH for 5–7 minutes, then garnish with mint or coriander leaves and serve with boiled rice.

Paprika lamb stew

Overall timing 30 minutes

Freezing Suitable: defrost and reheat on HIGH for 10–12 minutes, stirring twice

To serve 4

1	Green pepper	1
1	Large onion	1
1	Garlic clove	1
4	Bacon rashers	4
1½ lb	Boneless shoulder of lamb	675 g
14 oz	Can of tomatoes	397 g
2 tbsp	Tomato purée	2x15 ml
1 tsp	Paprika	1x5 ml
1 tsp	Sugar	1x5 ml
½ pint	Stock	300 ml
	Salt and pepper	
4–5 tbsp	Soured cream	4–5 x15 ml

Seed and slice the pepper. Peel and chop the onion. Peel and crush the garlic. Dice the bacon and put in a casserole dish with the pepper, onion and garlic. Cook on HIGH for 5 minutes.

Cut the meat into 1 inch (2.5 cm) cubes and add to the casserole. Chop the tomatoes and add them with their juice to the meat. Mix in the tomato purée, paprika, sugar and stock and season well. Cover and cook on MEDIUM for 20 minutes. Leave to stand for 5 minutes. Serve with soured cream for everyone to spoon over the top of the stew, and boiled potatoes.

Piquant kidneys

Overall timing 10 minutes

Freezing Not suitable

To serve 2

8 oz	Lamb kidneys	225 g
2	Bacon rashers	2
1	Onion	1
1 tbsp	Butter	1x15 ml
1 tbsp	Plain flour	1x15 ml
½ pint	Beef stock	300 ml
2 tsp	Tomato purée	2x5 ml
¼ tsp	Dried sage	½x2.5 ml
	Salt and pepper	

Prepare and thinly slice the kidneys. Dice bacon; peel and chop the onion. Put the bacon and onion in a bowl with the butter and heat on HIGH for 3–5 minutes. Add the kidneys and cook for a further 2 minutes. Stir in the flour and gradually blend in the stock. Add the tomato purée and sage and season well. Cook on HIGH for 5 minutes, stirring once. Serve spooned over hot buttered macaroni.

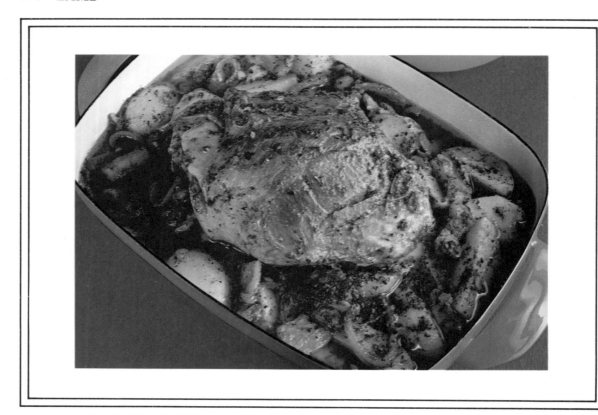

Casseroled lamb

Overall timing 1 hour

Freezing Not suitable

To serve 6

2	Large potatoes	2
2	Onions	2
1	Carrot	1
4 oz	Mushrooms	100 g
1	Garlic clove	1
1 oz	Butter	25 g
2½ lb	Boneless shoulder of lamb	1.1 kg
14 oz	Can of tomatoes	397 g
½ pint	Red wine	300 ml
¾ pint	Hot stock	450 ml
1 tsp	Ground coriander	1x5 ml
1 tsp	Ground cumin	1x5 ml
	Salt and pepper	
1 tbsp	Cornflour	1x15 ml
1 tbsp	Chopped parsley	1x15 ml

Peel and finely dice the potatoes. Peel and slice the onions, carrot and mushrooms. Put all the vegetables in a casserole dish with the peeled and crushed garlic and the butter. Heat on HIGH for 5 minutes. Place the meat on top of the vegetables. Chop and add the tomatoes and their juice, the wine, stock, spices and seasoning. Cover and cook on HIGH for 10 minutes, then LOW for 45 minutes, turning and basting the meat once.

Remove the meat from the juices and wrap in foil, shiny side in. Mix the cornflour to a paste with a little water and stir into the casserole. Cook on HIGH for 5 minutes. Return the meat to the casserole, sprinkle with chopped parsley and serve with broccoli.

Greek lamb stew with spinach

Overall timing 28–30 minutes

Freezing Not suitable

Serves 4–6

1½ lb	Boneless lamb	675 g
1	Large onion	1
1 oz	Butter	25 g
14 oz	Can of tomatoes	397 g
2 tbsp	Tomato purée	2x15 ml
	Dried oregano	
	Salt and pepper	
½ pint	Hot stock	300 ml
1 lb	Leaf spinach	450 g

Cut the lamb into bite-size pieces. Peel and thinly slice the onion. Put in a casserole dish with the butter and heat on HIGH for 3 minutes. Add the lamb, tomatoes and their juice, tomato purée, pinch of dried oregano, salt, pepper and the stock, stir and cover the casserole with a lid. Cook on MEDIUM for 20 minutes.

Shred spinach, add to the casserole and cook on HIGH for a further 5–7 minutes. Taste and adjust seasoning before serving with hot crusty bread.

Roast ginger chicken

Overall timing 45 minutes

Freezing Not suitable

To serve 4

1	Tart apple	1
1 inch	Piece of ginger root	2.5 cm
5 oz	Cooked long grain rice	125 g
¼ pint	Natural yogurt	150 ml
1½ oz	Softened butter	40 g
	Salt and pepper	
3 lb	Chicken	1.4 kg
	Chicken seasoning	

Peel, core and grate the apple. Peel and finely chop or grate the ginger and add to the apple with the rice, yogurt, half the butter and seasoning. Mix well together and use to stuff the chicken.

Place the chicken on a meat roasting rack, spread with the remaining butter and sprinkle with chicken seasoning. Cook on MEDIUM for 30 minutes. Leave to stand wrapped in foil, shiny side in, for 15 minutes. Serve with a green or mixed salad.

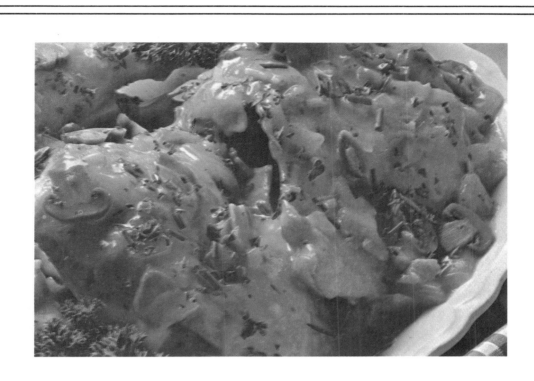

Alsatian chicken

Overall timing 40 minutes

Freezing Not suitable

To serve 4—6

8	Chicken pieces	8
1	Garlic clove	1
2	Onions	2
2 oz	Bacon rashers	50 g
1 oz	Butter	25 g
4 oz	Mushrooms	100 g
½ pint	Dry white wine	300 ml
2	Bay leaves	2
2 tbsp	Chopped parsley	2x15 ml
2 tbsp	Chopped chives	2x15 ml
	Salt and pepper	
1 tbsp	Arrowroot	1x15 ml
¼ pint	Single cream	150 ml
	Sprigs of fresh parsley	

Rub the chicken all over with the halved garlic clove. Peel and chop the onions, dice the bacon and put them in a casserole dish with the butter. Heat on HIGH for 3 minutes. Slice the mushrooms and add to the casserole with the chicken. Pour over the wine, add the bay leaves, half the chopped parsley and chives and the seasoning. Cover and cook on MEDIUM for 30 minutes. Remove the chicken pieces from the juices and arrange on a serving dish. Cover with foil to keep warm.

Mix the arrowroot with a little cold water and add to the juices. Heat on HIGH for 5 minutes, when the sauce should have thickened. Stir in the cream, taste and adjust seasoning and heat for 2 minutes. Pour the sauce over the chicken, sprinkle with the remaining parsley and chives and garnish with sprigs of parsley.

Chicken à la king

Overall timing 12 minutes

Freezing Not suitable

To serve 4

1 lb	Boneless cooked chicken	450 g
1	Onion	1
1	Green pepper	1
2 oz	Butter	50 g
1½ oz	Plain flour	40 g
½ pint	Milk	300 ml
	Salt and pepper	
	Grated nutmeg	
2 tbsp	Sherry	2x15 ml

Cut the chicken into bite-size pieces. Peel and chop the onion. Seed the pepper and finely chop half of it; cut the remainder into rings and reserve. Put the onion and chopped pepper in a bowl with the butter and heat on HIGH for 5 minutes, stirring twice. Stir in the flour and gradually blend in the milk, beating well. Heat on HIGH for 2 minutes, then stir well. Season with salt, pepper and nutmeg and stir in the chicken. Heat on HIGH for 5 minutes, stirring once.

Stir in the sherry, adjust seasoning to taste and serve with boiled rice or buttered noodles, garnished with the green pepper rings.

Mustard chicken casserole

Overall timing 50 minutes

Freezing Not suitable

To serve 4

3½ lb	Roasting chicken	1.5 kg
1	Onion	1
1 lb	Potatoes	450 g
2 oz	Smoked bacon	50 g
1 oz	Butter	25 g
1 tbsp	Vinegar	1x15 ml
2	Cloves	2
1	Bay leaf	1
¼ tsp	Grated nutmeg	½x2.5 ml
1 tsp	Powdered mustard	1x5 ml
¼ pint	Chicken stock	150 ml
8 oz	Can of tomatoes	225 g
	Salt and pepper	
2 tsp	Cornflour	2x5 ml

Wipe the chicken and cut into eight portions. Peel and finely slice the onion. Peel and finely dice the potatoes. Dice the bacon and put in a casserole dish with the onion, potatoes and butter. Cook on HIGH for 8 minutes. Add the chicken portions, vinegar, cloves, bay leaf, nutmeg, mustard, chicken stock, chopped tomatoes and their juice. Season well. Cover the dish with a lid and cook on HIGH for 30 minutes.

At the end of cooking, mix the cornflour with a little water and stir into the casserole. Cook on HIGH for 2 minutes, then leave to stand for 10 minutes before serving. To serve, remove bay leaf and adjust seasoning to taste.

Duck with oranges

Overall timing 45 minutes

Freezing Not suitable

To serve 4

4 lb	Duck	1.8 kg
1 oz	Butter	25 g
	Sweet paprika	
1 tbsp	Redcurrant jelly	1x15 ml
½ pint	Chicken stock	300 ml
4	Oranges	4
2 tsp	Cornflour	2x5 ml
¼ pint	Red wine	150 ml

Prick the duck all over with a fork. Rub with butter and sprinkle with paprika. Place on a meat roasting trivet and cook on MEDIUM for 28 minutes. Wrap in foil, shiny side in, and leave to stand for 15 minutes.

Meanwhile, make the sauce by heating 1 tbsp (1x15 ml) of duck juices with the redcurrant jelly and stock on HIGH for 2 minutes. Grate the zest and squeeze the juice from 2 oranges, then add to the sauce. Mix the cornflour to a paste with the wine and add to the sauce. Heat on HIGH for 1½–2 minutes, stirring once. The sauce should have thickened slightly; if not, heat for a further ½–1 minute.

Unwrap the duck, carve into portions and arrange on a warm serving plate. Spoon a little of the sauce over the duck. Peel and section the remaining oranges and use to garnish the duck. Serve with sautéed potatoes and peas and the rest of the sauce served in a sauce or gravy boat.

Prawn pilaf

Overall timing 30 minutes

Freezing Not suitable

To serve 4

2	Large onions	2
2	Fresh green chillies	2
2	Garlic cloves	2
8 oz	Bacon rashers	225 g
7 oz	Long grain rice	200 g
14 oz	Can of tomatoes	397 g
	Salt	
¾ pint	Chicken stock	450 ml
1 lb	Shelled prawns	450 g
2 tbsp	Chopped parsley	2 x 15 ml
2 tbsp	Grated Parmesan cheese	2 x 15 ml

Peel and finely slice the onions. Seed and finely chop the chillies. Peel and crush the garlic; chop bacon. Put the onions, chillies, garlic and bacon in a 4 pint (2 litre) casserole dish and cook on HIGH for 5 minutes, stirring once.

Stir in the rice, tomatoes with their juice, salt and chicken stock. Cover the dish and cook on MEDIUM for 12–15 minutes. Stir in the prawns and cook on HIGH for a further 5 minutes. Stand for 5 minutes, then sprinkle with parsley and cheese and serve immediately.

Fish paella

Overall timing 33–40 minutes

Freezing Not suitable

To serve 6

1	Large onion	1
2	Garlic cloves	2
1	Red pepper	1
1 tbsp	Oil	1x15 ml
14 oz	Can of tomatoes	397 g
4	Saffron strands	4
1¾ pints	Chicken stock	1 litre
	Salt and pepper	
1½ lb	White fish fillets	675 g
14 oz	Long grain rice	400 g
8 oz	Frozen peas	225 g
14 oz	Can of artichoke hearts	397 g
14 oz	Can of kidney beans	397 g

Peel and chop the onion. Peel and crush the garlic. Seed and chop the pepper. Put the onion, garlic and pepper in a large casserole dish with the oil and heat on HIGH for 5 minutes. Add the tomatoes and their juice, saffron, stock and seasoning. Heat on HIGH for 8–10 minutes, then leave to stand for 5 minutes.

Cut the fish into bite-size chunks. Add to the casserole dish and stir in the rice and peas. Heat on MEDIUM for 12–15 minutes. Drain the artichokes and cut in half lengthwise. Drain the kidney beans, stir into the rice with the artichokes and heat on HIGH for 3–5 minutes. Fluff the mixture with a fork, taste and adjust seasoning. Serve immediately.

PASTA

Cannelloni with tuna fish

Overall timing 19–21 minutes

Freezing Suitable: defrost for 10 minutes, reheat on HIGH for 5 minutes

To serve 4

12	Sheets of lasagne	12
1 tbsp	Oil	1x15 ml
2	Onions	2
2	Garlic cloves	2
7 oz	Can of tuna fish	200 g
2 oz	Capers	50 g
4 oz	Soft breadcrumbs	100 g
1 tbsp	Lemon juice	1x15 ml
1	Egg	1
2 tbsp	Chopped parsley	2x15 ml
	Salt and pepper	
14 oz	Can of tomatoes	397 g
2 tbsp	Grated Parmesan cheese	2x15 ml

Place the lasagne in an oblong dish, cover with boiling salted water and the oil. Heat on HIGH for 6 minutes, then leave to stand for 5 minutes.

Peel and finely dice the onions; peel and crush the garlic. Drain the tuna fish oil into a bowl, add the onions and garlic and heat on HIGH for 3 minutes. Add the capers and flaked tuna, followed by the breadcrumbs (reserving 2 tbsp (2x15 ml)), lemon juice, egg, parsley and seasoning. Mix well. Drain the lasagne, place some of the mixture in the centre of each sheet and roll up. Place, join side down, in a shallow oblong dish.

Press the tomatoes and their juice through a sieve, season and spread over the lasagne. Sprinkle with reserved breadcrumbs and then the Parmesan cheese. Heat on HIGH for 10–12 minutes. If desired, brown the top under a preheated grill.

Corsican spaghetti

Overall timing 21–23 minutes

Freezing Suitable (sauce only): defrost and reheat on HIGH for 8–10 minutes, stirring frequently

To serve 2

8 oz	Ripe tomatoes	225 g
1	Onion	1
1	Garlic clove	1
1 oz	Butter	25 g
8 oz	Minced beef	225 g
1	Small dried chilli pepper	1
	Salt and pepper	
8 oz	Spaghetti	225 g
1 tbsp	Oil	1x15 ml
6	Pitted green olives	6
2 tbsp	Grated cheese	2x15 ml

Cut tomatoes in half and place on a plate cut side down. Heat on HIGH for 2 minutes, then peel off skins and chop flesh. Peel and finely chop the onion. Peel and crush the garlic. Put in a basin with the butter and heat on HIGH for 3 minutes.

Put the tomatoes, onion mixture, beef, chilli pepper and salt in a casserole dish. Cover with a lid and cook on MEDIUM for 8–10 minutes. Leave to stand while the spaghetti is being cooked.

Put the spaghetti in a large bowl with the oil and plenty of hot boiling water. Cook on HIGH for 8 minutes, stirring twice. Drain and pile into a warm serving dish. Remove the chili from the sauce, taste and adjust seasoning. Slice the green olives and stir in. Pour sauce over the spaghetti and serve with the grated cheese handed separately.

Spaghetti alla carbonara

Overall timing 15–17 minutes

Freezing Not suitable

To serve 4

12 oz	Spaghetti	375 g
	Salt and pepper	
2 tbsp	Oil	2x15 ml
4 oz	Button mushrooms	100 g
4 oz	Bacon rashers	100 g
1 oz	Butter	25 g
2	Eggs	2
¼ pint	Single cream	150 ml
2 oz	Grated Parmesan cheese	50 g

Put the spaghetti in a large bowl with 1 tsp (1x5 ml) of salt and the oil. Cover with plenty of boiling water. Heat on HIGH for 8 minutes, stirring twice, then drain.

Slice the mushrooms, put them in a bowl with the diced bacon and butter and heat on HIGH for 4 minutes. Stir in the eggs, cream and cheese and heat on MEDIUM for 1½–2 minutes.

Put the spaghetti in a suitable serving dish and top with the sauce. Reheat on HIGH for 2–3 minutes, stirring twice. Serve immediately.

Ratatouille

Overall timing 26–27 minutes

Freezing Suitable: defrost on HIGH for 10 minutes, stirring frequently

To serve 4–6

1	Large aubergine	1
1 lb	Courgettes	450 g
	Salt and pepper	
2	Large onions	2
2	Garlic cloves	2
1	Large green pepper	1
1	Large red pepper	1
1 lb	Ripe tomatoes	450 g
2 tbsp	Olive oil	2x15 ml
1 tsp	Sugar	1x5 ml

Cut the aubergine into 1 inch (2.5 cm) chunks. Cut courgettes into quarters lengthwise and then into 1 inch (2.5 cm) pieces. Put the vegetables in a colander and sprinkle with salt. Leave for 30 minutes.

Meanwhile, peel and thinly slice the onions. Peel and crush the garlic; seed and slice the peppers. Cut the tomatoes into quarters and place on a plate. Heat on HIGH for 1–2 minutes until the skins can be removed easily.

Put the onions, garlic and peppers in a casserole dish with the oil and heat on HIGH for 5 minutes. Wash the salt off the aubergine and courgettes and add to the onion mixture along with the tomatoes, sugar and plenty of pepper. Stir well, then cover with a lid and cook on HIGH for 20 minutes. Taste and adjust seasoning and serve hot, or serve cold with salads.

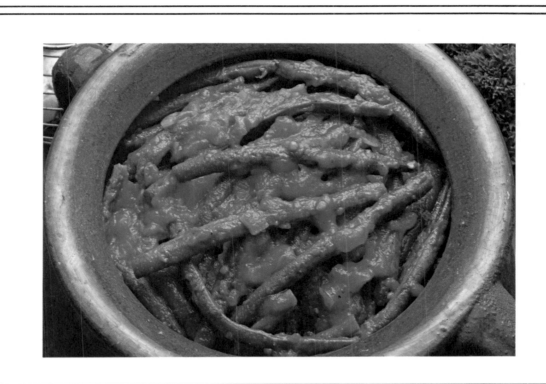

Venetian green beans

Overall timing 16 minutes

Freezing Suitable: cook from frozen on HIGH for 8 minutes

To serve 4–6

1¼ lb	Green beans	575 g
14 oz	Can of tomatoes	397 g
1	Medium onion	1
1	Garlic clove	1
1 oz	Butter	25 g
¼ tsp	Dried marjoram	½ x 2.5 ml
	Salt and pepper	

Trim beans and remove strings if necessary. Drain and chop the canned tomatoes. Peel and thinly slice the onion. Peel and crush the garlic. Put the onion, garlic and butter in a medium-size casserole dish. Cook on HIGH for 3 minutes. Add the beans, tomatoes and marjoram. Cover the dish with a lid or with pierced cling film. Heat on HIGH for 8 minutes, then leave to stand for 5 minutes. Season lightly at the end with salt and pepper.

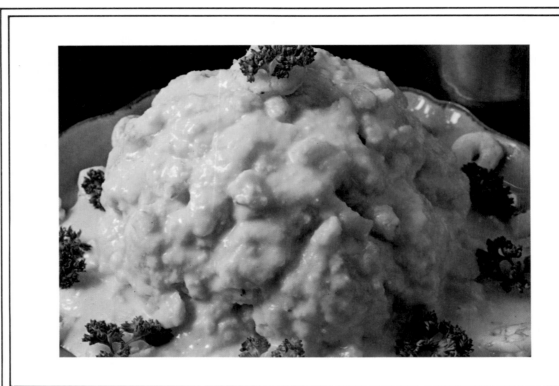

Norwegian cauliflower

Overall timing 11–13 minutes

Freezing Not suitable

To serve 4

1	Cauliflower	1
1½ oz	Butter	40 g
4 oz	Soft white breadcrumbs	100 g
½ pint	Milk	300 ml
	Salt and pepper	
4 oz	Shelled prawns	100 g
	Pinch of sugar	
1 tbsp	Brandy (optional)	1x15 ml
3 tbsp	Single cream	3x15 ml
	Sprigs of parsley	

Remove any leaves from the cauliflower and trim the stalk. Put the cauliflower in a straight-sided soufflé dish with 4 tbsp (4x15 ml) water. Cover with cling film, pierce and cook on HIGH for 6–8 minutes. Leave to stand for 5 minutes.

Meanwhile, put the butter in a jug and melt on HIGH for 1 minute, stirring once. Add the breadcrumbs and the milk and season. Heat on HIGH for 2 minutes. Set aside a few prawns for garnish, add the remainder to the sauce along with the sugar and brandy, if used. Heat on HIGH for 2 minutes. Lastly stir in the cream.

Drain the cauliflower and put on a warmed serving plate. Pour over the sauce and serve hot, garnished with reserved prawns and parsley.

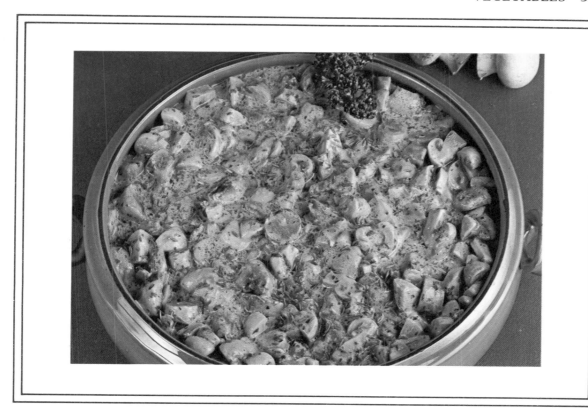

Moravian mushrooms

Overall timing 8 minutes

Freezing Not suitable

To serve 6

1¼ lb	Button mushrooms	575 g
1½ oz	Butter	40 g
½ tsp	Salt	1x2.5 ml
1 tsp	Cumin seeds	1x5 ml
1 tbsp	Finely chopped parsley	1x15 ml
1 tbsp	Plain flour	1x15 ml
1 tsp	Lemon juice	1x5 ml
¼ pint	Milk	150 ml
2 tbsp	Double cream	2x15 ml

Trim and quarter the mushrooms. Put them in a casserole dish with the butter, salt, cumin seeds and parsley. Cook on HIGH for 5 minutes. Stir in the flour and gradually blend in the lemon juice and milk. Heat on HIGH for 2 minutes, then stir in the cream and heat for 1 minute. Serve hot with toast.

Celery in yogurt sauce

Overall timing 18–20 minutes

Freezing Not suitable

To serve 4–6

1 lb	Celery	450 g
1	Onion	1
1 oz	Butter	25 g
½ pint	Chicken stock	300 ml
Sauce		
1 tbsp	Butter	1x15 ml
1 tbsp	Plain flour	1x15 ml
¼ pint	Natural yogurt	150 ml
¼ pint	Soured cream	150 ml
	Grated nutmeg	
	Salt and pepper	

Trim celery and cut into short lengths. Peel and slice the onion and put in the base of a shallow oblong dish with the butter. Heat on HIGH for 3 minutes. Arrange the celery on top, pour over the stock and cover with a piece of cling film. Pierce film and cook on HIGH for 12 minutes. Leave to stand for 5 minutes.

To make the sauce, heat the butter in a jug for 30 seconds on HIGH, then blend in the flour. Drain ¼ pint (150 ml) of cooking juices from the celery and mix into the butter and flour. Heat on HIGH for 2–3 minutes, stirring twice. Add the yogurt, soured cream, pinch of nutmeg and seasoning and stir until smooth. Heat on HIGH for 1–2 minutes, then pour over the celery and serve hot.

Pears in chocolate sauce

Overall timing 15 minutes

Freezing Not suitable

To serve 6

6	Firm pears	6
½ pint	Water	300 ml
1 tbsp	Lemon juice	1x15 ml
2 oz	Sugar	50 g
1	Vanilla pod	1
4 oz	Plain chocolate	100 g
1 oz	Butter	25 g
	Vanilla ice cream	
	Crystallized violets (optional)	

Peel the pears and remove the stalks. Stand the pears in a casserole dish. In a jug, mix together the water, lemon juice and sugar and heat on HIGH for 2 minutes. Pour over the pears. Put the vanilla pod in the base of the dish and cover the dish with cling film. Pierce and cook on MEDIUM for 10 minutes, then leave to cool.

Put the chocolate in a jug and add 4 tbsp (4x15 ml) of juices from the pears. Heat on HIGH for 3 minutes, stirring every minute. Beat in the butter until the sauce is smooth.

Drain the pears and arrange on a flat dish or plate. Pour over the sauce. Serve with scoops of vanilla ice cream and decorate with crystallized violets, if liked.

Chocolate mousse

Overall timing 3 minutes plus 3 hours chilling

Freezing Not suitable

To serve 4

6 oz	Plain chocolate	150 g
3 tbsp	Strong black coffee	3x15 ml
1 tbsp	Orange juice	1x15 ml
1 tbsp	Rum or brandy	1x15 ml
4	Eggs	4

Put the chocolate, coffee and orange juice in a bowl and heat on HIGH for 2 minutes, stirring once. The chocolate should have melted; if not, heat for a further 1 minute. Stir until smooth. Add the rum or brandy.

Separate the eggs and add the yolks to the chocolate, beating well. Allow the mixture to cool.

In a clean bowl, whisk the egg whites till stiff peaks form. Fold 1–2 tbsp (1–2x15 ml) of the egg white into the chocolate, then gently fold in the remainder with a metal spoon or spatula, taking care not to let the mixture become flat and heavy.

Pour into a serving bowl and chill for 3 hours before serving.

Sherry trifle

Overall timing 5 minutes

Freezing Not suitable

To serve 6–8

3 tbsp	Custard powder	3x15 ml
2 tbsp	Sugar	2x15 ml
¾ pint	Milk	450 ml
6 slices	Sponge cake	6 slices
2 tbsp	Raspberry jam	2x15 ml
1 lb 13 oz	Can of sliced peaches	800 g
6 tbsp	Sherry	6x15 ml
¼ pint	Double cream	150 ml
2 oz	Toasted split almonds	50 g

In a large heatproof jug, blend the custard powder, sugar and a little milk to a paste, then mix in remainder of the cold milk. Heat on HIGH for 2 minutes, stir and heat for a further 2–3 minutes until thick. Put to one side to cool, covering the surface with damp greaseproof paper to prevent a skin forming.

Cut sponge into small pieces and spread with jam. Arrange around the bottom and sides of a serving dish.

Drain the peaches. Mix 3 tbsp (3x15 ml) of the juices from the can with the sherry and sprinkle over the sponge. Reserve a few peaches for decoration and arrange the rest on top of the sponge.

Remove the greaseproof paper from the cool custard and beat well. Pour over the peaches and chill for at least 1 hour.

Whip the cream until stiff, then pipe onto the trifle. Decorate with the reserved peaches and sprinkle with the almonds.

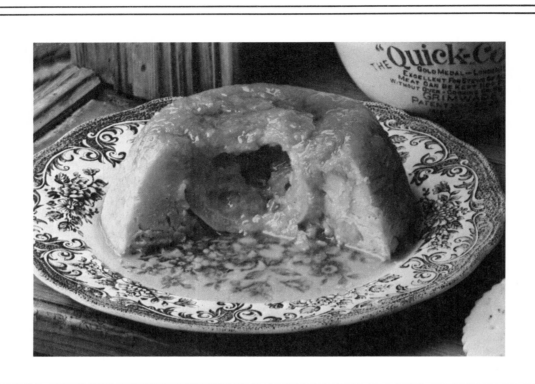

Sussex pond pudding

Overall timing 6–7 minutes

Freezing Not suitable

To serve 6–8

8 oz	Self-raising flour	225 g
2 oz	Shredded suet	50 g
¼ pint	Water	150 ml
4 oz	Butter	100 g
4½ oz	Brown sugar	125 g
4 oz	Currants	100 g
1	Large thin-skinned lemon	1

Mix the flour and suet in a large bowl. Add the water a little at a time to form a soft but not sticky dough. Knead the dough lightly. Roll out three-quarters of the dough to line a greased 2½ pint (1.1 litre) pudding basin.

Cream together the butter and sugar till light and fluffy, then stir in the currants. Put half into the base of the pudding. Prick the lemon all over with a fine skewer and press into the butter. Top with the remaining butter mixture.

Roll out the remaining dough and cover the filling, sealing well at the edges. Cook on HIGH for 6–7 minutes. Unmould and serve immediately with custard.

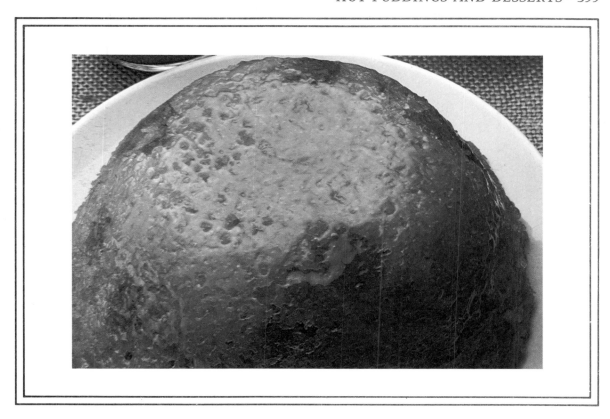

Cherry pudding with jam sauce

Overall timing 10 minutes

Freezing Not suitable

To serve 4–6

4 oz	Butter	100 g
4 oz	Sugar	100 g
2	Eggs	2
6 oz	Self-raising flour	150 g
3 oz	Glacé cherries	75 g
8 tbsp	Milk	8x15 ml
½ tsp	Almond essence	1x2.5 ml
Sauce		
2 oz	Raspberry jam	50 g
8 tbsp	Water	8x15 ml
1 tsp	Arrowroot	1x5 ml
1 tbsp	Lemon juice	1x15 ml

Cream together the butter and sugar until pale and fluffy. Gradually beat in the eggs one at a time. Fold in the sifted flour and cherries. Add the milk and almond essence to give a soft dropping consistency. Place in a lightly greased pudding basin and cook on HIGH for 5–6 minutes. Leave to stand while the sauce is cooking.

Put the jam and water in a jug and heat on HIGH for 3 minutes. Mix the arrowroot and lemon juice together and add to the jam. Heat on HIGH for 2 minutes. Stir well. Unmould the pudding onto a plate and pour over a little of the sauce. Serve the remaining sauce separately in a sauce boat.

Wholewheat bread

Overall timing about 1 hour

Freezing Not suitable

Makes 2—4 loaves

1 tbsp	Brown sugar	1x15 ml
1½ pints	Lukewarm water	900 ml
1 oz	Dried yeast	25 g
3 lb	Wholewheat flour	1.4 kg
1 tbsp	Salt	1x15 ml
2 oz	Lard	50 g

Dissolve 1 tsp (1x5 ml) of the sugar in ½ pint (300 ml) of the water in a bowl. Sprinkle the yeast over and leave in a warm place to go frothy. This will take about 10 minutes.

Mix the flour, salt and remaining sugar in a large bowl and rub in the lard. Add the frothy yeast liquid and the rest of the warm water and mix to a dough. Knead the dough thoroughly until it feels firm and elastic and is no longer sticky. This should take 5—10 minutes. Shape into a round and place in an oiled plastic bag. Put into the bowl for support and prove using the microwave. Heat on HIGH for 15 seconds, stand for 10 minutes, repeat three times until the dough has doubled in size.

Turn onto a floured surface and knead again until firm. Divide into two or four, shape into loaves and put in suitable containers. (Remember that if you wish to prove in the microwave you must use non-metallic containers.) Prove each loaf individually until doubled in size and cook. A 1 lb (450 g) loaf will take 3—5 minutes on HIGH. If a crisp crust is required, cook bread in the conventional way in an oven preheated to 450°F (230°C) Gas Mark 8 for 30—40 minutes.

Coffee ring cake

Overall timing 4–5 minutes

Freezing Suitable

To serve 16

6 oz	Butter	150 g
6 oz	Sugar	150 g
	Pinch of salt	
2	Eggs	2
1	Orange	1
1 tbsp	Instant coffee powder	1x15 ml
6 oz	Self-raising flour	150 g
¼ tsp	Ground cinnamon	½x2.5 ml
2 oz	Plain chocolate	50 g
Icing		
6 oz	Icing sugar	150 g
2 tsp	Instant coffee powder	2x5 ml
1 tsp	Cocoa	1x5 ml
2 tbsp	Hot water	2x15 ml
	Vanilla essence	

Cream the butter, sugar and salt till light and fluffy. Gradually add the eggs and beat well. Grate orange rind and add to the mixture.

Squeeze the juice from the orange and mix with the coffee. Sift the flour and cinnamon and add alternately with the coffee mixture. Grate the chocolate and fold in. Add more orange juice or water to give a soft dropping consistency.

Spoon the mixture into a lightly greased 8 inch (20 cm) ring mould and cook on HIGH for 4–5 minutes. Leave to cool for 5 minutes before turning out onto a wire rack to cool.

To make the icing, sift the icing sugar into a bowl. Dissolve the coffee and cocoa in the hot water, then add to the icing sugar with a few drops of vanilla essence. Mix well until smooth. Pour over the cooled cake and smooth surface with a knife. Transfer the decorated cake to a serving plate and leave to set before cutting.

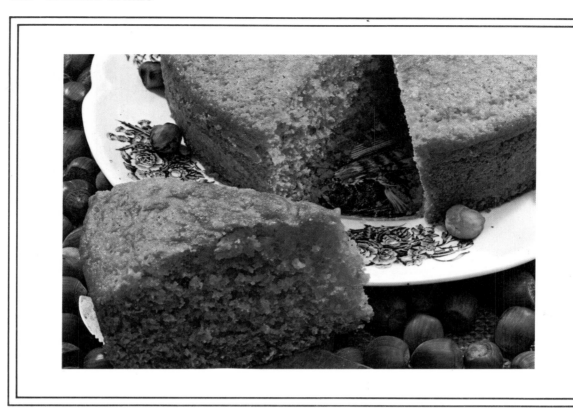

Hazelnut and honey cake

Overall timing 8–9 minutes

Freezing Suitable

To serve 8

6 oz	Butter	150 g
5 oz	Dark soft brown sugar	125 g
2 oz	Clear honey	50 g
3	Eggs	3
8 oz	Wholewheat self-raising flour	225 g
	Pinch of salt	
4 oz	Toasted hazelnuts	100 g
8 tbsp	Milk	8x15 ml

Cream the butter with the sugar and honey, then beat in the eggs, one at a time. Fold in the flour, salt and chopped hazelnuts alternately with the milk.

Turn into a 7–8 inch (18–20 cm) soufflé dish which has been base lined with greaseproof paper. Cook on HIGH for 8–9 minutes. Cool for 5 minutes, then turn onto a cooling rack. Coat with fudge frosting if a more elaborate cake is desired.

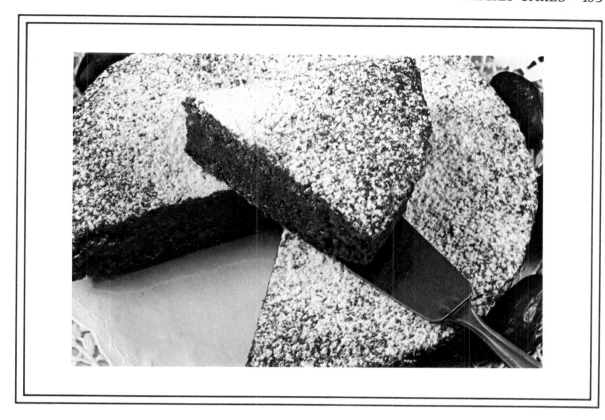

Moist date and ginger cake

Overall timing 8½–9½ minutes

Freezing Suitable

To serve 12

8 oz	Stoned dates	225 g
1 tsp	Baking soda	1x5 ml
¼ pint	Boiling water	150 ml
4 oz	Butter	100 g
4 oz	Dark brown sugar	100 g
2 tbsp	Black treacle	2x15 ml
1 tbsp	Golden syrup	1x15 ml
2	Eggs	2
8 oz	Self-raising flour	225 g
2 tsp	Ground ginger	2x5 ml
2 tbsp	Icing sugar	2x15 ml

Chop the dates and place in a small bowl. Sprinkle with baking soda, then pour on the boiling water. Leave to cool.

Cream the butter with the sugar until light and fluffy. Beat in the treacle and syrup, then add the eggs one at a time, beating well. Sift in the flour and ginger and add the dates and soaking liquid. Stir till well blended.

Line the base of a 9 inch (23 cm) round dish with greaseproof paper and pour in the mixture. Cook on HIGH for 8½–9½ minutes. Cool in the dish for 5 minutes before turning onto a wire rack to cool. When cool, sprinkle the top with sifted icing sugar and serve.

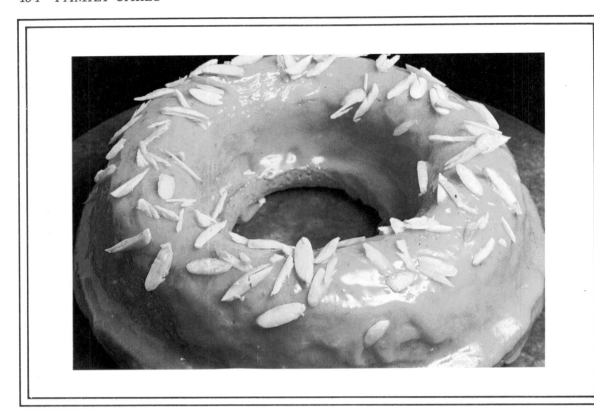

Caramel ring cake

Overall timing 6–7 minutes

Freezing Suitable: ice cake after thawing

To serve 12

4 oz	Butter	100 g
4 oz	Brown sugar	100 g
2	Eggs	2
1 tbsp	Golden syrup	1x15 ml
6 oz	Self-raising flour	150 g
1 tsp	Ground cinnamon	1x5 ml
	Pinch of salt	
¼ tsp	Baking soda	½x2.5 ml
8 tbsp	Milk	8x15 ml
	Vanilla essence	
	Flaked almonds	
Icing		
1½ oz	Butter	40 g
2 tbsp	Golden syrup	2x15 ml
1 tbsp	Milk	1x15 ml
1 tsp	Vanilla essence	1x5 ml
8 oz	Icing sugar	225 g
1 tsp	Ground cinnamon	1x5 ml

Cream the butter with the sugar and beat in the eggs and golden syrup. Sift in the flour, cinnamon and salt and beat well. Mix the soda with the milk and a few drops of vanilla essence and add to mixture. Place in a lightly greased 9½ inch (24 cm) ring mould and bake on HIGH for 5–6 minutes. Cool for 5 minutes in the dish before turning onto a wire rack.

For the icing, put the butter and the syrup in a jug and heat on HIGH for 1 minute. Stir in the milk and vanilla. Stir in half the sifted icing sugar and the cinnamon and beat well. Stir in rest of sifted sugar.

Pour icing over cake and smooth with spatula dipped in hot water. Sprinkle with the flaked almonds and transfer to a serving plate.